The Woman of Reason

The Woman of Reason

Feminism, Humanism and Political Thought

Karen Green

Continuum • New York

1995

The Continuum Publishing Company
370 Lexington Avenue
New York, NY 10017

Printed in Great Britain
This edition first published by Polity Press, 1995

Library of Congress Cataloging-in-Publication Data

Green, Karen.
The woman of reason : feminism, humanism, and political thought/
Karen Green.
p. cm.
Includes bibliographical references and index.
ISBN 0-8264-0821-4
1. Feminist theory. 2. Rationalism. 3. Liberalism.
HQ1190.G74 1995
305.42'01 – dc20   94-24016
                                                     CIP

Contents

Acknowledgements

I would like to thank John Bigelow, Linda Burns, Leslie Caust, Leslie Connell, Jennifer Hornsby, Jeanette Kennett, Genevieve Lloyd and Philip Pettit for advice and encouragement in the production of this book, and Siobhan Lancaster for her editorial assistance.

Some of the material in chapters 1, 5 and 8 has appeared earlier in 'Reason and Feeling: Resisting the Dichotomy', *Australasian Journal of Philosophy* 71 (1993), pp. 385–99, and the main argument of chapter 3 with some of chapter 2 is published as 'Christine de Pisan and Thomas Hobbes', *Philosophical Quarterly* 44 (1994), pp. 456–75.

Introduction

For this is humanism: meditating and caring, that man be human
and not inhumane, 'inhumane,' that is outside his essence. But in
what does the humanity of man consist?

                                        Heidegger, 'Letter on Humanism'

It is only during the past couple of decades that feminism has become
an accepted area of political philosophy. In order for this to happen, a
change had to be effected in the accepted definition of 'politics'. When
it was published in 1970, Kate Millett's book *Sexual Politics* introduced
a radical new contention:[1] sexual relations are political relations, and
sexuality a nexus for the expression of power and the domination of
women by men. The essence of politics is power, said Millet, and the
society we live in is one in which the female half is controlled by the
male half. She coined the term 'patriarchal' to describe such societies,
introducing a new use for an old word. Since Kate Millett's ground-
breaking work a huge amount has been written on feminism and on
patriarchy, but there is still much disagreement over the nature of
patriarchy, its specific connections with capitalism and its origins. During this period, feminism has undergone a number of changes in orientation and developed in a confusing proliferation of directions. In the early
seventies the most theoretically sophisticated feminists were heavily
influenced by Marx's dialectical materialism and de Beauvoir's *The
Second Sex*. But by the late seventies, at least three new influences
emerged; one was Freudian psychoanalysis, another radical feminism
and a third post-structuralism. These three influences have cross-
fertilized each other in complex ways, resulting in a break with traditional Marxism and liberalism, and an attempt to build feminism from
a completely independent feminist perspective. This proliferation has
lead to a great richness and diversity in feminist points of view and to
a certain confusion over directions for feminist political action.[2] Most

feminists agree that patriarchy is ubiquitous but there is little agreement over the form that a non-patriarchal society might take, or even over the fundamental epistemological issue of whether a legitimate answer can be given to this question.

At one level, the aim of this book is to contribute to the task of bringing order to this proliferation and to lay the groundwork for an answer to the question, 'How can society be organized in order to transform patriarchy and promote the good of women, rather than merely the good of men?' In order to answer this question we need to be clear about the choices available and the way in which women have fitted into past political theories. At another level, the book offers an answer to this question which is grounded in the tradition of feminst humanism. In order to justify such an approach we need to meet a challenge, posed by post-structuralism, which seems to suggest that such questions cannot be given non-authoritarian answers. I will argue that this challenge can be met from the perspective of feminist humanism.

The many different feminisms, or strands within feminism, sometimes contest each other's right to be considered the legitimate feminism.[3] In this book I will resist this tendency and begin with a very broad definition of feminism, attempting to clarify what is at issue between the different strands. 'Feminism', as I will use it, refers to all theories of the good society which begin with the explicit recognition that women are as much ends in themselves as are men, and which incorporate the expressed aim of improving the lot of women.[4] 'Masculinism', by contrast, either explicitly or implicitly aims for the good of men and treats women as part of the means of achieving this good. Given this broad definition, there are many feminisms and the central problem of feminist political theory is to ascertain which is most viable.

Feminism is often taken to be a rather recent movement, which emerged during the late nineteenth century and flowered in the latter half of the twentieth. It is a presupposition of this work that feminism is much older than this, being, in fact, implicit in humanism and contemporaneous with it. Humanism immediately gives rise to questions that tend to lead to feminism: questions like, 'Is there a single human nature, the same in both sexes?', 'If men and women are equally human, why are they not social equals?' and 'What constitutes justice in the realm of sexual relations?' These questions have not, however, always been given feminist answers. Many male philosophers, writing within the broad humanist tradition, have redeveloped Aristotle's view that women are in an important sense lesser humans, and therefore appropriately treated as means to humanity's (men's) greater ends. Nevertheless, an examination of literary and philosophic texts since the Middle Ages reveals an on-going, if marginalized, preoccupation with the implications of sexual difference for humanism and a significant change in western notions of womanhood, marriage and the family. Many of the questions raised by recent feminists have been touched upon in greater or lesser depth by earlier men and women. Yet at the same time, the implications of feminism for humanist political theory have not been fully worked out.

The relation between feminism and humanism is currently a matter of some controversy and the possibility of salvaging feminist humanism has been questioned by feminists working within a number of differing traditions. In the first chapter of this book I examine the underpinnings of the recent mistrust of humanism and argue that it is misplaced. I hope to demonstrate that a careful adherence to the methods of humanism, and a scholarly reappraisal of past feminist humanists, while it shows the inadequacy of masculinist humanisms, offers an alternative viable form of gynocentrism, a feminist humanism. This gynocentrism is non-essentialist in so far as it rejects the idea that there is a biologically given feminine nature, or a universal feminine essence, which *determines* social possibilities. But it also takes issue with those post-structuralists who assert that gender identity is always merely a normative injunction imposed by 'established political contexts'.[5] There are commonalities in women's experience which have a biological origin, and biology places *constraints* on possible social forms and their acceptability. Women, I will argue, should be interpreted as having constructed their own identity through their interpretations of the more or less similar situations in which they find themselves. The position I develop is gynocentric, in that it takes women's points of view seriously, but it rejects those strands of gynocentrism which too hastily associate women with the rejection of rationality and representationalism. Indeed, it will be argued that out of the philosophical tradition, a distinctive feminine conception of rationality and objectivity that can provide the basis for feminist political theory can be seen to emerge.

Kate Millett and other feminist writers have brought the personal into the political arena. Sexuality and family relations, which orthodox twentieth-century political philosophy had consigned to the realm of the private and personal, are to be brought under public scrutiny, for it has been recognized that they are just as much an integral part of political society as are the impersonal relations between rulers and ruled. They too are areas in which justice and oppression can apply. But it would not be true to say that the personal has never been recognized as being part of political theory. Indeed the foundational texts of western political theory, Plato's *Republic* and Aristotle's *Politics*, have a good deal to say concerning marriage and the family, and it is worth while sketching the positions that they take, for in many ways they offer two alternative visions of the place of women and the family in society that emerge again and again.

In part vi of *The Republic* Plato discusses women and the family in his ideal society.[6] Plato's ideal society arguably constitutes a paradigm of an elitist society in which there is equality of opportunity. It is a meritocracy in which the rulers, called Guardians, are those whose wisdom, strength and virtue makes them most fit to protect and rule the community. Plato believes that private interests lead to the corruption of rulers; those who ought to be governing in the interest of the whole society tend to succumb to the temptation of benefiting themselves and their own families. Thus he makes it a condition of guardianship that the Guardians should have no private property, and even more strongly than this, no specific private interest in any of the children of the society. The Guardians will engender their children in state-run orgies, so that none of them will know which children are theirs. Plato is not generally egalitarian, but he believes that a capacity for philosophy or for fighting is the same in a woman as in a man and that many of the disabilities that women show are due to their not having been given the education or opportunity to compete with men.[7] In this context he gives an argument in favour of equality of opportunity, which still stands. He says that women are weaker in all areas than men, but this is still compatible with the strongest women being strong and with some women being good at mathematics and philosophy. So even if there are natural differences between men and women, in a meritocracy, whose members are all to do what they are best suited to do, it would be unjust if women did not have the same opportunity to develop their natural capacities as men. Therefore, Plato would give women the same opportunity to be Guardians as is accorded to men. He then implicitly recognizes that one major disability that women face in competition with men is being expected to care for children, and he so conceives of the children of Guardian women being taken away and cared for in state-run nurseries, without their mothers, any more than their fathers, being able to determine which child is theirs. What is particularly interesting about Plato's sketch of an ideal society is that, like many feminist writers, he seems to see women's lack of equality as bound up with their status as childcarers within the private realm of the family, and he thinks that justice in the state and equality of opportunity for women require the abolition of the family and the institution of a system of wives and children 'in common'.

Aristotle objects to Plato's scheme for a number of reasons, which can be summed up in the claim that it is neither possible nor desirable to abolish the private sphere of the family.[8] First he claims that even if one attempted to force people to rear children in common, people would still be able to tell which were theirs, and would naturally attempt to favour their own. Secondly, one of the major motives for caring for someone or something is that it is one's own. In a society in which children were held in common, looking after them would be a duty that people would tend to leave to someone else, leading ultimately to the neglect of all children. Thirdly, one of the strongest human motives is love, and love is a particular passion that cannot be felt for a multitude. People do things for others because they love them, but, Aristotle claims, in Plato's society nobody would love anybody, since none would identify any other person's interests with their own. People would be indifferent to the plight of others and hence, in the end, not motivated to do things for the society.

Aristotle goes on to give a classic justification for patriarchal society. He takes the family to be the natural private foundation of society and makes the father the head and ruler of the family. Political life becomes the organization of society by, and distribution of power between, men who are heads of families. The ultimate goal of political life is the production of good men. Women, children and slaves have only defective reason, therefore it is proper, according to Aristotle, that husbands should rule over their wives, children and slaves within the household.[9] Men participate in the public sphere of politics, women are relegated to the private sphere of the household. This way of construing the relationship of women and men to private and public life respectively has remained ubiquitous for the last two thousand years.[10] It is only recently that feminism has begun to challenge it.

At the same time, while no feminist could accept the Aristotelian justification for patriarchy, many of the things that Aristotle has to say in criticism of Plato are likely to strike a chord with women. Motherhood, love of one's own children, private passion; these are surely all important goods that ought to be preserved in a society that is just and promotes human happiness. Plato's perfect society, constructed on purely rational grounds, leaves something out. If Aristotle is correct, it leaves out of account the realities of human nature. The very idea that there is a human nature is contentious and needs to be carefully scrutinized. Yet surely Aristotle has a point. It is no good constructing utopias, if real people, with actual human desires, could not live in them. Love, a private realm of action, the opportunity to bring up one's own children; these do seem to be natural goods. One of the problems that feminist political theory must face is how to preserve what is good in them without preserving patriarchy.[11]

In writing this work I have not attempted to deal comprehensively with every writer who has had something of interest to say on the status of women. Rather, I have chosen a few of the most notable and influential authors in order to illustrate how at each period developing humanist ideas have had implications for the status of women and political theory which have been partly perceived and then largely ignored. Indeed, it is the thesis of this work that humanist political philosophy takes on a completely different cast when it begins with the observation that humans are sexual beings, who are born helpless, and its theory of justice aims, in the light of these facts, for the good of both women and men.

I have not limited my discussion to female or even feminist authors. Nevertheless, where I have discussed the views of male theorists, it has been in an attempt to place the work of the more influential feminists in the philosophical context in which it was written and to develop their thoughts, in order to draw out their implications for the present day. Having, in chapter 1, defended the method and preoccupations of the book, I turn in chapter 2 to the thought of Christine de Pisan, whose writing is important for a number of reasons. She is the earliest feminist whose work we know, and she expresses a concern over masculine sexuality that is reminiscent of the attitude of many later feminists. Her views on women are integrated into a sophisticated medieval political philosophy, within which the subordination of women to their husbands constitutes not an aberration, but rather a model of the appropriate subordination of self to the requirements of one's social position and the pursuit of peace. The reading of Christine de Pisan casts a new light on Hobbes's political philosophy. In chapter 3 I examine Hobbes's political thought and recent feminist criticisms of it. Feminist critics of liberal political theory have tended to equate Hobbes's social contract theory with liberalism, rejecting liberalism because of objections to Hobbes's framework.[12] In this chapter I clarify the substance of these objections, and argue that they amount to objections to Hobbes's moral psychology. I argue that, in fact, this moral psychology is not an essential component of liberalism and, further, that Hobbes is not an archetypal liberal, but a transitional figure who was the last exponent of a version of the political philosophy of subordination found in de Pisan. It is on the issue of moral psychology that de Pisan and Hobbes disagree. And I claim that the moral psychology assumed by de Pisan is compatible with liberalism and has interesting affinities with that expected by those who maintain that women have a different ethical voice.[13]

For later exponents of social contract theory, particularly Locke and Rousseau, women pose a particular problem, since, if women are human, and all humans are equal, their subordination within the family appears to be an injustice. It is Rousseau who tackled this problem in greatest detail, giving rise to nineteenth-century orthodoxy on the role of women in the democratic state. Chapter 4 examines Rousseau's thoughts on women and sets the scene for the next chapter, in which Wollstonecraft's critique of Rousseau is examined. Her liberal feminism is defended against the charge that, having shown that Rousseau's philosophy is inconsistent, she fails to appreciate that without this incon- sistency, masculine democratic theory collapses. Nevertheless, two issues emerge from Wollstonecraft's writing which have become central to the feminist debate and which are only hinted at by her. These are socialism and sexuality. In the subsequent chapter I sketch the develop- ment of these interconnected themes through the work of Engels, Freud, Reich, Marcuse, Fromm and Firestone, and I contrast these early thoughts on the place of sexuality in the liberation of women with the more recent arguments of Andrea Dworkin, Sheila Jeffreys and Catharine MacKinnon.

In chapter 7 de Beauvoir's claim that woman has been Other, even for herself, is examined and ultimately rejected, because it undermines the possibility of taking earlier feminists seriously, and leads to the bizarre and rather arrogant view that it is only in the late twentieth century that women have acquired the capacity to judge their own interests. In this chapter I return to the issues raised in the first, and fill out an argument for rejecting the association of feminism with the critique of reason inspired by post-structuralism. I argue that, despite the fact that she wrote within the humanist tradition, de Beauvoir's thinking paved the way for recent feminist claims that in order to speak as women we need an entirely new 'logic' or entirely new language. These claims are, I sug- gest, ambiguous. On the one hand, they may merely indicate the need for new conceptions of rationality which are freed from the metaphorical masculinization of the past. This would involve not the rejection of rationality and good argument, but their feminization, and a demonstra- tion of their affinity with sympathy and emotion. On the other hand, the claims suggest a need to speak outside all past discourse. But this project, I argue, is self-defeating and impossible. The most fruitful way forward from de Beauvoir's thought is not to attempt to speak from the impossible position of the Other of discourse, but to discover our own feminist subjectivity and reason in the cultural legacy left to us in the writings of women. In the last chapter of the book I build on the interpretation of the writings of the historical feminists discussed, in order to offer a reconceptualization of humanism and the rational subject.

Throughout my discussion I have kept in mind recent claims that all western philosophy has been imbued with dichotomous modes of thought within which reason is opposed to emotion, culture to nature, woman to man. In the light of Derrida's critique of western logocentrism (which Derrida associates, via the work of Lacan, with phallocentrism, thus giving rise to the concept of phallogocentrism) and in the light of his deconstruction of the dichotomies inner/outer, sensible/intelligible, signifier/signified, some feminists have claimed that feminist modes of thought need to transcend dichotomous ways of thinking.[14] In my discussion of feminist thinkers, and of the philosophers who have influenced them, I have pointed out that far from operating with simple dichotomies, many of the writers that I consider, particularly those who wrote before Hegel, were heavily influenced by Plato's conception of the tripartite soul. The three parts of the soul – reason, spirit and appetite – correspond in later writers to reason, conscience and appetite. As in Plato's image of reason as a charioteer driving an unruly black horse and a virtuous white one, spirit, conscience or love of the good is conceived of, in this tradition, as an emotional drive that is allied to reason, appetite as an irrational drive in conflict with it. Neither Christine de Pisan nor Mary Wollstonecraft operated with a simple dichotomy between reason and emotion, and both were, I argue, committed to moral philosophies that conceived of the possibility of a harmony between reason and feeling. Love, in particular, was implicitly conceived of by Christine de Pisan as a rational passion that is a powerful motive for doing good. For instance, in her romantic parable of the duke of true lovers, love makes the true lover prepared to undergo even the deprivation of not seeing his beloved, rather than doing her harm.[15] And despite her criticisms of Rousseau's glorification of nature, Wollstonecraft was no cold rationalist but hoped that women would develop an educated sensibility and a reason enlivened by the imagination.[16]

There are considerable metaphysical difficulties with the Platonic concept of the tri-partite soul as it has come down to us in the Christian tradition. Some of these persist in a common assumption that there is an underlying human (or female) nature which is good. Nevertheless, in the conclusion of this book I argue that the best prospect for developing a coherent vision of a non-patriarchal society lies in the development of a feminist humanist tradition which has from its earliest exponents been based on a vision of a moral society as one in which reason and emotion are brought into harmony.

1

Against Feminist Anti-humanism

This book mounts a defence of feminist humanism. It builds on the work
of a number of feminist authors in order to argue that a distinctively
feminine concept of the rational individual already exists. The idea that
women have the capacity to offer a more thoroughly human, rational
and ethical vision than men is not new. Hilary Rose argued, in 1983,
for a more humane science that integrated hand, brain and heart.[1]
More recently Michèle Le Doeuff has brought up the possibility of a
'female version of rationality', and has offered a characterization of
humanism that emphasizes the mutual recognition of humanity among
subjects, in contrast to Sartre's masculine vision of the isolated
individual.[2] Yet many feminists have rejected humanism as masculine
hegemony, which assumes a universal model of rational man, who is
implicitly male. And this feminist critique of masculine humanism seems
to be in step with the post-structuralist deconstruction of universal
mankind. Yet a fairly simple argument suggests that feminist critics of
philosophy may have been precipitous in extending their rejection of
liberalism and other humanist philosophies, as developed by men, to
include the forms espoused by past women. Many critics of masculine
humanism have relied on psychoanalysis as a means to explain the content, or character, of the masculine point of view. Among others, Jane
Flax, Jane Gallop, Susan Bordo and Luce Irigaray have postulated that
many of the perennial preoccupations of western philosophy, particularly the conception of an immaterial rational self, the attempt to
ground objective knowledge in reason, and a way of characterizing
reason according to which it is opposed to the bodily and feminine are
the result of masculine gendered subjectivity.[3] Another group of writers
has similarly relied on psychoanalytic theory to account for the fact that

women experience themselves as connected to others and take a different moral or epistemological stance; the most influential of these are Carol Gilligan and Evelyn Fox Keller.[4] Yet another group has suggested that past feminist writers, working within the dominant philosophical paradigms of their time, have analysed woman's condition from within a masculine point of view.[5] It is the claims of this last group which are particularly problematic.

Characteristically, critics of past egalitarian or humanist feminisms rely on features of the content of these theories which are taken to be indicative of a masculine point of view (for instance faith in reason and objective truth, the demand for equal rights or the pursuit of transcendence) in order to ground their claim that these thinkers are 'masculine'. But, given the psychoanalytic explanation for the difference in masculine and feminine gendered points of view, this is difficult to justify. For these preoccupations, when they appear in the writings of men, have not been criticized on the basis of their content or implications, but only explained as the expected results of masculine psychosexuality. The shift from difference grounded in the actual sex of the speaker to that grounded in content takes place particularly clearly in Sarah Ruddick's 'Remarks on the Sexual Politics of Reason'.[6] Because she is aware that a mere gender difference, under conditions of patriarchy, cannot by itself be the basis for a critique of the masculine outlook, Ruddick chooses to see the two moral voices as identified by cognitive modality, not by gender. But, if we make this identification, it becomes obscure why women should be criticized for speaking in a 'masculine voice', since nothing yet shows that the voice, contingently identified with the masculine gender, is cognitively defective. Furthermore, it has been implicitly assumed by feminists that masculine gender identity has remained sufficiently constant, throughout the period of development of philosophy from Plato to Descartes and Sartre, for it to explain recurrent images in western philosophy. Female gender identity might be expected to have shown a similar constancy. Yet when the writings of historical women are examined it is assumed that, because some of their preoccupations are inherited from their male contemporaries, they have expressed a masculine rather than a feminine point of view. This cannot be justified on the evidence presented, for if gender identity expresses itself so vividly in the texts of men, why should we not also expect to find it expressed in the texts of historical women?

There are three strategies which might be adopted to deal with this conflict. One would involve giving up the claim that we should expect to find any interesting cross-cultural differences in content between

masculine and feminine moral and epistemological stances. This would
be to deny that we should expect to find or encourage any deep differences between the sexes. This outlook has been equated by Susan
Okin with feminist humanism; although this is a different usage from
the one that I adopt.[7] Another strategy would involve giving up the
claim that feminists in the past have adopted a masculine standpoint.
The last, which is the most common, introduces the contention that past
feminists have adopted philosophical personae alien to their real selves.
In this work I argue for the adoption of the second of these alternatives.
The claim that there are differences between masculine and feminine
gender identity will be provisionally upheld, using historical evidence for
a different emphasis within the writings of feminist philosophers to those
of their male counterparts. However, the differences are more subtle
than the those which have been predicted by psychoanalysis, and
amount to a different characterization of reason and its relationship to
emotion, rather than implying a way of thinking which is opposed to
the rational. Moreover, as should be expected, feminist humanist conceptions of the self change, as society and woman's place in it change.

The assumption that past women writers within the humanist tradition have unwittingly adopted patriarchal and logocentric values seems
hard to justify if the explanation for the existence of those values in the
writings of men is to be found in their psychosexual orientation. But a
further argument may well seem to strengthen the case for assuming that
in the past women writers were incapable of expressing opinions which
were authentically feminist. Patriarchy, like any other system of power,
can be presumed to have upheld itself through an ideology which makes
the social inequalities of the system appear natural. Women, in the past,
have not been in a position to situate themselves outside this ideology,
since to do so would have involved an impossible leap beyond all existing modes of thought. It is only as the social structures change that past
theories can be revealed for what they were, projections of the preoccupations of the ruling class. So the attempt to discover an authentic
expression of the interests and preoccupations of women, within the
writings of past women, is doomed to fail. It is, I believe, an argument
along these lines which lies behind the common expectation that past
egalitarian feminists must have fallen into ways of thinking that were
inherently masculine. In chapters 6 and 7 I will deflect the force of this
objection by arguing that political questions concerning real interests, of
the sort which concern feminists, cannot be solved if we assume the
ubiquity of ideology. There, Foucault's doubts about the concept of
ideology will be used to undermine its usefulness for political debate; my

ultimate conclusions will, however, differ from Foucault's.

Even if the foregoing is accepted, and the critique of patriarchal modes of thought is not automatically applied to women writing within patriarchy, it may be argued that there are reasons, quite independent of feminism, for rejecting humanism. If humanism is inherently flawed, quite independently of its being the expression of a masculine psychosexuality, then feminists should avoid its mistakes. In what follows I will attempt to throw some doubt on contemporary critiques of humanism. This will fall far short of a complete rehabilitation of humanism. There are too many strands of contemporary critique for them to be dealt with in depth in one chapter, but I hope that the following comments will show that the case against humanism is not impregnable. Marxism, psychoanalysis, post-structuralism and radical feminism are all associated, in some of their forms, with criticisms of humanism. What is being criticized differs markedly, both between these areas, and among different writers within each of them. This is perhaps not surprising, since 'humanism' is a grab-all term with vague boundaries and covers a broad spectrum of positions, each of which incorporates ethical, political and epistemological elements. Liberalism is usually thought of as a kind of humanism, and there are Marxist, Christian and existentialist humanisms; rationalism is an aspect of some humanisms, empiricism an aspect of others. It has been suggested by Michel Foucault that 'the humanistic thematic is in itself too supple, too diverse, too inconsistent to serve as an axis of reflection'.[8] But this rejection seems too hasty, for despite the diversity of its manifestations, two propositions appear to be central to humanism and to the objections of those who would leave it behind. The first is that there is some basis of commonality, a 'human nature' or 'human condition', which links all humans, despite their considerable differences, and which can provide the basis for ethical agreement. The second is that human faculties, including reason and perception, are capable of grounding some access to truth. In some writers this turns into an overweening faith that they are privileged with a direct access to the underlying pattern of the universe, or the mind of God, and this arrogant over-evaluation of reason has been justly criticized by feminists and post-structuralists.[9] But in others there is merely a presupposition that we have a fallible and incomplete access to the way things are; one which may be intersubjective, rather than absolutely objective. The generality of these propositions leaves open a huge scope for argument over human nature and the justification of belief. But put together they ground the possibility of giving reasoned answers to political questions of the sort which concern feminists.[10]

There are at least four major strands to recent critiques of such humanism. The first emerges out of the Marxist tradition and attacks the idea that there is a pre-social human nature. It argues that there is no human subject which exists independently of a particular historical and cultural moment; no timeless unchanging 'essence of humanity'. Thought of this way, the dispute between humanists and anti-humanists could be characterized as one between essentialists and constructionists.[11] If one allows that the existentialist claim that man is essentially free perversely involves a kind of essentialism, then Michèle Le Doeuff's early criticism of de Beauvoir fits in with this way of understanding feminist criticisms of humanism. Under the rubric 'humanism as an epistemological obstacle', she argues that existentialism is ultimately inadequate as a basis for understanding woman's oppression because it is incapable of taking seriously the way in which social formation constrains individual choice.[12] But from another perspective, this difference between essentialists and constructionists should be located within humanism, for one very ancient strand of humanism opposes human nature to the nature of other biological kinds, emphasizing human freedom, agency and self-creation.[13] What is at issue between essentialists and constructionists would then be the accepted account of human nature; essentialists claiming that there is a biological human nature, which remains the same in all cultures and which places constraints on all possible forms of the good life and the good society; constructionists arguing that since humans are (essentially) social creatures, whose sense of identity has a specific history, and is expressed in a language the meaning of which changes, human nature changes and there are no timeless constraints on human behaviour.[14] Social constructionism has, however, become a more radical critique of humanism through its marriage to a popular epistemological outlook, which might be called anti-representationalism.[15] The Marxist critique of humanism that has been considered so far introduces a distinction between the nature of humans and the nature of other biological kinds. A frog or a flower has a nature determined by its biology, which determines its capacities. A human being has a nature which is rooted in biology and is also the result of a historical process of past material development and class conflict. Somewhat paradoxically it involves as well the capacity to construct the self through interaction with the environment and with the givens of history. These two aspects of constructionism stand in some tension. Emphasizing the first tends to lead towards the denial of human agency, and has been deemed anti-humanist; emphasizing the latter gives Marxism a more humanist cast.[16] But what is important to note, for the moment, is that all of this could be said within a representationalist epistemology, according to which, as humans develop, their theories of the world get closer and closer to a truth which exists independently of them. This epistemology is, however, partly undermined by the following thought. If humans are socially constructed, then so too are their beliefs. Why should we expect the beliefs of one period to represent the world better than the beliefs of another period, rather than just representing it differently, and more appropriately, given the material conditions and class structures of the historical moment? Quite independently, the structuralist account of language, developed by Saussure, also tends to undercut the representationalist theory of language and leads to a second strand within anti-humanism.[17] This is essentially a critique of representationalism and its concept of truth.

According to a naive representationalist theory of meaning, simple sentences are made up of two kinds of expression: names, which pick out objects, and predicates, which pick out properties. Objects and properties are two kinds of thing existing in the world, and simple sentences (those without negation or other connectives) are true when they say of objects that exist that they have the properties that they do. Structuralism challenges this representational model. Saussure's primary interest was in language thought of as a system of sounds, and he was struck by the fact that the phonemes, which make up the physical elements of language (the signifiers), are not universal. Each language imposes its own spacing on what is in fact a phonetic continuum. Language brings into existence a structure of significant differences whereby a certain segment of the phonetic continuum comes to be recognized as a phoneme. Similarly, Saussure argued, the conceptual side of a sign (what is signified) does not exist independently of the structure of language but comes into existence with it.[18] If each language brings its own way of dividing up the world, its own conceptual scheme, truth cannot consist in accurate representation of an already existing structure of reality but must rather be thought of as what is acceptable within a scheme. Since our conception of ourselves as subjects is itself developed within language, it too is a construct determined by language. Lacan's anti-humanism applies this insight to Freud's psychoanalysis, objecting to 'humanist' and biologistic versions of Freud and interpreting the Oedipus complex as describing the way in which the ego is constructed through being 'inscribed' within the structure of language. Here 'inscription' is thought of in terms of a placing in relation to a privileged signifier, the phallus.[19] Briefly, one either is (feminine) or has (masculine) the phallus. Taking seriously the existence of the unconscious, Lacan also objects to the unity of the subject in standard philosophical thought. The subject is not the unitary, transparently knowable, rational consciousness of the Cartesian tradition, but irrevocably split, constructed through an imaginary identification with an image, first in the mirror, later in the Other of language.

A frontal attack on post-structuralism would take the form of a critique of the structuralist account of language which it presupposes. The theory of language is an area of great dispute, and it is beyond the scope of this book to develop a refutation of structuralism. Nevertheless, it seems clear that the structuralist claim that concepts come into existence out of the play of differences overplays the importance of language for the existence of properties and objects in the world. Since language is itself an evolved biological capacity which enables humans to communicate their expectations with regard to the regularities in the world, it seems plausible to assume that its evolution was grounded in the existence of properties, structures and regularities in the world which existed before language. Some common perceived world seems to be required for language learning and for translation. But to develop a thorough critique of structuralism, a whole treatise on reality and representation would be needed. It is enough in this context to indicate that the assumption that structuralism is true is a large one.[20]

Foucault's 'archeology' and 'genealogy' apply elements of the structuralist perspective to knowledge and the history of ethics respectively.[21] Since there cannot be, within this perspective, any progress of science towards a language-independent truth, the study of the history of science becomes a meticulous account of replacement of one 'game of truth' by another, organized along different principles.[22] For Foucault, as for Marxist constructionists, there is no timeless human nature, rather 'man is an invention of recent date.'[23] However, it would be a mistake to read his work as involving a complete break with humanism. In 'What is Enlightenment?' Foucault expresses his commitment to a general ethos associated with one aspect of Enlightenment thought, that in which 'the critique of what we are is at one and the same time the historical analysis of the limits that are imposed on us and an experiment with the possibility of going beyond them.'[24] And in his latest writing this 'experiment with the possibility of going beyond' the limits imposed upon us by our history becomes an ethics of life as a work of art, a free creation. This is close to Sartre's existentialism and closer still to Nietzsche. Which indicates that just as humanism is extremely vague in its boundaries, so too is the post-modernism that is opposed to it. Since on this view the goal of humanity is still freedom, and discourses constrain action, we are only truly free when we create ourselves by going beyond the shackles imposed by past 'games of truth'.[25] According to Foucault we must exercise this aesthetic of the self without recourse to truth, for to take seriously the idea that we might be making our lives beautiful, through following the truth about the good life, or that we might have discovered true beauty, would be once again to subordinate ourselves to an authorial discourse.

Terminology is likely to become confusing here since, whereas Foucault is critical of humanism but retains a faith in one element of the ethos of the Enlightenment, post-modernism is often characterized, following Lyotard, as involving 'a breakdown in the metanarrative of the Enlightenment'.[26] However, Lyotard's rejection of metanarratives of legitimation, like the one he associates with the Enlightenment which 'is cast in terms of a possible unanimity between rational minds', is in fact quite similar to Foucault's acceptance that at most we have 'games of truth' which can be described, played or displaced, but not justified from any timeless metaperspective.

The third strand of recent critiques of humanism derives from Derrida and his tactical use of structuralism, which he takes beyond itself, in an extension of Heidegger's destruction of metaphysics called 'deconstruction'. Structuralism, as I have characterized it, questions the relationship between words and the world, arguing that the structure that we use to organize our experience comes into being with the structure of the language that we use to express that experience. Deconstruction self-reflexively applies this strategy to the relationship between signs and language. The structuralist assumes that there *is* something, such as the meaning of the phallus, which is determined by the structure of language. But this assumes that the structure of language exists independently of the way in which we represent it, when, applying the structuralist insight consistently, we should accept that the structure of language comes into existence with the emergence of the system of differences that 'represents' it.[27] Thus, in *Of Grammatology*, Derrida criticizes Saussure for having treated writing as an inessential and exterior sign for an already existing phonemic language, just as naive representationalists treat sounds as inessential and exterior signs of already existing concepts. Applying the structuralist move to language itself, we see that there is just writing, a structure of differences, which is interpreted in more writing. Just as structuralism showed that there were no properties or essences independent of our means of 'representing' the world, so this strand in post-structuralism shows that there are no meanings independent of our means of 'representing' language.[28] Derrida introduces the key terms, *'différance'* and *'logocentrism'* to convey his thought. *'Différance'* is a portmanteau word made up from 'difference' and 'deferral' and is used by Derrida to capture the thought that the articulation of a structure of differences, in a material medium, constitutes the condition of possibility of the deferred thought, in the present, of an absent object. 'Logocentrism' captures the central myth of western metaphysics; the idea that the meaning of a word can be fully present to the rational mind. Even structuralists retain vestiges of logocentrism, according to Derrida. Thus he is able to accuse Lacan of phallogocentrism, for assuming a fixed and present significance for the phallus and an identifiable significance of 'femininity'.[29]

Within feminist writings Derrida's technical term *différance* is often replaced by the ordinary notion of difference, so that perfectly traditional difficulties, such as the complex issue of when the pursuit of equality should be over-ridden by real differences in people's needs, tastes and situations, come to be interpreted as implying the adoption of post-structuralism or post-modernism.[30] This tendency is also encouraged by Derrida, who, in response to the accusation that deconstruction is nihilistic and apolitical, has responded that in fact deconstruction is a new rationalism and an affirmation of alterity. So there seems to be a certain hiatus between what appear to be the implications of Derrida's more radical epistemological and metaphysical views and his express political commitments. What has seemed to many to involve the denial of the possibility of a rational consensus appears to others to involve the rational acceptance of plurality.

Derrida's thought has its origins in a highly complex intersection between Hegel's dialectic, Husserl's phenomenology, Heidegger's introduction of temporality as the clue to the question of the meaning of Being, and Saussure's structuralism. Although it is difficult to tease apart the complex interweavings of these threads, at least the following can be said. Derrida's critique of logocentrism is a critique of a certain way of conceiving reason and has elements in common with Heidegger's destruction of metaphysics. But just as Heidegger's 'destruction' of metaphysics still remains in a certain sense metaphysical, so too the critique of reason that is implied by the rejection of logocentrism still remains within reason. It is reason which suggests to us that meaning is invested in material signs and that our capacity to think of the past depends on the iterability of such marks. Derrida responds to Heidegger's thoughts on the historicity of *Dasein* with the following observation: 'The iterability of the trace ... is the condition of historicity.'[31] This observation lies behind his complex thoughts on *différance* and his rejection of all attempts to explain meaning in terms of a historical origin or transcendental signified. Martin Heidegger's commitment to the historicity of *Dasein* is developed in *Being and Time*, where he says: 'In analysing the historicality of *Dasein* we shall try to show that this entity is not "temporal" because it "stands in history", but that on the contrary, it exists historically and can so exist only because it is temporal in the very basis of its being.'[32] Derrida announces his commitment to a form of historicity in *Acts of Literature*: 'Contrary to what some people believe ... I consider myself very much a historian, very historicist – from this point of view ... Deconstruction calls for a highly "historian's attitude" (*Of Grammatology*, for example, is a history book through and through).'[33] But Derrida's history is not one which we can look back to, in order to discover the originary meanings of words. It exists in the material traces which are texts.

I will not attempt to resolve the complex question of whether this implies a complete overturning of reason, or a critique of one way of understanding it, for Derrida's comments on historicity and the trace suggest the following. If our humanity is to be understood not in spiritual or transcendental terms but in terms of the material and iterable trace, then women should find their identity not in some ahistorical essence, but in the traces women have left in the history of ideas. Either deconstruction fails as the basis for an emancipatory politics, or it offers us a conception of our humanity which makes it an on-going product of its own self-representation. Such a view would suggest that woman's identity is not something given but something to be created in writing. So, without endorsing the linguistic idealism that is incipient in this view, one way of understanding this book would be as part of the project of 'creating' woman's past in order to shape our future.

Many elements of these critiques of humanism have been absorbed, developed and transformed by feminist writers. Joined to the assumption that it is the ruling class who determine the structures of language, and the observation that men are the ruling class, structuralism leads to the conclusion that we live in a world created by men.[34] What might then seem to be required is a 'new language', a 'new logic', one which is created by woman and expresses her subjectivity.[35] In Luce Irigaray's writing 'phallocentrism' comes to stand for the hypothesis that the structure of language as we know it, the search for unitary meaning and objective truth, maps the morphology of the male body onto the language, and thus determines the construction of the subject within language.[36] She writes to promote the development of a different feminine subjectivity which would no longer be constrained by this masculine logic. Yet this thought is problematic within the framework of structuralism and post-structuralism. For, if structuralism is right, there is no such property as being a woman independently of the actual structure of language, and if post-structuralism is right there is not even a stable concept.[37]

Irigaray has been interpreted as one of the major feminist post-humanists, significantly influenced by Derrida. Alice Jardine asserts that Derrida is her 'primary text'. Liz Grosz suggests that she makes considerable use of Derrida's notion of *différance*, Carolyn Burke says more ambiguously that she may be 'situated in relation to Derridean deconstruction', and Toril Moi claims that 'her analysis of male specular logic is deeply indebted to Derrida's critique of Western philosophical tradition'.[38] So I will use her writing to highlight the problems of adapting these post-humanist themes to feminist ends. One way of reading Irigaray suggests the following thought. The difference between the sexes has often been constructed so as to associate masculinity with reason, and femininity, which is marginalized and repressed, with unreason. If the feminine is opposed to reason, an allegiance to feminism can appear to be allied to the post-structuralist deconstruction of reason's pretensions and the avoidance of rationalist methodology. Feminism thus becomes identified with a rejection of all past humanisms, which are characterized as phallocentric, particularly in their quest for objectivity and truth, and in their assumption of the unity and authority of the author.[39] But the consequences of this reading need to be examined with care for at least three reasons. Together these difficulties suggest that either the reading is uncharitable, or it is correct, but the position it leads to is untenable. Feminism requires the possibility of speaking of women as an identifiable group with identifiable interests. But if Foucault is right and man is a recent invention, woman too is an invention brought into existence by the discourse that studies her. Since we have been largely studied by men, this leaves us with no identity apart from that given us by men, the identity as Other, which I will discuss in chapter 7. It also tends to leave the project of deciding on our interests, and the future development of our conception of our identity, unconstrained. If we are just whatever we freely choose to make ourselves through our discourse, what is to guide us in our choice? These are particular manifestations of the general problem that post-humanism is itself fraught with paradox, and provides at best a problematic basis for any coherent emancipatory politics. For despite Derrida's disclaimers, deconstruction appears to undermine categories like justice, truth and human nature which many feminists take for granted.[40] Because truth at a particular stage in history is identified with the ways of organizing the world implicit in the institutions and discourses of those in power, emancipation becomes a process of permanent revolution or of proliferating cultural configurations.[41] In contrast with this, we will see that the writings of women often focus on aspects of life which remain relatively constant throughout history, among them morality as connected with love, sentiment and imagination, the ethical development of children, and the duties of parents. Since babies are not yet socially constructed, concentrating on them as paradigm humans offers the possibility of discovering truths about the way people become motivated to live peaceably and justly. It offers a 'universal' perspective which takes into account the fact that we are both constructed and embodied. It is true that often appeals to nature are disguised justifications of the *status quo*. But this need not make us think that we have no nature, or that we cannot understand what constitutes better or worse ways of living.

The reading of Irigaray that we have been considering associates her thought with deconstruction. But it is not clear that this is the most charitable or cogent interpretation of her writing. Accepting the connection between women and unreason involves accepting a way of reading the distinction between the sexes which is itself part of our patriarchal past. In her reading of Plato's myth of the cave Irigaray suggests that woman, the cave/womb, becomes the place from which the male subject differentiates himself; she is the ground and precondition of his transcendence into the light, but is not acknowledged as such. Rather than proper recognition being given, and the debt being paid, to the womb from which he emerges, the mother takes on the character of the mere bodily other, outside representation, which is left behind in man's progress towards reason, God or the light.[42] At times it appears as though Irigaray herself is caught up by the image of woman, excluded from the rational order, which is the legacy of patriarchal thought. But accepting that woman is the beyond of reason is accepting that woman is what she is for this patriarchal philosophy: its repressed Other. The very possibility of woman speaking then becomes paradoxical, for it can seem that the only position available from which to conceptualize oneself as a subject is the masculine one.[43] A woman can mimic either the woman of patriarchal discourse, or the man, but there is no place from which she can authentically speak. This feature of Irigaray's thought contrasts with her clear commitment to the possibility of women speaking among themselves, and her endorsement of the development of a woman-to-woman sociability.[44] She clearly articulates the need for women to have access to images of themselves as cultural beings enmeshed in a genealogy of women. And she suggests women's potential for developing a different rationality. Margaret Whitford suggests that we solve the difficulty of interpretation that this presents by understanding Irigaray as speaking sometimes of woman as she has been defined by men and at other times of the possibility of a new symbolization of woman: one which is no longer woman as the Other of man.[45] In searching for this new symbolisation it turns out that Irigaray does not go beyond all logic and language, but rather looks back to those images of woman as nature which come from a past time at which, it seems, patriarchal genealogies took over from matriarchal.[46] In finding images of woman in these myths Irigaray shows herself quite happy to take on some aspects of the image of woman that has come down to us in the tradition. She accepts a certain natural relationship between women's bodies, their natural cycles and the rhythm of the universe.[47] Making this move, she distances herself from post-modern and anti-humanist suspicion of nature, speaking of the possibility of a natural economy and of nature as a basis from which we continue to create culture, and lamenting the fact that deconstruction 'gives little thought to the constitution of a new rationally founded identity'.[48] Women's symbolization of themselves no longer seems to require the impossibility of speaking outside all past logics in a language which has no proper meanings, as some of Irigaray's early work suggested, but now involves an articulation of a shared understanding of ourselves as sexually differentiated, cultural and natural beings.

The shift in emphasis which can be clearly traced in Irigaray's writing indicates some of the difficulty in accommodating post-structuralist anti-humanism to feminist ends. When one turns from the critique of masculine 'truths' to the attempt to articulate positive political proposals, it seems that one is forced to rely on the possibility of communicating a relatively clear and precise message, one that can be shared and be the basis of collective action. Derrida's apparent commitment to the contention that no such sending of a precise message is possible undermines one of the features of society that we take for granted. Similarly, the rejection of the existence of any human nature which can provide the basis for an emancipatory politics, common to Derrida and Foucault, undermines the possibility of agreeing that some particular form of society is, or is not, in our real interests.[49]

Sharing with Irigaray the belief that for women to articulate their own subjectivity they need to construct their own genealogies and their own understanding of their place in the world 'through images of [themselves] already deposited in history', I have tried to capture the specificity of women's thought through an examination of the writings of actual historical feminists and their characteristic differences from their male contemporaries. Unlike Irigaray, I do not believe that the result is a woman's voice which undoes logic or proper meaning. At the same time there is, implicit in women's writing, a critique of a certain conceptualization of reason and the suggestion of an alternative. Moreover, the conception of reason implicit in the feminist tradition ought to be congenial to Irigaray's desire to overcome what she sometimes calls the 'schiz' required by a conception of reason and logic which is opposed to desire, emotion and the bodily.[50] For it is, I will argue, much more embodied and more closely tied to the emotions than that characteristic of male philosophical texts.

A critique of reason can be a critique of a certain kind of reason, or a rejection of rationality altogether. Where there is no attempt to provide a positive characterization of rationality, the first kind of critique can come to look very like the second. Given this distinction, this book can be thought of as an attempt to supplement the critical movement of feminism, which has pointed to the limitations of the masculine conceptualization of rationality, by providing a genealogy of feminist rationality. As should be evident by now, the humanist tradition is extremely broad. Most feminist work on the history of philosophy has concentrated on the metaphors used by male authors in their development of notions of reason.[51] The problematic metaphors are then assumed to infect feminist humanism. What I hope to demonstrate is that there are significant differences between the feminist and masculinist humanist traditions which make the first a less problematic basis for contemporary feminism than has recently been assumed.

I want to conclude this chapter by discussing one last element in recent criticisms of humanism, particularly those with a feminist orientation. But this element, although it has been identified with anti-humanism, effectively amounts to a debate within humanism. A number of writers have categorized feminisms into those that are 'gynocentric' and those that are 'humanist', often being influenced in their description of the character of these feminisms by recent versions of psychoanalysis.[52] A rough way of understanding this debate is in terms of answers to the question, 'Is there a single human nature?' Humanist feminists are taken to be those who answer the question in the affirmative, and who then argue for equality between the sexes. Gynocentric feminists, by contrast, emphasize the differences between the sexes and argue for a re-evaluation and empowering of the feminine. This way of understanding the contrast must be seen as only provisional, for it apparently implies a commitment to the idea that there is a biologically given human nature, while many of the writers in this tradition recognize that our gendered identities are socially constructed, not biologically given. However, this does not affect the fact that the dichotomy tends to result in a debate within which gynocentric feminists criticize humanist feminists for adopting conceptions of human nature which are implicitly masculine, while humanist feminists argue that the notion of difference is dangerous, because any understanding that we now have of a gynocentric point of view is inevitably infected by patriarchal characterizations of the feminine which may in turn be grounded in biological explanations of woman's inferiority.[53]

There are a number of difficulties with this way of opposing feminism to humanism, the first of which emerges once one recognizes that both answers to the question 'Is there a single human nature, the same in both sexes?' can be given a feminist or an anti-feminist slant. This is most obvious in the case of writers who emphasize the differences between the male and female nature. At one extreme we have Aristotle who makes women clearly inferior.[54] At the other, Mary Daly takes women to be superior.[55] In between there are those who attempt to articulate the troublesome notion of equality with difference. Among writers who have emphasized that men and women participate in a shared humanity, there are those who, like Plato, are rightly accused of having given a model of what it is to be a human being which is implicitly so masculine that it can only be attained by aberrant women.[56] Plato allows both women and men to be Guardians in his ideal society, but in order for the female Guardians to develop their human virtues fully they have to be liberated from all normal womanly activity, except child-birth. Other writers, particularly in the liberal tradition of Mary Wollstonecraft, Harriet Taylor and John Stuart Mill, begin with a concept of humanity which is less obviously male, but they too have been accused of implicitly taking men to be the norm.[57] It would also be theoretically possible for a humanist to espouse the existence of a single human nature, beginning with a model of humanity clearly drawn from women, and whilst I know of no writer who explicitly sets out to do this, it will be part of the enterprise of this book to demonstrate that traditional humanist feminists have, in fact, implicitly written in this way. Dichotomizing humanist and gynocentric theories leads to a discussion within which views about the sameness or difference between the sexes become central to distinguishing true feminism from false rivals. Yet, because there are anti-feminists of both persuasions, the discussion is liable to trap us in an impasse. A more complex categorization of the issues at stake therefore appears worthwhile.

Those who emphasize the equality of the sexes nevertheless implicitly recognize that there are some sexual differences which should be taken into account by society. And those who emphasize difference usually recognize some similarities between the sexes and ways in which they should be treated equally. It is therefore more fruitful to avoid speaking as though we should expect a single, clear-cut distinction between 'humanist' and 'gynocentric' points of view.[58] Indeed, the interesting question may be not whether men and women are equally human, for clearly they are, nor whether there are essential differences between them, for clearly there are at least the gross and apparent differences in reproductive physiology. The more important question concerns the implications that the differences between the sexes have for our notion of the just society, for political theory and for philosophy and epistemology in general. Questions of difference become more complex, when we move from the perspective of dealing within a theory with perceived differences between the sexes, to questions of differences in theoretical outlook between the sexes; but even here, what it seems most reasonable to expect are elements of similarity and of difference.

It is perhaps worthwhile emphasizing this point by making some obvious remarks, which are sometimes overlooked, about the logic of the words 'same' and 'different'. When we ask the question 'Is this the same as that?' we are sometimes asking a question about identity, but more often we are asking whether two non-identical things are equal or equivalent in some respect, for instance in value, colour, weight or beauty. To ask whether they are different is also usually to ask whether they are different in some particular respect, made clear by the context. This implies that there is no single answer to the unmodified question 'Are men and women the same?' They surely are equal in intrinsic value; or at least, it must be constitutive of feminism that women are of equal, or greater, value than men, but this may be compatible with their being different in character, in conception of the good life, and even in the way they conceive of themselves and their relationship to the world.[59]

'Humanism', as I am using the term, has two elements. One is epistemological and accepts that human faculties are capable of discovering some truths, particularly truths about what is better or worse for humans. I am not going to argue directly here for such 'representationalist' views. However, I hope to demonstrate that accepting them does not imply any commitment to a theory of human nature which is implicitly masculine, and to indicate why the price of rejecting them is too high. The other element of humanism involves the acceptance that there is a shared human nature which constrains what is to be judged as a good life. Once again, this is very broad and could, but need not, involve biological theories of human nature, rationalist conceptions which conceive of humans as essentially disembodied minds, the existentialist view which sees us as human only to the extent that we are free, or Marxist conceptions according to which our nature is determined by the material conditions of the historical moment. The conception of human nature which, I will argue, emerges from the feminist tradition is different from any of these. It is a conception of humans as self-conscious, social, rational and passionate beings who are both constrained by biology and circumstance and ethically responsible. The human self which emerges from the writings of feminist humanists is not the same self that emerges from the writings of male humanists, nor is she a completely different being. She is rational but also thoroughly aware of herself as an embodied and emotional being. The next chapter will begin to explore her preoccupations and conception of her own humanity as they are articulated in the writing of Christine de Pisan.

2

Women of Virtù

It is significant that the first feminist book we know of was written at the very dawn of the humanist period. Christine de Pisan, author of *The Book of the City of Ladies*, written in 1405, makes it clear from the outset that she writes as a female humanist, who aims to show that women can exercise all the quantities assigned to the man of *virtù*. She begins her defence of women, against the near universal misogyny of medieval authorities, by remarking that for many years she was puzzled by the discrepancy between the evidence available to her, as a natural woman, and the testimony of notable men. Since so many famous men could not be wrong she had been led to accept their assessment of women, distrusting her own intellect and relying on the judgement of others, rather than on what she herself felt and knew.[1] This account is probably historically accurate, for in her poem, *Le Livre de la Mutation de Fortune*, she describes herself as having been changed by fortune into a man.[2] This suggests that, at the time of writing this work, she accepted that only a woman 'turned man' could write a poem worth reading. Her purpose in *The Book of the City of Ladies* is, by contrast, to establish that women are, of their own nature, as virtuous and capable as men. Here, Reason, Rectitude and Justice come to guide her and exhort her to construct the city of ladies, within which women will be fortified against the slanders of men.

Deftly, she establishes that, from the humanist stance, her own educated reason is as good a guide to truth as any other. Women are not denatured by excelling in the pursuit of reason. She would, after all, be denying humanism were she to believe the classical authorities rather than Reason. And she drives home her right to speak by pointing out that one should not have absolute faith in philosophers who contradict each other.[3]

Christine de Pisan was born in 1365, in Venice. Her father was a doctor, who had been educated at the University of Bologna. While Christine was a child he was invited to take up a post with Charles V in Paris, and hence Christine moved there and spent the rest of her life in France. Though, as she relates in *The Book of the City of Ladies*, she had been given a fuller education in the sciences than was usual for a woman of her time, she would probably never have taken up serious writing but for the fact that, at the age of 25, her father being already dead, she found herself widowed with at least two children. She therefore turned, possibly first to copying, and then to writing as a means of making her living.[4] Her work is specially significant for feminism for two reasons: it demonstrates how easily humanism, when pursued by a woman, becomes feminism; and in her writing de Pisan eloquently develops a view of women, love, sexuality and their place in the world which, imbued with a stoical Christianity, arguably corresponds closely to the self-assessment of many generations of Christian women.

The Book of the City of Ladies and its sequel *The Treasure of the City of Ladies* are the culmination of a series of works on women and the way they are portrayed in literature, which began with de Pisan's criticism of the courtly poem *The Romance of the Rose*. This poem is the work of two authors, Guillaume de Lorris and Jean de Meun. It is the later additions, by Jean de Meun, which offended de Pisan. In the poem, the Lover, enslaved by the God of Love and overwhelmed by an all-consuming passion for the Rose, discourses with Reason, a Friend, a Duenna, Nature and Genius, among others, who elaborate, in their own specific ways, their views on the subject of love and illicit sex. Reason exhorts the Lover to give up his irrational sensual folly and to replace his desire for the Rose with a higher love, friendship.[5] According to Reason, carnal love and fortune are false friends; she advises the Lover to become, like Socrates, a lover of wisdom.[6] She develops the worth of this rational higher love by arguing that it is more valuable than justice. For if there were universal love there would be no need of justice, whereas justice without love would be destructive.[7]

Jean de Meun's Lover, however, rejects Reason's advice, arguing that she has discredited herself by using lewd words. She has used the word 'cullions' (testicles) in relating a story about the introduction of love to the world. Reason defends her language by pointing out that these words refer to things that God has made. The evil in the word must derive from the thing named, since it is not intrinsic to any word, but since the thing was made by God, neither it nor the word can be bad. The Lover then requests Reason not to censure *him* and turns his attention to the advice of his Friend, who most helpfully describes the strategies he might use to satisfy his desire.[8] The point of this exchange is that since Reason cannot deny that God made our sexual organs, there can be nothing wrong with pursuing the path dictated by them. De Meun partly obscures his intentions by making it unclear which of the opinions voiced in the poem he endorses. But there is much therein to substantiate de Pisan's charge that the poem is an incitement to illicit love. In fact the last few pages in which the conquest of the Rose is described fall not far short of pornography.[9]

Earlier on, the Lover's Friend has put it to the Lover that he should use all the means at his disposal – bribes, gifts, lies – to get what he desires. He urges the time-worn claim that a bit of force will be justified; for women really want sex, though they do not like to admit to it:

> Lay hands upon your Rose with might and main;
> And prove yourself a man when with the time
> The place and the occasion both agree.
> Nothing, perhaps, will please them more than force
> Employed by one who understands its use.
> There's many a one whose nature's so perverse
> That what she dares not give she'll yield to strength
> And feign that what she would permit and wish
> Has ravished from her been against her will.[10]

And it seems the Lover has taken the Friend's advice, for at the end of the poem he notes, having spilt his seed at the centre of the bud, that:

> Of course she did remind me of my pledge
> And say I was outrageous in demands,
> And that I had done what I should not have done;
> But, ne'ertheless she never did forbid
> That I should seize and strip and quite deflower
> Both trunk and limbs of every leaf and bloom.[11]

The naturalness of heterosexual sex is argued for by Genius in his exhortation to fecundity.[12] And infidelity is promoted by the Duenna, with arguments that almost have a modern ring:

> Women are freeborn; they've restricted been
> By law, that takes away the liberty
> That Nature gave them. Nature's not so fond,

> As we should see if her intent we scanned,
> That Margot she would bring into the world
> Solely for Robichon, nor Robichon
> Solely for Agnes, Margot or Perette.
> Rather, fair son, we're made, beyond all doubt,
> All women for all men, and all the men
> For all the women interchangeably.[13]

The poem in long and rambling fashion unfolds, in the build-up to the seduction, the faults and foibles of women and of men in love. Along the path to the conquest of the Rose there are scattered many passages which express conventional, misogynistic claims of the type that are repeated to this day. The Jealous Husband rails against his wife, calling her 'foul woman, ribald hussy, lecherous bitch', and exclaims:

> All women are, have been, and ere will be,
> In thought if not in deed, unvirtuous;
> Though some may hesitate to do the act,
> None can restrain their wish. All women have
> This great advantage: they their purpose hold.[14]

Ultimately, Nature aids the Lover to gain his prize, and the overall impression of the poem is that women are by nature sexual, devious and lascivious, so men should be encouraged in their pursuit of the delights of carnal love.

The notion that woman is particularly carnal and dominated by sex was hardly unusual in the Middle Ages, or later. But de Meun's apparent advocacy of illicit love was. Indeed, it is likely that de Meun left his intentions unclear in order not to offend the conventions of his time. De Pisan's objections to the work are twofold. First, like Ovid's *Art of Love*, it is really a treatise on how to seduce women without being trapped by them into marriage.[15] Secondly, women are vilified and consequently marriage is depicted, when it is discussed, as a terrible state in which men are cuckolded by greedy wives, who use their husband's fortunes to adorn themselves, or who entice their husbands to reveal their deepest secrets in order to be able to blackmail them into obedience.[16] Even in one of the passages most complimentary to women, an account of the relationship between Abélard and Héloïse, the point is to demonstrate the unhappiness that marriage brings.[17] In the letters which make up her contribution to the Quarrel of the Rose, de Pisan argues against contemporary defenders of the poem, who contend that the work is meant merely to describe rather than endorse immoral behaviour, that it really is immoral and unjust to women. Here she first expresses a number of ideas which recur in her longer works.

The attitude that de Pisan evinces towards profane love is worth examining in detail, for like many feminists since, she was extremely suspicious of masculine sexuality. Love, in the philosophical tradition, comes in three forms. There is sexual or profane love, Christian love, as epitomized in the injunction to love one's neighbour as oneself, and Platonic love of wisdom. Within the medieval Christian tradition, Christian love and Platonic love had fused, following the lead of St Augustine, who argued that the Platonic Good is virtually identical to the Christian God.[18] Platonic love of wisdom is a desire for knowledge of the Good, while Christian love is grounded in the desire for knowledge of God. Knowledge of God is knowledge of his love for all and hence of the injunction to love others as oneself, as he does. In de Meun's poem, Christian love is advocated by Reason, but Reason's words are discredited, and instead carnal, profane love wins out. De Pisan, by contrast, advocates in all her writings chastity and adherence to Christian love. By chastity she means abstinence outside marriage and fidelity within it. Chastity is the manifestation of Christian love within marriage, but the importance of Christian love is much wider than this, for she sees it as an ideal which if it is adhered to brings peace and stability to society, binding wife to husband, servant to master, subject to king.

De Pisan's counter-text to the *Romance of the Rose* is her *Duke of True Lovers*, in which a young nobleman falls in love with his 'cousin', who is already married to a domineering and suspicious husband. As a true lover, he has no desire to act in any way which would dishonour his beloved, but only to enjoy her company. Ultimately, even this is not possible, since it is impossible for the lady to preserve her honour and to remain above suspicion while seeing her beloved. Her former companion writes to her in the same vein as the governess who advises the wayward princess in *The Treasure of the City of Ladies*, pointing out that as a princess she has a duty to act in such a way that there can be no question as to the legitimacy of her heirs, that she should recognize that her behaviour might be spoken of in foreign lands, bringing ill-repute to her country, and that it provides a bad example to her inferiors. The lover, being true, has no desire to act in such a way as to harm his beloved, so accepts the restraint on his freedom to see her, and lives out his desire by increasing his fame and worth so that his lady might hold herself loved of a brave man.[19]

In *The City of God* St Augustine had argued that since God created nature, nature is good.[20] Evil is the result not of God's creation but of human free will, and evil is, by this reasoning, unnatural. Sex within marriage is therefore not intrinsically evil, and would have occurred as the natural means of procreation even in paradise. Yet, since the Fall, sex has been associated with lust, which is evil.[21] De Meun adopts the idea, orthodox since at least St Augustine's time, that nature is good, but puts it to new use, arguing that our natural tendency to promiscuity is also good. The naive naturalism pursued by de Meun has become more and more influential in the centuries since he wrote, and is one of the bases for the contemporary sexual revolution. But it is interesting to note that it is only valid if it is assumed that nature is the creation of a good God. If nature is construed naturalistically, then it is intrinsically neither good nor evil, since there is natural evil as well as natural good. De Pisan, like de Meun, echoes St Augustine's view that what is natural is good, and in particular 'the great love which, through the will of God, Nature places between a man and a woman' is good, so men who attack women are unnatural and corrupt.[22] But she disagrees that promiscuity is natural, claiming that a woman is by nature 'decent, mild and modest'.[23]

Yet de Pisan does not let her defence of chaste, Christian love rest with its naturalness. Rather, she argues for its value on prudential grounds. *The Treasure of the City of Ladies* contains seven principal teachings of Prudence, which amount to the teaching that it is in a woman's best interest to be patient, loving, self-controlled and generous, for through the intelligent exercise of these virtues she will give others no justification for harming her.[24] This is not a philosophy that applies only to wives. Ladies of the court are advised to love their mistresses,[25] and princes as well as princesses are advised to behave in a way which will lead their subjects to love them. De Pisan's views concerning the importance of the Christian virtues of clemency, pity, charity and love were of particular relevance in her time, when, as she judged the situation, the venality and lack of wisdom of Queen Isabella were abetting the dangerous rivalry between the French barons that ultimately led to the humiliation of an uncrowned Dauphin and the tragedy of civil war. In her 'Epistle to the Queen of France', written in 1405, she exhorts Queen Isabella to follow other wise queens, and, through the forces of conciliation, charity and love, to avert the impending crisis. In general she attaches particular importance to the role of queens and princesses as mediators within the court who can achieve a great deal towards maintaining the peace.[26]

According to Jean de Meun, love is a natural passion opposed by reason and cultural constraint and associated with the venal feminine. This series of oppositions occurs frequently in western philosophy.

Nature is opposed to culture, passion to reason, the feminine to the masculine, the heart to the mind. Indeed, it been argued that western notions of reason have been constructed in opposition to the feminine and that femininity itself has been partly constituted through a process of exclusion of reason.[27] It is noteworthy that de Pisan does not recognize these oppositions. For her, Christian love is a rational passion to be contrasted with false, venal love. Love of the good is a natural inclination, which reason dictates should be fostered for the sake of peace and social harmony. And women, partly because of their lack of strength, show a particular and laudable propensity to act in accordance with the dictates of this rational passion and to be peace-makers and conciliators.[28]

The Book of the City of Ladies draws together all the threads of the defence of women that were inspired by de Pisan's reaction to *The Romance of the Rose*. In it she sets out to defend women against all unjust allegations and to demonstrate, from the works of the ancients and from more recent history, how women are virtuous and chaste and have nobly served men as wives.[29] She begins by refuting the best-known medieval arguments for the inferiority of women.[30] First she mentions the widespread view (which can be traced back to Aristotle) that women are created in the womb when there is weakness, so that women are deformed or at least not fully formed men.[31] She refutes this by pointing out that since God created the body of woman it cannot be a deformed thing. Rather, it was created out of the same substance as man's body in the terrestrial paradise. Moreover, in so far as man was created in God's image, so too was woman, since it is the soul that is in God's image, and this is the same in both men and women. Here she has in mind those writers who denied that woman was created in God's image in the same sense as man.[32] She argues that the value of a person has nothing to do with the sex of their body; rather, it stems from their virtue. So a woman is better than a man when she is more virtuous and the man of greater value when he is the more virtuous. Next she deals with a conventional challenge to this, which would make woman inferior due to Eve's sin. She argues that taken together the sin of Eve and the immaculate conception of Mary have led to God's becoming man. This event, which could not have come about without women, is one of which men and women should be glad.

In calling her book *The Book of the City of Ladies*, de Pisan surely intends her readers to recall St Augustine's *The City of God* and to avail herself of the support of his authority for men's and women's spiritual equality.[33] She refers to him in reverent tones, pointing out that it was his mother's tears which converted him to Christianity.[34] She might equally have quoted his declaration that 'A woman's sex is not a defect, it is natural' in support for her claim that woman is not a defective man.[35] In the final pages of her work she equates the City of Ladies with the City of God, making clear her intention of establishing that the production of virtuous women is as much God's divine intention and the end of a good community as is the production of virtuous men. She elaborates her view thus:

> The common good of a city or land or any community of people is nothing other than the profit or general good in which all members, women as well as men, participate and take part . . . There is not the slightest doubt that women belong to the people of God and the human race as much as men, and are not another species or dissimilar race, for which they should be excluded from moral teachings.[36]

The bulk of *The Book of the City of Ladies* is filled with examples drawn from the ancients, and from more recent history, to show that women are capable of exercising all the virtues which common opinion denies them. She begins with examples of wise female rulers, women who have been strong warriors and women of great learning. Then she turns to the arts and skills that women, according to mythical tradition, have introduced to the world, and argues that natural prudence is as common among women as among men, giving a number of examples. She considers those writers who have deplored the state of marriage because of the evil of women, and refutes them by relating examples of woman's strength and constancy in love. She introduces the stories of Portia and Curia as counter-examples to Jean de Meun's charge that women cannot be trusted with secrets. Then she deals with examples of women who have given their husbands good advice and have brought about great good for their people and for society, and in this context she urges the value of education for women, giving herself as an example. The slander that all women are unchaste and that they really want to be raped is denied, as is the claim that women are inconstant. Here she alters her method, giving the examples of Nero and Claudius to demonstrate the even greater inconstancy of men, rather than only referring to admirable women. She completes her work, the roofs and towers of the City, with stories of women martyrs and saints, concluding with the example of the Virgin Mary, who presides over all.

There are elements of de Pisan's philosophy, however, which are not congenial to modern feminists; in particular, her devout Christianity and her strong defence of the holy estate of marriage, which is typified by

the concluding remark of *The Book of the City of Ladies*: 'And you ladies
who are married, do not scorn being subject to your husbands, for
sometimes it is not the best thing for a creature to be independent.'[37]
This is a theme which is taken up at greater length in *The Treasure of
the City of Ladies*, and Mathilde Laigle, who wrote the first scholarly
study of this book, argues on the basis of such comments that it is
a mistake to deem de Pisan a feminist at all.[38] More recently Sheila
Delany has endorsed this dismissal of de Pisan's claim to be a feminist,
although she notes the similarity between her views and those of contemporary feminist critics of pornography.[39] However, given the very
broad definition of feminism that I have introduced, de Pisan is clearly
a feminist. Her starting point, the way in which women are treated in
literature as mere objects of desire to be conquered, makes her an early
precursor of Kate Millett, and her aim is clearly the amelioration of
woman's reputation and position. The incompatibility between her views
and modern notions of women's rights within marriage stems rather from
fundamentally different notions about the nature of the good society. In
particular, she can be read as implicitly defending the view that a just
'patriarchy', in which those in authority have responsibilities of a parental kind for those with less power, is compatible with woman's interests.

The conception of the nature of the good society that de Pisan accepts
stems from her reading of the ancient and medieval authorities. Among
these St Augustine, Aristotle and Boethius clearly played a significant
part. Her Justice, who 'dispenses according to each man's just deserts',
echoes Plato's statement that justice is 'to give every man his due'.[40] Yet
it seems unlikely that de Pisan had read Plato's text, since had she done
so she would have had something to say about his thoughts on the
family. Moreover, in *Le Livre du Corps de Policie* she attributes to
Aristotle the view that justice is a measure which gives each his due.[41]
Plato develops this idea in such a way as to end up with a definition
of the just state as one in which all persons perform the function that
suits them best, and see this as compatible with women ruling.[42] De
Pisan develops this line of reasoning in a way more reminiscent of Aristotle in order to explain why women do not hold the same positions of
authority as men.[43] And in regard to the institution of marriage, she is
also more in accord with Aristotle and St Augustine than with Plato.
Like them she sees marriage as natural, and she implicitly goes further
and deems it an institution which is to the benefit of women. This is not
to say that she idealizes marriage; she recognizes that there are bad
husbands and describes the situation of women 'who because of their
husband's harshness live in the bond of marriage in greater suffering than

if they were slaves among the Saracens'.[44] But she sees the position of wife as one which brings with it duties which can be fulfilled with excellence and which is compatible with a happy and virtuous life. Though husbands may be lacking in virtue and fail to fulfil their duties, this should be seen as analogous to the case of kings who fail their subjects. For de Pisan, the evil of others is not a justification for failing to act righteously oneself. Here the influence of Boethius, which she reports elsewhere, is manifest.[45] Her morality is first and foremost concerned with personal virtue and salvation, and this is incompatible with rebellion against God's institutions. Just as monarchy is in her eyes a good institution which can be perverted when monarchs fail in their duty to govern their subjects wisely, so too marriage is a potentially good institution, which may be perverted by evil men. She advocates for women the benefits of performing well the duties of a wife, no matter what the faults of their husbands, but at the same time argues that princes should make themselves loved by their subjects, implying that the best way for a husband to secure his wife's loyalty is through kindness and taking note of her advice.[46]

One might develop de Pisan's point by distinguishing virtue from the virtues. Virtue is consciously doing what is right, whereas virtues are certain kinds of disposition which are prima facie conducive to doing what is right. We consider courage, sympathy, patience, even-temperedness and intelligence to be virtues, but, as this list should make clear, many virtues are appropriately exercised only in certain contexts. Sympathy is inappropriate when it leads one to protect dangerous criminals, courage is useless when one is confronted by the needs of a whining child. Which virtues are appropriate depends largely on the social situation one is in. Obedience is a virtue in children but a vice in adults who obey the orders of wicked superiors. De Pisan's point can then be put in the following way: since the natural function of women differs from that of men, and since this implies different social roles, women and men can be equally virtuous through the pursuit of different virtues. It is not always best to be independent, and the virtues that can be exercised by a loyal subject are as important as the virtues that can be exercised by a prince.[47]

'Patriarchy', as Kate Millett uses the term, refers to the rule of women by men, and this usage has become widespread. But 'patriarchy' in its original sense referred to the rule of fathers over their sons, daughters, wives and other members of the household. The society within which de Pisan lived was thoroughly patriarchal. Political authority was thought of as analogous to parental authority, and people at all levels of society were taken to have duties to those either above or below them, which were similar to the duties of children to parents or of parents to children. Though women were subject to their husbands, as the people were subject to the monarch, women were also subject to certain women above them in the social hierarchy. Indeed, the hierarchy of men was mirrored by a complementary hierarchy of women. Daughters were subject to mothers, servants to their mistresses, mistresses to queens. Moreover, men of lower estate were subject to women. Included in the advice to women in *The Treasure of the City of Ladies* are directions to women on the management of their estates, and to baronesses on the defence of their lands.[48] A woman of noble degree had to know how to fulfil her duty as subject to her husband, but she also needed to be able to fill his place as ruler of their estate in his absence.[49] Thus, although married women were subject to their husbands, and husbands were chosen for girls by their parents, women were by no means powerless. Women of high social position had significant power over those below them in the social hierarchy, and the wise running of a kingdom or estate depended almost as much on the influence of the queen or mistress as on that of the king or master.

Little in the literature of her time tended towards the criticism of such social institutions, and in this sense de Pisan is a creature of her age. At the same time one can find in her work, given this context, a plausible defence of marriage. Her own experience was one of a happy arranged marriage in which she was financially and emotionally secure, followed by many difficult years fending for herself as a poor widow. Thus she had no doubt that marriage was an institution within which women could be happy. Although she does not object to the right of husbands to rule their wives, it is clear that she conceives of a good husband as like a good king, one who consults with his subjects and leaves them free to do what they think best, so long as they do no wrong. She advocates an education that will enable women to be truly active partners in marriage and insists that a woman should acquaint herself with her husband's business and the running of his estates, not only so as to be able to manage them well during his absence, but also in order to be able to defend her rights should she be widowed.

In speaking to widowed ladies, de Pisan makes it clear that she does not take marriage to be unalloyed bliss and she does not recommend remarriage as the obvious solution to a widow's problems. For a young woman, she admits, it may be necessary, or at least very convenient.[50] Older women, she implies, ought to have the self-confidence to trust in their own intelligence and certainly not make fools of themselves by

marrying young men. Her aside concerning younger women suggests
that she well recognizes the sexuality of young women, and sees marriage
as necessary in order to provide a secure environment for child-birth and
the care of children. In discussing the prejudice which makes parents
welcome the birth of a son over that of a daughter, she acknowledges
the widespread fear that daughters will be deceived while young and get
themselves into trouble, while arguing that if they are properly brought
up they are as likely to be of benefit to their parents as are sons.[51] And
in relating the story of Ghismonda she shows some sympathy for the
plight of a young woman prevented by her father's possessiveness from
marrying.[52] The necessity of marriage for young women lies, then, in
the fact that the majority of young women, like the majority of young
men, are sexual beings, and marriage provides an environment within
which children can be legitimately fathered and properly nurtured.

For de Pisan women are as intrinsically valuable as men, so if one is
to make the aim of the good society the production of good people, the
production of good women is as important as that of good men. At the
same time she accepts an interpretation of the nature of the good life
which appears heavily indebted to Boethius, whose *Consolations*, she
reports, led her to recognize that nothing is truly good except virtue; the
only thing that can never be taken away by fortune.[53] Virtue is individual and pertains to the soul. It can be attained in any position of society
and consists in the exercise of general virtues such as truthfulness,
chastity, charity and courage and in the fulfilment of the duties peculiar
to one's station.

The institution of marriage is therefore not incompatible with the production of women of *virtù*, as the tales of *The Book of the City of Ladies*
demonstrate. But the distorted image of themselves that is held up to
women by men discourages women from seeing themselves as valuable.
It is used to rationalize men's attempts to seduce them from the path of
virtue, and it justifies the neglect of women's education which prevents
women from fully developing their potential and enables the myth of
female inferiority to be perpetuated. It is therefore by the practice of virtue and self-improvement that de Pisan urges women to defend their
place in society.

As has already been indicated, de Pisan is no social radical; indeed,
she is rather the opposite, deploring the introduction of new liberties in
dress which allow rich merchants' wives to wear ladies' gowns, and suggesting the revival of restrained and Christian court manners.[54] Delany
sees this conservatism, so evident in de Pisan's reaction to the Caboche
rebellion, as further indication that de Pisan was no feminist.[55] But to

do this is to wed feminism to current socialist theory, and to foreclose too quickly the possibility of seeing her as a serious feminist. She wrote in opposition to the new and radical way of thinking that was implicit in de Meun's poem, and which ultimately led to the triumph of naturalism and the sexual revolution, because she thought that it undermined individuals' sense of their moral duty. She was against rule by the people because she saw authority as bringing with it moral responsibility and as requiring wisdom. Yet there are also seeds of radicalism in her thought, which took a number of centuries to germinate. If, as she claims, women are as much ends in themselves as men, wherein lies the justification of their subjection to their husbands? It was not until the eighteenth century that this question was widely discussed, but it stands out as a problem, as de Pisan is at least partly aware, and she answers it in a way that is quite unsatisfactory. In particular, when husbands are bad men and their wives virtuous, why should not women rebel? Her response to this is that prudence dictates the appropriate obedience even to a bad man, since he might otherwise throw his wife out, ruining and shaming her and leaving her worse off. Moreover, a consistent and public show of wifely devotion is most likely to bring the husband around to appreciating her worth.[56] These are counsels directed at women whose livelihoods depend on the good graces of their husbands, and whose honour depends on their being seen to be chaste. But they do nothing to answer the humanist who is seriously questioning the justification of this economic dependence, sexual constraint and the subjection that goes with it. Furthermore, the position de Pisan advocates is unstable. What she demands is equality of respect for women without equality of power. Yet it is plausible that the lack of respect which men show women in their writings is part of the mechanism for maintaining the subordination of women. Those who have power will quickly attempt to justify the subordination of others through claims of superiority. And those who do not have the power to command respect are likely to get mere chivalrous deference rather than the real thing.

Nevertheless, in her defence of women de Pisan marshals many of the arguments put forward by later authors. And she expresses an outlook which remained influential for many centuries. Mary Poovey argues that as late as the eighteenth century women understood their duty to fulfil their place in society as providing a model of the proper relationship of subordination to social superiors and ultimately to the will of God.[57] And de Pisan also sees woman's virtue as exemplary. Women are men's equals or superiors in virtue and in spiritual value, yet have an appropriate role to play as wives who are rightly subject to the authority of their husbands. Chastity and fidelity are central to woman's virtue, and men's sexual advances are among the greatest dangers to her honour. Women's interests are best served by the imposition of sexual restraint on men, but this is only to be acquired by an even greater regard for sexual propriety on the part of women. Since the enormous influence of Engels's *The Origin of the Family, Private Property and the State*, it has been usual for feminists to interpret chastity as a virtue imposed on women by men in order to ensure the legitimacy of their offspring. But chastity and modesty are also values which have been constantly extolled by women for both women and men. De Beauvoir, developing Engels's views, takes this as evidence that women have internalized men's view of themselves as mere objects whose end is to make themselves as attractive as possible to men. But this is surely not de Pisan's thinking. She is centrally interested in women as moral subjects and extols the life of contemplation as the highest life, but she also recognizes that most women will be moral subjects living with the realities of sexual desire, pregnancy and the need to make ends meet.[58] In such circumstances an emphasis on woman's right to chastity and on men's obligation to enter into a contract to care for wife and children before having sexual relations is in accord with women's interests, whether those interests are to be left free from sexual molestation or to enter into sexual relations. The case of Christine de Pisan, who is by no means unrepresentative of women's views, suggests that the explanation for the persistence of patriarchal marriage over time and through cultures lies, at least partly, in the fact that within it woman's desire for the security of her offspring, and man's desire to have offspring that he knows are his own, converge.

This view is likely to be resisted by some feminists, for it suggests woman's complicity in the construction of the patriarchal family and possibly in the capitalist societies which have been founded on it. In many ways it is much more comfortable to accept the analysis offered by Engels and de Beauvoir, according to which women have been mere pawns in a historical development of class struggle played out by men. But the cost of this interpretation is that women are denied any understanding of the development of their own historical consciousness. Instead, I take the view that de Pisan's political philosophy and her attitude towards sex and marriage form a coherent whole. Political society is thought of as an organic whole. The prince is the head, and the moral and material welfare of the body depend on his virtue.[59] The obligation of princes to their people is characterized in terms of the

model of parental obligation. Here I use 'parental' advisedly, for in contrast to that of male writers in the patriarchal tradition, there are
interesting maternalist elements in de Pisan's thought. Like a mother, the
good prince is responsible for the moral welfare of his subjects and has
a duty to act as a moral exemplar to them. In contrast to Machiavelli,
who answers the question 'Is it better for a prince to be loved or feared
by his people?' in favour of fear, de Pisan advises the princess that it
is the love of her subjects which is her surest protection and which she
should work to deserve.[60] This has interesting connections with her
advice to the governess of a young princess, who, she suggests, will have
more success in extracting obedience from her charge if she has won her
love than by any harsh measures of punishment. De Pisan's enlightened
views on education are plausibly seen as deriving from practical traditions of child-rearing, and are extended in the sphere of government to
the status of a general principle; that subjects will be more strongly
motivated to please and obey rulers whom they love and respect than
those they fear and despise.[61] Within a good family, the position of
child is not more onerous than that position of parent. Though the child
owes its parents obedience, it is free of the responsibilities that go with
parental power. The more power that individuals have, the greater their
responsibility for the moral and material welfare of those within their
charge, and it is in the light of these views that de Pisan can both be
considered a feminist and consistently judge that women should not
scorn their lack of independence.

The central problem for feminist politics is that the maternalist ethic,
which is plausibly found in de Pisan's writing, can easily transform into
a quietist acceptance of virtuous subordination when it is pursued by
those who lack power. While from the ethical point of view it may be
exemplary, from the political point of view it is impotent in the face of
ruthlessness. Feminism requires that women are equal not just in the
respect offered them, but also in the power they wield, for without equal
power respect is in jeopardy. Yet, since power is a prerogative of certain
powerful groups, and is often upheld in opposition to what is ethical,
the acquisition of power seems to require the abandonment of feminine
virtue. This dilemma was, perhaps, not so evident in de Pisan's day, in
which the hereditary power of princes and princessess was, like the
power of parents, conferred by birth. But in a society in which power
is the result of success in competition for power, de Pisan's advice seems
to condemn the virtuous woman to powerlessness. Yet perhaps it is
unfair to extrapolate, since modern liberal notions of the state differ

radically from the medieval ideas which guided de Pisan. In the next
chapter we will turn to the origins of these modern notions in the writing
of Hobbes.

By contrasting de Pisan's thoughts on political authority with those
of Hobbes we will be led to articulate more clearly a central difference
between her understanding of reason and that which comes down to us
from Hobbes. De Pisan extends a familial model of maternal authority
from the private realm to the public realm of princesses and princes
(though this way of putting it is anachronistic, since no sharp distinction
between the public and private realms is recognized by her). Hobbes by
contrast extends his model of civil society, as based on contract and
upheld by force, from the public realm of relations between men to the
private realm of the family. De Pisan's political thought thus can be considered to contain an early description of what Virginia Held has called
a 'non-contractual society'.[62] Interestingly, just as Held believes that a
non-contractual conception of society would take the mother–child relationship as a paradigm, it is arguable that de Pisan's ideas on the responsibility accruing to those in power for the moral and material wellbeing
of those with less power is an extension of the presuppositions of
motherhood. Her experience as a mother perhaps also lies behind her
understanding of moral psychology and her emphasis, both at the level
of parents with children, and at the level of princes and subjects, on the
responsibility of those in power for the development of the ethical
attitudes of others. It is here that one of the central differences between
de Pisan and Hobbes emerges. As I have already mentioned, she
accepted a version of a Christian Platonic moral psychology in which
we have a natural disposition to love the good. However, this disposition has to be fostered in childhood, and she is aware that it is by kind
treatment, through coming to love others and through example that the
tendency to desire to do good is developed. She thus accepts that there
is a moral inclination, or love of the good, which is part of human
nature, and she presupposes that part of the reproduction of the good
society lies in the fostering of such moral sentiments. Hobbes, by contrast, rejects all talk of natural ethical motivation and argues that the
motivation for ethical action is no more than prudential self-interest.
This difference in their thought is linked to another. For de Pisan there
is little difference between the relationship between mother and child,
husband and wife, lover and beloved and that between prince and subject. Sexual relations and political relations are seen as equally both
political and ethical. The same virtues are advocated in these different
realms – centrally, self-restraint and the exercise of one's obligations to

others – and the same rewards are offered for the exercise of these virtues; knowledge of one's own virtue, salvation and the love and respect of others. Hobbes, as we will see, also equates parental and political relations, but for him the ethical is submerged by the political in a manner which is ultimately untenable.

3

Hobbes, Amazons and Sabine Women

Hobbes is often claimed to be the originator of the modern social contract tradition, but this is in some ways misleading. The idea of the social contract can be found in much earlier writers, including Christine de Pisan.[1] What is distinctive about Hobbes's treatment of the subject is that, impressed by the scientific advances of his time, he applied the scientific method of reasoning from experience and first principles to the question of the justification of political institutions. This led him to attempt to reduce moral truths to truths of reason, and to argue that morality is identical with rational self-interest. He began with the premise that by nature humans are equal and each equally interested first and foremost in the preservation of her or his own life and liberty.[2] Since people are equal and want the same things this leads to conflict, a war of each against all. Such a conflict is in no one's interest and it is for this reason that people contract with each other to be governed by one sovereign, either a monarch or an assembly, who will uphold civil laws and defend them against other nations. Like de Pisan, Hobbes was not a liberal and his aim was to justify the absolute authority of the sovereign.[3] Nevertheless, the method of reasoning from first principles that he made central to political philosophy became fundamental to Enlightenment political thought, and the development of social contract theory played an important part in the genesis of the French and American Revolutions. Later social contract theorists, such as Locke and Rousseau, argued that since sovereign power is justified by contract, the people must retain a right to renew or rescind that contract, thus paving the way for constitutional monarchy and modern representative democracy.

Hobbes's thought has played an important role in the feminist rejection of liberal humanism, for he epitomizes a version of rationalist humanism which has little time for the sentimental. In this chapter I will argue that the legitimate feminist rejection of the moral psychology which Hobbes develops does not show that all versions of social contract theory are defective. Hobbes's moral psychology is in fact independent of social contract theory, and it led him to develop an ultimately untenable argument for political and moral subjection. In some ways Hobbes is a transitional figure who, like the medieval Christine de Pisan, is interested in justifying political subjection to the monarch, rather than in asserting the sovereignty of the subject. The comparison of their views on moral and political subjection results in the hypothesis that at the heart of the perceived difference between masculine and feminine voices is a dispute over moral psychology. This will lead me, in chapters 5 and 8, to develop the possibility of a feminine, or 'maternalist', contractualism, which retains the insights into moral psychology that are typical of women theorists and combines them with the rational justification of political equality that is the legacy of the contractarian tradition.

Hobbes's method is to ask first what the nature of humankind is. Although Aristotle had also argued in this way, the conclusions that Hobbes draws are significantly different, for unlike his predecessor, Hobbes believes that humans are by nature equal. In particular humans are all equally possessed of reason, the desire to preserve their own life above all things, and the capacity to preserve it. The standard interpretation of his argument is that since the state of nature is a state of war, it is in the interests of individuals to enter into a social contract and give up their freedom in exchange for the protection which the state provides. Thus the existence of the state and its laws is justified in the light of the rational egoism of all humans. Reason leads to the recognition that the best way to preserve one's own life and goods is to submit to the power of a state that will protect them.[4]

Feminists have pointed out that the existence of women and children poses a number of difficulties for Hobbes's political views.[5] Yet unlike Aristotle, he does not deny that women are men's equals. Nor does he claim that marriage is natural. Indeed, with admirable consistency, Hobbes insists that in the state of nature men and women are equals and that any authority that husbands have over wives is the result of civil society. He points to the possibility of a society like that of the 'historical' Amazons, who, tradition alleges, contracted with a neighbouring tribe of men for intercourse and gave them any boy children who might be born, retaining exclusive control over their daughters.[6] In the state of nature, Hobbes argues, authority over children rests with mothers exclusively, for, without the social structures that ensure paternity, paternity cannot be proved, and 'since every man by law of nature, hath right or propriety to his own body, the child ought rather to be the propriety of the mother, of whose body it is part until the time of separation.'[7] Nevertheless, it is not generation but preservation which entitles the mother to dominion over her child, and should she expose it and it be brought up by some other, the right of dominion would pass to that other.[8] Having made these observations, Hobbes says nothing explicit regarding the justice of the usual relationship of husbands to wives in the society in which he lived. He observes merely that for the most part civil law gives dominion over children to the father because commonwealths have been erected by the fathers and not by the mothers of families.

Given that this is so, one is entitled to ask why it is the case. If Hobbes's premises were true and if society were founded on a social contract between equals, we would expect women to be among the contractors as well as men. Individual women are not, as Hobbes admits, necessarily weaker than individual men, and in any case, weak men as well as strong ones are party to the contract that founds society. It seems therefore that something must be missing from Hobbes's story.

A number of feminist critics of liberalism have suggested places where this account of the origin of society falls down. Many have objected to Hobbes's premises concerning human nature and in particular the claim that humans are rational egoists. Some have modified this claim by suggesting that only men are rational egoists and that consequently the view of human nature that Hobbes offers is distorted and purely masculine.[9] In defence of the first of these criticisms it can be pointed out that Hobbes's story is not borne out by anthropology. Before the creation of communities large enough to be considered states, with codified laws, rights to private ownership of land and recognized authorities for administering laws, people lived in tribal groups within which property was largely communal, and law was embodied in myth and tradition. Such egalitarian modes of social organization suggest that humans are naturally social beings with altruistic impulses, and this can be backed up by consideration of our pre-social ancestors. Many other primates live in social groups and are, at least in some measure, group altruists. They are prepared to aid other members of their own group, in particular their own offspring. Indeed, in order for infants to survive, mothers must be, at least partly, altruistic. So, it can be argued that Hobbes's assumption of universal rational egoism is not supported by the facts.[10]

It is not clear, however, that these observations by themselves take us very far as criticisms of Hobbes. Humans may not be total egoists, but they are not total altruists either. Although most people act altruistically towards some individuals, particularly their own children, friends and relations, many cannot be relied upon to extend this behaviour to a very wide group. If they could, there would be no need for laws and institutions to protect our rights. As Hobbes himself observed, in response to contemporary objections to his jaded assessment of human nature, we shut our doors when we go to sleep and defend our coasts, thus manifesting our belief that others will not necessarily treat us altruistically.[11] And, in fact, all that Hobbes needs to assume for the sake of his argument is that even if we are by nature reasonably altruistic to those who are close to us, by blood relationship, by proximity, or in virtue of some other trait that excites our sympathy, we place our own self-preservation very high among our interests, and, in general, it is over-riding.[12] At the end of this chapter I will return to the criticisms of Hobbes's moral psychology and develop the idea that the important axis along which feminist and masculinist characterizations of the rational individual can be distinguished concerns the relationship of human motives such as love and sympathy to reason. But to indicate that there is this difference in assumptions concerning moral psychology is not to have shown that one or other is better. In order to pave the way for rejecting Hobbes's characterization of human rationality and its relation to ethics, I will first show how his reasoning breaks down even given the weak characterization of his assumptions which makes them most plausible.

Another common and related criticism of Hobbes is that his premises are flawed because there never was a state of nature in which people lived as isolated individuals. One reading of Hobbes's story does suggest that he was committed to the implausible hypothesis that there once was such a state of nature, yet in other places he clearly thinks of it as populated by family groups, who exist in conflict with each other, and are brought together into a commonwealth by the social contract. This suggests the following development of the feminist critique of Hobbes. Either he accepts the unrealistic hypothesis that there was a state of nature in which humans lived as isolated atoms, or he must admit that the family constitutes the first society and that the family is held together by natural altruistic sentiments.[13]

Hobbes, however, can be read as having pre-empted this criticism and as having rejected it on the grounds that natural ties of affection are not sufficient to hold families together. He speaks of the families of 'the savage people in many places of America' being held together only by 'natural lust',[14] and also of there existing in the state of nature, 'the natural inclination of the sexes, one to another, and to their children'.[15] But, he says, such ties are weak and easily broken. The family must therefore be held together by a compact that reflects in miniature the compact that founds civil society.[16] Members of a family consent to the absolute authority of the family head in exchange for the protection provided by membership. Since children owe their lives to the protection and nurture of the one who has brought them up, who need not be a natural parent, that person has dominion over them derived from the child's consent, 'either express or by other sufficient arguments declared'.[17] So civil society depends on a two-stage process. Individuals come together in family groups which are, as a matter of fact, usually patriarchal, and then patriarchal family heads contract together to form a commonwealth. The state of nature that exists in an abstract and theoretical sense between individuals exists historically as a state of war between families and exists even now between nations.[18]

This two-stage interpretation of the development of society allows us to attribute to Hobbes the following explanation of the inequality of women in civil society. Commonwealths are set up by fathers, and civil society accords dominion to fathers because mothers are already subjugated within patriarchal families; and this seems to be close to the actual historical situation with regard to the formation of states.[19] But this only pushes back the apparent inconsistency a step. For how is it that fathers have obtained dominion over mothers and hence over their children? One answer might be that Hobbes is simply wrong about the natural equality of all individuals and that men and women are not equal in natural liberty.[20] Indeed Hobbes himself equivocates over the equality of men and women in the state of nature and at one place admits that the equality he has in mind is possessed by 'all men of riper years'.[21] This admission would be strengthened if one took into account the fact that, although an individual man may not be stronger or more able than an individual woman, women as a group are less strong than men. It is also plausible given the particular disadvantages women suffer because of pregnancy. Pregnancy is, at least to some extent, physically debilitating. Since the survival of infants depended, historically, on their being suckled by women, pregnancy meant that at any time some women would have infants in tow and would be disadvantaged in combat. Women wishing to preserve their infants' lives are likely to surrender in the face of a threat to their children, even if they could sacrifice the infant and then possibly vanquish their aggressors. And, because of the possibility of pregnancy, women are subject to a kind of attack, rape, that will have consequences for them different to any that a man will ever suffer. Pregnancy also has another consequence. So long as children are seen as an asset, women will be a valuable resource and so be treated as booty, rather than as enemies, in war. There is historical evidence that the first slaves were women captured in battle and spared the death that automatically awaited the men of their vanquished tribes.[22] The theft of women seems to be common to many societies, confirming that men have little motivation to kill women, and women have therefore little to gain by attempting to vanquish men. A development of Hobbes's reasoning along these lines is taken up by Rousseau.[23] Hobbes himself makes little explicit mention of the natural disadvantages that women face due to child-bearing, but they remain in the background of his account.

According to Hobbes, 'by right of nature, the conqueror is lord of the conquered.'[24] A conqueror acquires dominion over those of the vanquished who agree, in exchange for their lives, to obey him or her. These become his or her servants. Given the above differences between the sexes, it is plausible that men will be more likely to conquer women than women are to conquer men. So the Hobbesian conclusion will be that woman's subjection is grounded in the superior strength of men. Or more accurately, it is grounded in consent, obtained in circumstances where there is a choice between consent to obedience, in return for protection, or being killed or enslaved.

In her book *The Sexual Contract* Carole Pateman considers a Hobbesian story of this sort and argues that it is not consistent with Hobbes's general assumption that people are rational egoists. If choosing to care for infants puts women at a disadvantage, and all individuals are rational egoists, then women will not care for infants and so the first generation will be the last.[25] But this is too quick a rebuttal of the Hobbesian story. Hobbes's individuals are interested, first and foremost, in the preservation of their lives. In the face of conflict with a potential enemy there are always three options: to flee; or, if it is too late for that, to submit to the other party and contract into their service; or to fight to the point where either the other is vanquished (killed or submits) or one loses one's own life. If it comes to battle some women may take the first, some the second and some the third course. Since the children of those women who take the option of fighting to the death are less likely to be born, if the woman is childless, and more likely to die, if she has children, over time there will be more children who are brought up by those women who have accepted submission. Such women will be likely to argue that it is rational for women to submit, and, presumably, will educate their children in this wisdom. So the assumption that the first aim of all is self-preservation leads to the conclusion that, in the state of nature, the women whose children survive will tend to be those who are prepared to accept submission in order to increase their children's chances of survival, and who are in this sense reasonably altruistic, at least towards their own children.

More recently, Pateman seems to have given up her criticism of the cogency of Hobbes's story and to have recognized in his work 'an early version of the argument, presented in the later nineteenth and earlier twentieth centuries in elaborate detail and with much ethnographic data, that civilisation and political society resulted from the overthrow of mother-right and the triumph of patriarchy'.[26] This may well be right. Hobbes, with his mention of the Amazons, shows some awareness of the very myths of the historic 'defeat of women' which fuelled later speculation about the existence of an original matriarchy. What Pateman fails to make clear is that interpreting Hobbes in this way throws into question the success of the Hobbesian project, and so demonstrates the inadequacy of the Hobbesian account of the nature of morality and society. Hobbes's project involves a demonstration of the rational justification of obedience to the state and the reduction of ethical motivation to rational self-interest, but his argument that prudence gives rise to ethical motivation relies on substantive assumptions which are undermined when we consider the position of women.

The Hobbesian framework can provide an explanation of the origin of women's subordination within the patriarchal family, but it cannot provide a justification for that subordination. Pateman's intention in her early rejection of the consistency of Hobbes's argument would seem to be to pre-empt any rationalization of the subjection of women which took it to be, like the subjection of servants to masters and of citizens to the state, grounded in consent, albeit consent obtained in circumstances of duress. Instead, she interprets women's historical situation as one of slavery imposed upon them by the fraternity of men in order to guarantee men's right of sexual access. She follows Freud in seeing the social contract as a contract between brothers, against the father, to secure the individual male's sex-right.[27] This interpretation has the advantage that it makes it clear that woman's position has been one of imposed subjugation, but it has at least three central difficulties. First, in Freud's story, women play no part in the genesis of society, not even a rational if submissive one, so one is left with the unanswered question of how and why women have allowed themselves to be enslaved. Secondly, Freud's story is based on no historical evidence and is little more than a fabrication of his imagination, intended to provide a historical, social counterpart for the Oedipal desire to kill the father that was central to Freud's theory of individual psychic development.[28] Further, Pateman's total rejection of social contract theory leaves nothing in place for the reconstruction of a feminist theory of justice. Although social contract theory may be flawed, properly interpreted it can provide a plausible account of many of our intuitions about justice as fairness. When, for instance, Rawls's thinking about justice is applied to the institution of the family, shared parenting and other feminist demands can be seen to be just, as intuitively they should.[29] And it is hasty to reject a theory which has won so many benefits for women while no better alternative is available. It is therefore worthwhile taking a rather longer route in order to see what is at fault with the Hobbesian rationalization of women's historical subjection.

Social contract theory is intended to provide a framework for understanding political relations which can serve to justify our political institutions. In so far as Hobbes implicitly assigns the basis of woman's civil subordination to her inferior strength, this attempted justification may assume very ancient origins. It is plausible that in ancient times, myths relating the foundations of a state or people served, in those societies, a function not dissimilar to that served by modern political metaphors, such as the state of nature or the social contract, in ours. They explain and justify the continuation of the society's political and social institutions by grounding them in a compact of reconciliation which had been preceded by a conflict that the citizens would not want to reproduce.[30] Both Athens and Rome, which were patriarchal societies that have had considerable influence on western thought, had foundation myths which, though they differ from each other in emphasis, bear striking resemblances to the Hobbesian explanation of the subordination of women as I have outlined it.

According to the Athenian myth, the early Athenians defeated the Amazons. These women were reputed to be warriors who lived without men to protect them, had their own queens, and partook in a number of battles. They have always fascinated women with feminist leanings, not the least Christine de Pisan, who relates their history in *The Book of the City of Ladies*, in her *Epistre d'Othea* and in *La Mutation de Fortune*.[31] According to the myth, the ancient Greek heroes went to the country of the Amazons, where they defeated the most noble of the Amazonian warriors and brought them back to Athens. The remaining Amazonians laid siege to Athens in order to liberate their princesses, but were defeated. The historical facts concerning the existence of the

Amazons are shrouded in mystery, but for our purposes it is unimportant whether or not they did exist. It is plausible that the function of this myth was to give a hypothetical explanation for an existing state of affairs, the inferior position of women in Athenian society. The barbarity of the defeated Amazonian world, in which there is no marriage, men and women fight to the death, and fatherhood does not exist, rationalizes the Athenian society in which women are subordinated and Amazonian tendencies repressed.

The story of the Sabine women shows a rather different group of women, though, once again, it serves to rationalize woman's subjection. It illustrates rather well the dilemmas facing women. According to this myth, as it is related by Plutarch and retold by de Pisan, the Sabines were the original inhabitants of the Tigris valley, and the Romans, in order to populate their new city, abducted and raped the Sabine women. Some time after their abduction their brothers, fathers and husbands came to do battle with the Romans in order to liberate the women. But the women, pregnant and carrying the children they had borne to their captors, interposed themselves between the two armies, suing for peace. Plutarch, puts the following speech into their leader Hersilia's mouth:

> Which shall we call the worse, Roman love-making or Sabine compassion? If you were making war upon any other occasion, for our sakes you ought to withhold your hands from those to whom we have made you fathers in law and grandfathers. If it be for our own cause, then take us, and with us your sons in law and your grandchildren. Restore to us our parents and our kindred, but do not rob us of our children and our husbands. Make us not, we entreat you, twice captive.[32]

They wanted neither the death of the fathers of their children, nor that of their own fathers and brothers. And one can have some sympathy with their plight. Were the Sabine men to win the battle, the children of the Sabine women would have been enemies in the Sabine camp; they might have been put to death, or, if allowed to grow old, have wanted to avenge the deaths of their fathers.[33] Were the Sabine men to lose, the Sabine women would have lost brothers and fathers. The women are portrayed as preferring subjection to their conquerors rather than revenge for their rape and abduction. In these myths, the Amazons defend themselves but are ultimately unable to defeat the superior strength of their male foes. The Sabine women accept subjection to their abductors, but preserve their own lives and their children's lives, instituting the rule of law and making their children the inheritors of Rome. In each case the myth acts as a rationalization and explanation for the subjection of women, within the rule of law.[34] In both cases woman's child-bearing capacity and relative lack of strength provide the rationale for pursuing the path of peace with submission in order to attain the end of survival. Interestingly, de Pisan sees a positive virtue in this submission which halts war and leads to the survival of Rome. She relates it as an example of the benefits which women have brought, and in many ways the story functions as a paradigm of the good wrought by women's exemplary subjection.[35]

There is, in the literature on Hobbes, some controversy over the interpretation of his intentions.[36] The most interesting interpretation is one which sees him as attempting to show that the natural moral law is a law of reason. It is with regard to this reading that, I argue, his reasoning can be shown to fail once women are included in the picture. On another traditional view, he gives a description of political society, based on what he takes to be scientific premises, which leads him into ethical relativism and the claim that might is right. He says that there is no justice outside civil society and that what is just depends on the civil law. This applies, in particular, to matrimony. The civil law is whatever is promulgated by the sovereign, and the sovereign gains its legitimacy from its power to protect the citizens subject to it. Subjection to the sovereign is rational because it is only through the consent of each individual to be ruled that peace can be preserved, and peace is the precondition for the preservation of life. The subjection of women to their husbands will be rational, by the same reasoning, if civil society has patriarchal laws. It will be rational in the state of nature also, in so far as it is a means of preserving peace. If might is right then, if one is not one of the mighty, obedience and service to the powers that be are the most reasonable and prudent course of action, the best way of maintaining the protection of the mighty and the benefits of their good favour. So if Hobbes is correct, women's traditional acceptance of submission is grounded in their desire for self-preservation and their consequent desire for peace.

Although this reading of Hobbes might appear to rationalize woman's historical subjection, it also has emancipatory implications. If men hold sway over women merely on the grounds of consent obtained through the use of force, and women are able to reverse the situation, perhaps because changing technology has altered the importance of muscle in the distribution of power and diminished the disadvantages of pregnancy, then women have a natural right to do so. All spoils will go to the victor in the battle of the sexes, and woman must be expected to retrieve her natural dominion over her children and the fruits of her labour whenever she can. But at the same time, this reading undercuts the possibility of articulating a satisfactory theory of justice between the sexes that could be acceptable to both men and women, because it denies that there is any justice beyond the laws which are upheld by those in power.

On the more interesting reading, Hobbes is arguing that there is a God-given natural law, the study of which is the science of natural justice, and this law is perceptible by the light of reason.[37] Such a law is ineffectual except when upheld by a civil authority, but, at the same time, a civil authority will ultimately be ineffectual unless it understands and obeys the natural law. Rational individuals subject themselves to the state in order to ensure that the natural law is upheld, and any state that is to preserve itself must have a civil law in keeping with the law of nature.[38] Because people enter civil society in order to preserve as many of their natural rights as is compatible with a recognition of the rights of others, a stable civil government will extend liberty to its citizens. Hobbes elucidates: 'By liberty, I mean, that there be no prohibition without necessity of any thing to any man, which was lawful to him in the state of nature; that is to say, that there be no restraint of natural liberty, but what is necessary for the good of the commonwealth.'[39] This reading of Hobbes has even more obvious emancipatory implications for women. For if, as Hobbes allows, women in the state of nature have dominion over their children and the right to their service, how can one justify their giving up these rights in civil society? If one gives the Hobbesian answer, outlined above, that most women have submitted to men at a stage of the development of society earlier than the institution of great states, we are still left with the question of how families were instituted in which women gave up their natural right of dominion over their children. But this now goes against the principle of natural law as spelt out by Hobbes, and so begins to look like a grave injustice.

A marriage that could be considered to fit with this edict of natural law would be one in which a woman gave up some liberty, notably the liberty to have sexual relations with any man other than her husband, in exchange for the protection of herself and her children. On his part the husband would give up some comparable liberty, presumably the liberty to dispose of his surplus production at will, in exchange for the secure knowledge of paternity. One could justify this as follows: traditionally, in order for there to be a family in which the husband's biological relationship to the children is similar to that of his wife, the wife's liberty to have sexual intercourse with all comers needs to be curtailed, but if the children are as closely related to the husband as to the wife, then his duty to care for them is as strong as hers and is equally necessary for the institution of the family to exist. Therefore, the liberties which are given up in marriage are those which must be given up for the institution to exist. If the institution is to conform to the natural law, as characterized by Hobbes in this quotation, it should involve the loss of no further liberties. So natural law would suggest that since this contract is between equals it should guarantee the parents' joint dominion over their children. At least one earlier English commentator seems to have seen the family in this way.[40] Hobbes, however, does not consider this possibility, for he assumes that either the husband or wife must rule, insisting that 'No man can serve two masters'.[41]

But this edict is a mere prejuduce. Since Hobbes is prepared to allow that an assembly may be sovereign of a state, there seems no obvious reason why two individuals should not be joint sovereigns of a family. True, since they are two there will be times when they disagree and, if they have equal power, there will be no easy way to decide between them. This might be a difficulty if one thinks, as Hobbes did, of the family as a mini-state. Yet the difficulty is surely not insurmountable. The couple could agree to abide by the casting vote of a judge in such situations, or take turns in having the determining say, or divide their spheres of influence. Something like the last compromise is implicit in de Pisan's acceptance that the wife will manage the household and her daughters' education while the husband will manage the estate and his sons' education. In fact, Hobbes's insistence, in this instance, that a man cannot serve two masters may have little to do with his thoughts on marriage as such, for this is a phrase which also occurs when he discusses an issue that occupies much more of his attention than does marriage; that is, the illegitimacy of the church's claim to temporal power.[42] Just as the 'marriage' of church and state cannot limit the sovereignty of the state, so too the marriage of woman and man cannot limit the sovereignty of the head of the family.

If we emphasize the normative elements in Hobbes's work, which stress the rational law of nature and each individual's equal right to those natural liberties that are compatible with a like liberty for others, the subjection of women to their husbands stands out as a manifest injustice. It is at this point that the situation of women suggests a fatal flaw in Hobbes's reasoning, which undermines his whole attempt to show how ethical behaviour and obedience to the state can be justified. What is interesting about the argument that Hobbes develops is that it seems to provide reasons for behaving ethically which are compelling *even for an egoist*. As I pointed out above, one does not need to attribute to Hobbes a belief in an implausible psychological egoism; he only needs to assume that a usually over-riding motive in human psychology is self-preservation. This does not detract from the claim that the argument, if good, will convince an egoist. For the achievement of all aims, whether they are egoistic or altruistic, almost always depends on one's own survival. However, whether one starts with the assumption that humans are by nature rational egoists, or with the weaker assumption that self-preservation is a primary motive, Hobbes's attempt to place obedience to the natural law on a rational foundation is flawed.

As already mentioned, a number of feminist writers have made the point that the attitude of the rational egoist comes more naturally to men than to women. But this observation by itself does not show that Hobbes's argument collapses. Indeed, the proffered explanation of woman's subordination suggests that women, more often than men, have had to seek their self-preservation through submission, and that this was particularly the case if their aims included the preservation of their offspring; but it offers no criticism of this situation, which is perpetuated at the expense of women. If we are to show the flaw in the argument we need to show that a situation which does not accord with the natural law, as Hobbes outlines it, nevertheless can perpetuate itself with the consent, under duress, of those who are deprived of their natural liberties.

Such intuitions are provided once it is admitted that women have as great a natural right to liberty as men. Since men do not have to take into account, to any very great degree, the threat that women pose to men's survival, they do not need to recognize the natural rights of women. For women as a group are disadvantaged in relation to men as a group. Women clearly could murder their fathers and husbands, as they do in one of Herodotus's stories.[43] But they are unlikely, given their average inferiority in physical strength, to be able to maintain men in a state of submission grounded in the threat of superior force, for if the men as a group were to rebel, they would be likely to achieve their ends. By contrast men, since they have little fear of women being successful in a rebellion, are able, as a group, to maintain women in a state of submission without fully recognizing their equal natural right to liberty. Hobbes attempts to show that adherence to the natural moral law is rational for both subject and sovereign, given that the desire for self-preservation and liberty is primary. The situation of women suggests that when the sovereign is a member of a group which is stronger than another group in the society, the sovereign can avoid such adherence in relation to members of the weaker group. This appears to be the historical situation of women, and of other subordinate groups or classes whose rights have not been recognized by the rulers of the societies in which they live.

At the root of this flaw in Hobbes's reasoning is an ambiguity in the concept of the equality of individuals. The argument that founds moral and political obligation on the desire for self-preservation depends crucially on a claimed equality of power, which is plausible so long as we think of people as isolated individuals; it breaks down, however, because real power is not merely an individual attribute, but belongs to individuals partly in virtue of the group to which they belong. At the same time, Hobbes recognizes an equality of natural right which exists independently of our power to enforce it. It is our moral intuitions grounded in this notion that enable us to recognize that there are situations in which individuals may be forced to consent to unjust pacts, and that consent of itself does not entail justice. It is the obviousness of this natural equal right to liberty which has been taken up by later feminists, and, it is important to note, it can be defended independently of implausible assumptions concerning our actual independence and equality in the state of nature or our intrinsic egoism. Modern social contract theory, like that proposed by Rawls, is quite independent of such assumptions.[44]

There are similarities worth noting between the political thought of Christine de Pisan and that of Hobbes. Both were writing at a time of civil war and both hoped that their work would contribute towards the maintenance of peace. Both adopted the dual strategy of pointing out to subjects the prudence of accepting their subjection, and to sovereigns the prudence of protecting their subjects' rights. There are also important differences. Although Christine de Pisan's Prudence points out to the powerful princess the dangers of self-indulgence and immorality in this world, she ultimately relies on the possibility of punishment in the world hereafter as the greatest danger courted by those who are rich and unjust. This may seem like a weakness in de Pisan's work, as compared to Hobbes's. For although Hobbes's reasoning in fact incorporates a belief in the existence of God, in that it involves the belief that there is a natural law which God has ordained, and which he has made it possible for us to recognize through the exercise of reason, Hobbes's arguments can be reconstructed so as to be independent of this assumption. Yet one could also interpret this feature of de Pisan's as resting on the honest recognition that those who are powerful and immoral are not always punished during their lifetimes, and that while it is essential to society that individuals, particularly those with great power, are ethically motivated, this ethical motivation cannot simply be reduced to personal prudence.

A more interesting difference, from our point of view, lies in their quite different views on human moral psychology. As was pointed out at the end of the last chapter, de Pisan clearly accepted the moral psychology handed down to her by Christian Platonism. In this tradition, virtue is an end in itself. This is associated in her writing with a profound sense of our dependence for our happiness on the goodwill of others. Virtue, in her scheme of things, makes that dependence more secure, and, in the last instance, is the one sure source of solace in the face of the changes of fortune that it is beyond our power to prevent.[45] Virtue makes one's situation more secure, partly through giving others no reason to hate one and partly because we are creatures who learn by imitation. By practising virtue we teach it to others, particularly our own children and servants, on whose virtue we ultimately depend. Just as importantly, the knowledge that one has acted virtuously brings inner peace and consolation in the face of adversity. By contrast, Hobbes begins with a state of nature in which it appears that we are all independent agents; morality is introduced as a restriction on our natural liberty, which we accept only because we are forced by a recognition of the strength of others to do so. Behind Christine de Pisan's philosophy it is plausible to find a thought of the following kind: it is in the interests of those who are relatively powerless to foster in others a sense of their duty towards them, for, being unable to force others to recognize their rights, the powerless are constrained to rely on reason and persuasion, on stimulating the sympathy or gratitude of others, or on teaching by example, in order to achieve their aims. Since we are all really relatively powerless, no matter how our good fortune might mask this fact at any time, we should all adopt this path. She suggests to princes that they should recognize that they are 'as frail as another man and no different from others except for good fortune'.[46] The political philosophy which results from this thought has a great weakness and a great strength. Its weakness is that the methods it suggests can be pursued for a long time without making the powerful change their ways. Its strength is that there is no conflict here between the means advocated to achieve the ultimate end and the end to which we aspire. The end is a society in which those with power recognize and fulfil their duty to exercise that power in defence of the wellbeing and liberty of all (with the exception of those who threaten the liberties of others). The means is simply to live, as far as possible, according to the principles that would be adopted were all to aspire to this end. Hobbes's reasoning, by contrast, is easily transformed into a rationalization of the use of force by the powerful, because his optimism that unjust subjection will be politically unstable is not borne out in reality.

Within the Platonic tradition it is assumed that the soul is divided into three parts. Two of these provide kinds of impulse, one a generalized impulse towards attaining the good, the other involving various impulses towards objects desired by the appetites. Reason, the third part of the soul, is allied with the desire for good, since it gives us the capacity to judge what is truly good. Love, in this tradition, is associated with the force that motivates us to do good. It can be love of the good, and the desire to do good to others, as well as love of the beloved for what is good in them. Sexual desire, on the other hand, is an appetite which may mislead by motivating one to pursue ends which are not genuinely good. Within this tradition it is assumed that all humans have a natural, God-given desire to do good, which needs to be stimulated and fostered, but which makes us by nature moral beings. Within Hobbes's psychology, however, all suggestion that there is natural moral motivation disappears. Humans' primary motivation is towards self-preservation, liberty and power. Morality is a system of rules which reason dictates it is in our interests to adopt, but morality is not an end in itself. It thus becomes extremely difficult to demonstrate why those who have freedom and power should bother about morality in the many situations in which their immorality cannot rationally be seen to threaten their self-interest. It is, I believe, ultimately to this feature of Hobbes's moral psychology that feminists are objecting when they reject his rational egoism.

Yet the alternative view held by Christine de Pisan, that virtue is an end in itself, is problematic when it is not backed up by the belief that there is a God who has endowed us with a faculty, conscience, which motivates us towards the good, and who has made it the case that what it inclines us towards is good. A host of empirical and epistemological problems will have to be solved before the intuition captured in the Christian Platonic moral psychology can be naturalized. Nevertheless, we have in the contrast between Hobbes's and de Pisan's thinking about morality, a difference which might well be thought to correspond to the different voices postulated by Gilligan and Ruddick.[47] While Hobbes believes that morality is grounded in reason, de Pisan is impressed by the connection between moral motivation and love. It is important to recognize that in her thought love is not opposed to reason or justice; rather, it adds an element missing in a moral landscape dominated by reason alone. This concern with moral emotions appears distinctively feminine, but, as we will see in discussing Rousseau, the same concern can be discovered in at least one male writer of a distinctly anti-feminist cast, and this throws into relief some of the dangers that lie in simply rejecting all talk of justice and replacing it with talk of the importance of care.[48] Some feminists, notably Nel Noddings, see an ethic of care as opposed to reason and justice, asserting that an ethic of care will involve 'the rejection of principles and rules as major guides to ethical behaviour'.[49] But, in rather different ways, the writings of both Rousseau and de Pisan suggest that this attitude involves throwing out the baby with the bathwater. Feminists need at least to be sure that the costs of the injunction to care are being distributed justly. De Pisan shows in her writing an ethical orientation of the kind predicted by views about feminine psychosexuality. She is far more concerned with our responsibilities for the ethical behaviour of others than is Hobbes, and she sees love as a central ethical notion. But in her writing these ideas are embedded within a general morality of submission which is hardly congenial to thoroughgoing feminism. This suggests that we need to combine a theory of justice with a moral psychology that incorporates love and care. Later in this book I will develop this suggestion, and argue that a distincively feminist conception of rationality can be extracted from the thought that certain sentiments play a constitutive part in the psychology of the rational moral individual.

In conclusion, it is worth noting that the political philosophies of de Pisan and Hobbes implicitly include women in the political realm as full citizens, and that, from the point of view of feminism, the developments introduced by Locke and Rousseau involve a distinct deterioration in women's status. This is connected with the fact that neither Hobbes nor de Pisan incorporates a clear public/private distinction. Both see the family and the state as analogous. De Pisan extends the model of the family, in which the mother is responsible for the moral and material welfare of her children, to the state. Hobbes extends the model of the state, in which subjects are governed by the power of force, to the family. Both see women as clearly both subjects and citizens, but this presumption is undermined by Locke and Rousseau, who introduce the public/private distinction into political thought.

Locke's introduction of this distinction is most explicit in the second of his *Two Treatises of Government*, but is already implicit in the first which criticizes *Patriarcia*, Sir Robert Filmer's defence, on traditional Biblical grounds, of the divine right of kings and the patriarchal authority of husbands and fathers over wives and children.[50] Locke developed, in the second of the treatises, one of the most historically influential outlines of social contract theory. In Locke's account, Hobbes's emphasis on the equality of power between individuals is taken over by what has become a more traditional emphasis on equal rights, which suggests quite clearly the injustice of woman's political and familial subordination.[51] Yet this injustice is largely ignored by Locke, who, although he does not deny that women are free, rational beings, says that where there are differences of opinion between husband and wife the decision will fall to the husband, 'as the abler and stronger'.[52]

Locke's own attitude towards the rights of women is ambiguous, but, through the distinction which he draws between political and parental power, he introduces into liberalism the public/private distinction which, in Rousseau's hands, justifies women's exclusion from the state. In refuting Filmer's argument that the divine right of kings is grounded in the absolute paternal authority of Adam, which Filmer suggests is captured by the Biblical injunction to 'honour thy father and mother', Locke makes the point that Filmer consistently deletes the reference to mothers in order to secure his position. Locke says:

> For had our A. [author] set down this command without Garbling, as God gave it, and joined *Mother* to Father, every reader would have seen that it had made directly against him, and that it was so far from Establishing the *Monarchical Power of the Father*, that it set up the *Mother* equal with him, and injoyn'd nothing but what was due in common, to both Father and Mother.[53]

Later Locke elaborates his views concerning parental power, which, he says, extends only so far as is necessary for parents to fulfil the duty of bringing up their children to maturity, when, their reason having developed, the children can use it for the free pursuit of their own ends.[54] Since paternal power is no more than parental power, it must be acknowledged to accrue to mothers as well as fathers: 'And will any one say, that the mother hath a Legislative Power over her Children? that she can make standing Rules, which shall be of perpetual Obligation, by which they ought to regulate all the Concerns of their Property, and bound their Liberty all the course of their Lives?'[55] Superficially, this may appear a laudable recognition of women, but read more carefully, Locke's logic is that since it is quite clear that women are not appropriate monarchs, the right to dominion cannot derive from parenthood, for women are as much parents as are men. This is a significant downgrading of women in relation to Hobbes's view of them. Hobbes recognized the absolute dominion of mothers over their children, which was only forfeited when mothers themselves became subject to others.

Locke insists, against a long tradition, that political power is not equivalent to parental power. It is arguable that as this became an accepted principle the real power of women was eroded, only to be wrested back in a new form by modern feminists. When Christine de Pisan wrote, she saw no difference between the public and private behaviour of women. She concerned herself mostly with the behaviour of princesses and noble women, and it was clear to her that their personal behaviour could influence matters of state. Moreover, she took it for granted that, as mothers, women would have an authority over their children, in particular over their daughters, which was only limited by the authority over them of their husbands, their sovereign and, most importantly, God and morality. Because political power was understood as equivalent to parental power, mothers had some share in political authority. They were deputies to their husbands, but like deputies, in the absence of their husbands, they were absolute monarchs over their subjects.

So, in denying that a mother can have legislative power over her children and in claiming that it is obvious that political power cannot be derived from parental power, since that would justify rule by women, Locke is voicing an opinion quite prejudicial to the interests of mothers. After all, the most obvious response to Filmer's omission is that he has failed to recognize the political power of queens, not that, because his philosophy clearly implies that queens have a right to political rule, there is something wrong with his philosophy. The most charitable interpretation of Locke may be that he is offering an *ad hominem* argument which panders to the anti-feminist prejudices of his audience. At worst, he sees some advantage in a justification of the origins of political right which does not automatically include women as bearers of that right. That the advent of democracy has been intepreted in this light can be illustrated by Mozart's *The Magic Flute*, in which the triumph of democracy involves the defeat of mother-right. There, the daughter of the Queen of the Night falls in love with Tamino and betrays her mother, becoming a subject of the new rational order established by free men.

It therefore seems fair to say that the defeat of patriarchy in the political sphere involved at the same time the abolition of the last vestiges of matriarchy. The complete disappearance of those traces of maternal power, which are to be found in societies where political right depends on family membership, eroded the potential power of mothers. But it would be too hasty to conclude that it was therefore necessarily to the disadvantage of all women. The liberation of sons from the power of their fathers brought with it a parallel liberation of daughters from the power of their mothers. This liberation manifested itself most clearly in the erosion of the parental right to determine whom daughters should marry. Daughters came to be seen as individuals who, once they had reached the age of maturity, had the right to make their own choices. Rousseau was among those who encouraged the belief in a daughter's right to choose her own husband, and the subsequent change in the conventions of marriage was one major consequence of social contract theory.[56] This was an increase of liberty for daughters. But whereas fathers retained their political rights as citizens in the new democratic order, mothers lost all vestiges of political authority and, at least in the short term, gained nothing in return.

Locke's political philosophy did have emancipatory implications for women, but it was to take a long time before those implications could be acted on. One was that women had a right to own property. Locke founds the right to property on individual labour, and this implies that women's right to benefit from their own production is as inalienable as is men's. It is therefore no accident that the first successes of nineteenth-century feminism involved the recognition of married women's property rights. At the same time, Locke's claim that 'the great and *chief end* therefore, of Mens uniting into Commonwealths, and putting themselves under Government, *is the preservation of their property*' was taken to imply that those who had no property to preserve had no interest in government.[57] Since nearly all women were in this position they were automatically excluded from the political rights of citizenship.

Hobbes and Locke are not explicit in regard to the status of women as citizens. Yet, had Hobbes spent more time discussing women, he might, like de Pisan, have upheld women as a model of citizenship. The Hobbesian citizen offers obedience in exchange for protection, and a Hobbesian account of the origin of the patriarchal family and the subjection of women suggests that since prehistory women have, like model citizens, played their role as obedient servants to the mini-sovereign who is head of the family. In Hobbes's *Leviathan* citizens are like wives and the sovereign like the *patria potestas* of the Roman family. Locke's views are more ambiguous. In so far as his citizens are property owners and women were largely propertyless, women are not citizens. In so far as women labour and hence have a natural right to property, they ought to have property and be citizens.

If Hobbes is right and citizenship involves acquiescence to the rule of the sovereign, and the first sovereigns are heads of families, then woman's acquiescence to her husband can be taken to be a paradigm of citizenship. Christine de Pisan remained unperturbed by women's subjection to their husbands just because she saw it in this light and as analogous to the rational and moral subjection of the citizen. But with the maturation of democratic theory and the transition from Hobbes to Rousseau there is a development in the concept of the citizen. For Hobbes, the citizen, after the founding of civil society, gives up his or her natural liberty and cedes absolute sovereignty to the ruler. For Locke, and more explicitly Rousseau, the citizen always retains his sovereignty. I use the male pronoun advisedly here, since there is much in Rousseau's writings that implies that citizens are men. In the next chapter I will argue that, on one reading of his work, this follows from his view that in a republic the citizens and the sovereign are one and the same, so citizenship requires the capacity to bear arms and protect the sovereignty of the state which is one's own. According to Rousseau the people are all 'individually *citizens*, insofar as they share in the sovereign power, and *subjects* insofar as they put themselves under the laws of the state'.[58] Citizens may elect or appoint a ruler or assembly to undertake the day-to-day business of government, but these individuals are not above the law and can always be removed by the sovereign people.[59] So, whereas for Hobbes the essence of citizenship is subjection, for Rousseau citizenship involves participation in sovereignty, and this participation is not extended to women. Mary Wollstonecraft, in 1792, wrote a *Vindication of the Rights of Woman*, where she explicitly develops the inconsistencies in Rousseau's position, extending the doctrine of equal rights to include women. The relationship between Wollstonecraft's thought and Rousseau's makes it all the more necessary to examine his writings closely, for not only is it against his opinions that Wollstonecraft explicitly directs much of her epoch-making work, but also, of all the expositors of social contract theory, he is the one who develops the most sophisticated rationalization for the exclusion of women from the rights of citizenship. His works encapsulate enduring and popular conceptions of the nature of women and their role in society. But, problematically for those feminist views which maintain that there is an incompatibility between masculine and feminine modes of thought, this rationalization is closely tied to his acceptance of a Platonic moral psychology, like that to be found in de Pisan, and a 'feminine' recognition of the importance of sentiment for moral motivation.

4

Virtuous Women and the
Citizen of Geneva

Rousseau initiated an interpretation of liberalism that developed in the nineteenth century into an explicit justification for the exclusion of women from full citizenship.[1] Yet, despite the deep sexism of some of his remarks, in the light of recent feminist emphasis on love, morality and the differences between the sexes, his views on women begin to look more complex and sophisticated than has been indicated by earlier feminists. Lynda Lange, for instance, points out that part of Rousseau's thought concerning women involves a critique of competitive individualism and should be congenial to those modern feminists who are concerned that liberal feminism merely extends an unacceptable masculine competitiveness to include women.[2] Rousseau makes women's position pivotal for democratic society, and, in placing a high value on woman's influence, he paved the way for nineteenth-century feminist appropriations of his views in favour of woman's suffrage, occasionally seeming to come close to them himself.[3] For instance, at the beginning of *Emile*, where he develops his theories concerning the importance of women as educators of children, and appeals to them to educate their young in such a way that they will grow into virtuous citizens, he says, in a footnote, that 'the laws . . . give too little authority to the mother.'[4] A feminist, agreeing with this observation, would quickly conclude that the way to remedy the situation is to make women participants in the legislature, but the general thrust of Rousseau's comments, his glorification of the seclusion of Greek women, his comments on the education of Sophie, and his discussion of the separation of the masculine and feminine spheres in *Politics and the Arts*, imply that he believes citizenship and participation in the law-making process to be purely masculine prerogatives. In fact there are a number of apparent contradictions in his utterances, and consequently in the interpretations placed on his work. Notoriously, he has been taken by different authorities to be both an arch individualist and a collectivist.[5]

Feminists, equally, are divided on the exact character of his anti-feminism. On the one hand Wollstonecraft suggests that it derives from too great a faith in nature and a consequent distrust of reason. She rightly perceives that his glorification of nature and the 'natural' family, in which the modest and subordinate wife tends the home of her robust and 'autonomous' husband, is inseparably linked with his dislike of women's higher education and dominance in public affairs.[6] On the other hand, Carole Pateman and Jane Flax are representative of a popular recent reading according to which Rousseau's thought fits into the western masculine dichotomous mould, in which all elements associated with the feminine, nature, passion and love are repressed in favour of the masculine, culture, reason and justice.[7] Pateman suggests that Rousseau believed women to be a 'permanently subversive force within the political order' because of their association with nature and love, which are opposed to reason and to the justice which results from the social contract.[8] Women, says Pateman, 'exemplify one of the ways in which nature and society stand opposed to each other'.[9] According to the first interpretation, Rousseau over-values nature and the importance of 'natural' woman to the social order. According to the second, nature, women and passion pose for him a constant threat to civil society.[10]

Despite these differences, which I will take up in greater detail below, the most obvious and influential interpretation of Rousseau's work is, briefly, as follows. The family is 'the oldest of all societies, and the only natural one'.[11] Within the family it is right and proper for woman's character and behaviour to be different from man's. The husband is to lead, to be the rational head of the family and to conduct its affairs in civil society. The wife is to care for him, and to make herself useful, a good mother to her children, a pleasing source of enjoyment for her husband, and an obedient servant.[12] Together, in these two mutually complementary roles, Rousseau argues, they will create a proper environment of love and affection within which to rear children. In Rousseau's democratic society, the structure of civil society, which is based on contract, law and justice, is rooted in the natural society of the family, which is based on love, sexual passion and the biological differences that make procreation possible. Rousseau, on this reading, implicitly agrees with Aristotle: a society must be founded in human nature, and sexuality is part of human nature, so a society must include a private sphere, the family, governed by love and sexuality, on which the public sphere, governed by reason and justice, can be erected.[13] At the same time, he agrees with Plato that private interest is inimical to good government.[14] So, in so far as woman's proper role is the maintenance of the private sphere of the family, her influence is pernicious in the public realm of administration of the law and the determination of the general will. Nature and passion are associated with femininity; civil society and reason with masculinity; and the containment of women within the private sphere reflects on a large scale the containment of passion by reason.[15]

But this reading of Rousseau cannot be quite accurate; it fails to come to terms with the distrust of reason that he sometimes conveys and with the positive value that he places on love. Indeed, Rousseau's views provide a number of dilemmas for modern feminists. On the one hand his insistence on the inadequacy of political theories, like that of Hobbes, which apparently treat of humans as pure rational egoists, should strike a chord with many feminist writers.[16] According to Rousseau, humans could not be rational egoists in the state of nature, for that state must pre-date the use of language, which is necessary for complex reasoning, and language itself presupposes social interaction. Rather, humans must be led to form society through their 'passions', which include, importantly, a natural tendency to be compassionate.[17] In his version of the emergence of the social contract, humans lived in the state of nature as isolated individuals and became social at least partly because of the potential they possess for sympathizing with others. At the end of the last chapter, I suggested that although Hobbes can be defended against the charge of having assumed an implausible total psychological egoism, it is nevertheless essential to his moral psychology that moral motives are the result of a rational calculation of the means of satisfying more basic drives.[18] This contradicts the Platonic moral psychology which makes the desire for the good a distinct force, connected, in a way which is still not very clear, with love. I suggested there was one possible interpretation of the distinction between Gilligan's ethic of justice and ethic of care, in the light of this older contrast. Rousseau's thought straddles this. He is clearly concerned with justice, particularly in texts like *The Social Contract*, but he also assumes that there must be some independent moral motivation and that its source is love. Part of his interest for us is that he partially attempts to naturalize this idea, and to show how the love of the good and the sociability necessary for men to live together can develop out of our natural self-esteem, which he calls 'amour de soi'.[19]

Although Rousseau's views on the origin of the family are sketchy, it seems that he believed that it is as the family develops that sexuality and reciprocal attachment begin to play a role in the formation of society. In *A Discourse on Inequality* he describes the family as it existed prior to civil society. It gave rise to 'The first movements of the heart . . . the sweetest sentiments known to man, conjugal love and paternal love', and was 'a little society, the more united because liberty and reciprocal attachment were the only bonds of its union'.[20] Since the origin of society lies, according to him, with human sentiments rather than in rational calculation, and since the corruptions of civil society are taken by him to reside in the corruption of our human nature, which is itself distorted by society, it is a misrepresentation of his thought to depict him as simply pitting passion and nature against reason and society. Wollstonecraft's recognition that Rousseau's opinions concerning the proper role of women are connected with his glorification of nature is more accurate. In societies like that in which he lived, aristocratic women had great power, and this power was the source of individual corruption, turning men into fops and flunkeys. Rousseau is not opposed to nature; rather he believes that a just society is one in which social institutions conform to human nature. In such a society individuals will become social through the proper development of their natural inclinations.

The idea that society is founded not on rational egoism but on a natural capacity for compassion, on sympathy, and in particular on the altruistic behaviour which women, like the females of other species, show towards their children has appealed to a number of women theorists.[21] Indeed, it is tempting to discern in this early essay on the origin of society an influence on Rousseau from Mme Dupin. For a number of years, Rousseau worked as secretary to Mme Dupin, a feminist aristocrat who was involved in a number of projects: a work on friendship, a work on women and a refutation of Montesquieu's *Esprit des Lois*. Rousseau's duties included reading, taking notes and taking down Mme Dupin's thought by dictation. Among the papers from the Dupin estate, dispersed in the late 1950s, the following criticism of Montesquieu's first chapter is reported: 'It is not true that man incessantly transgresses the laws established by God; if he transgresses them, this is not because he is intelligent, but because his intelligence is limited. Sensibility and passion are as necessary to man as is reason.'[22] Some of Rousseau's early writings on women show, as well as this early recognition of the importance of sensibility and passion, a rather positive portrayal of women.[23] However, despite this, the ideal society that Rousseau imagines, based on these premises, is one within which women maintain the integrity of the private world of passion by living through their love and devotion to husband and children. They are to be excluded from the public world of the citizen and are to be educated to a life of obedience, charm and sexual service.[24] To the extent that this makes men ends in themselves while women are conceived of as mere means to men's ends, such a society is incompatible with feminism no matter how broadly characterized.

At the same time, Rousseau's work is rich with insights into the development of moral psychology and he by no means undervalues the traditional role of women. Part of his originality lies in the importance that he places on education as the means for forming the character of the citizens who will populate the just state. He thought that since the moral character of those citizens depended on their upbringing, women, as the most natural educators of children, had a particularly important role to play in the foundation of a just state.[25] It is in *Emile* that he thoroughly develops his theories concerning the proper method of forming the character of the ideal citizen. And here he also develops his thoughts concerning his ideal wife, Sophie. Yet nothing could be more irritating to a woman of feminist consciousness than remarks like those which follow, concerning the proper character of Sophie, the ideal wife, that Rousseau imagines for his Emile. Whereas the whole education of Emile has been aimed towards creating an autonomous being, who will do whatever he believes right, and is sufficiently independent never to need to consider how his actions will appear to others, Sophie is to have a different training. For:

A woman's honour does not depend on her conduct alone, but on her reputation, and no woman who permits herself to be considered vile is really virtuous. A man has no-one but himself to consider, and so long as he does right he may defy public opinion; but when a woman does right her task is only half finished, and what people think of her matters as much as what she really is. Hence her education must, in this respect, be different from man's education. 'What will people think' is the grave of a man's virtue and the throne of a woman's . . . A woman's education must therefore be planned in relation to man. To be pleasing in his sight, to win his respect and love, to train him in childhood, to tend him in manhood, to counsel and console, to make his life pleasant and happy, these are the duties of woman for all time, and this is what she should be taught while she is young.

. . . habitual restraint produces a docility which woman requires all her life long, for she will always be in subjection to a man, or to man's judgement, and she will never be free to set her own opinion above his. What is most wanted in woman is gentleness; formed to obey a creature so imperfect as man . . . she should learn early to submit to injustice and to suffer the wrongs inflicted on her by her husband without complaint; she must be gentle for her own sake, not his. . . .

Cunning is a natural gift of woman, and so convinced am I that all our natural inclinations are right, that I would cultivate this among others, only guarding against its abuse. . . .

The search for abstract and speculative truths, for principles and axioms in science, for all that tends to wide generalisation, is beyond woman's grasp.[26]

It is these passages, and the manifest discrepancy between Rousseau's love of autonomy and his prescriptions for women, which continue to offend feminists, and which were at least partly responsible for spurring Wollstonecraft to develop her very different views on the education of women in her *Vindication of the Rights of Woman*. But before completely condemning Rousseau on the basis of these passages quoted out of context, it is worthwhile considering his justification for these views in greater detail. For although he believes that women should be different from men and should not aspire to 'masculine' virtues, he also ascribes a very important place to them in society, and for each derogatory quotation a more flattering counterpart could be supplied. For instance he asserts:

women are the natural judges of a man's worth. Who would be scorned by women? . . . And do you suppose that I, who tell them such harsh truths am indifferent to their verdict? . . . What great things might be accomplished by their influence if only we could bring it to bear! Alas for the age whose women lose their ascendancy, and fail to make men respect their judgement! This is the last stage of degradation . . . Every great revolution began with a woman.[27]

. . . the best managed homes are those where the wife has most power.[28]

Lovable and virtuous women of Geneva – the destiny of your sex will always be to govern ours.[29]

These passages have been taken by Susan Okin to be vestiges of the earlier feminist Rousseau who is discussed by Joel Schwartz, and is known to us only from fragments.[30] She interprets Rousseau's later work as reverting to Aristotle's view that woman has different natural capacities to man, which suit her to motherhood and obedience within the family. This seems to be implicit in the derogatory quotations above. But there is more to Rousseau's thoughts on women than a simple reliance on natural difference. It is true that he begins *Emile* with the very Augustinian pronouncement 'God makes all things good; man meddles with them and they become evil',[31] and he suggests that where education and society try to stifle nature there is strife and unhappiness. He concludes that the fundamental principle that should be followed in educating a citizen, or planning a society, is to attempt to bring education and society into harmony with nature. Nature has made woman mothers and given them breasts with which to suckle their infants, so they must be educated to perform the duties for which nature has designed them, motherhood and child-rearing. Rousseau's rather hypocritical insistence on the duty of a mother to suckle her own babies flows from this. His emphasis on this matter is remarkable, given the fact that he sent his own five children to be tended by the public wet nurses of the *enfants trouvés*, but it is presumably related to the regret he later felt over having abandoned his children in this way.[32] Whatever the origin of this insistence, it seems clear that Rousseau was of some importance in promoting the abandonment of wet nursing.[33] Yet attention to these natural duties does not by itself require patriarchal marriage, or subjection to men, since, on Rousseau's own account, these duties were performed very early in the development of society, which he conceives of as a time in which men and women lived independently and in which the first family, based on mutual affection, came into existence.[34]

At the same time, Rousseau does not merely assert that woman's nature is different from man's; despite his differences with Hobbes, he offers a story which constitutes a slightly modified version of the Hobbesian rationalization for the subjection of women, discussed in the last chapter. He argues that even if one concedes that woman's nature is the same as man's, in the sense that they are both rational beings, nevertheless women ought to be trained to show different virtues, to behave differently from men and to use different strategies for gaining the ends they require.[35] He claims that even if the natural differences between the sexes are no more than that women bear and men only engender children, this is sufficient to justify socializing and educating them to fulfil different roles. Since women will be indisposed by pregnancy, and since they will want to care for their children, they will at some stage in their life have to depend on men. Therefore, it would be self-defeating for them to attempt to compete with men on equal terms. What they have done, and should continue to do, is to manipulate men's passions in order to achieve the ends they desire. Hence their love of dress is natural and should be encouraged. Their first object should be to please. Their fate will be to obey, so they should learn docility, but also to develop their natural cunning in order to be allowed their own way in the face of obstacles that cannot be overcome by force. They should appear chaste yet be sufficiently coquettish to inflame their husband's desire and hence hold sway over him through his passions.[36] It is thus that Rousseau is able to claim that women's subordination is dictated by both nature and reason. His position is closer to Christine de Pisan's than to Aristotle's, for he assumes not that women are by nature inferior to men, but only that they are different, and that therefore reason will dictate different behaviours. Susan Okin obscures this difference by assuming that in advocating women's chastity and modesty, Rousseau has abandoned any feminist sympathies.[37] The case of Christine de Pisan demonstrates that this is not necessarily so. It is at least possible that a culture of sexual restraint is in women's interests, but the discussion of the importance of woman's sexual liberation to feminism must wait for a later chapter.

As we saw above, feminists are divided over whether, in developing this story about the relations between the sexes, Rousseau devalues or over-rates nature and the feminine. We can explain this puzzle by recognizing at work in his writing the influences of Christian Platonism which were so obviously important to Christine de Pisan.[38] We have already seen in the first pages of *Emile* the influence of the Augustinian tradition, according to which nature is good because God-given. So human nature must be virtuous, and it is the task of reason to unfold our true nature. Nevertheless, virtue is not automatic. We may be led astray by our senses. We need reason in order to strip away the barnacles from the statue of Glaucus and discover the form that nature intended us to have.[39] And reason is not necessarily on the side of virtue; it may become the ally of sensuality and unnatural vice. Rousseau's education of Emile is intended to solve the contradictions inherent in the twofold aim of educating in accordance with the natural tendency to live for oneself and with the unnatural requirement that one lives for one's society.[40] His method depends on a faith that leaving nature to unfold itself, with as little of the corrupting influence of civil society as possible, will lead to the desired end. The confession of the vicar of Savoy, inserted into the text of *Emile*, which can be presumed to constitute Rousseau's own religious belief, makes it evident that this faith rests on the belief that nature has endowed us with conscience which gives us the desire to pursue the good. Thus, far from operating with a simple dichotomy within which nature is opposed to culture, and reason to passion, we should interpret Rousseau as accepting the Platonic concept of the tripartite soul. This is particularly clear in the following passage:

> Having thus deduced from the perception of objects of sense and from my inner consciousness, which leads me to judge of causes by my native

reason the principle truths that I require to know, I must now seek such principles of conduct as I can draw from them . . . Still following the same method, I do not derive these rules from the principles of the higher philosophy, I find them in the depths of my heart, traced by nature in characters which nothing can efface. I need only to consult myself with regard to what I wish to do; what I feel to be right is right, what I feel to be wrong is wrong; conscience is the best casuist; and it is only when we haggle with conscience that we have recourse to the subtleties of argument . . . We think we are following the guidance of nature, and we are resisting it; we listen to what she says to our senses, and we neglect what she says to our heart; the active being obeys, the passive commands.[41]

We should conclude, therefore, that for Rousseau the three elements of the human psyche are reason, which he associates with the head, conscience, which he associates with the heart, and the passions, which he associates with the body. Both conscience and the passions are, in a sense, the voice of nature; indeed Rousseau claims conscience is to the soul what instinct is to the body.[42] But in so far as our nature is truly human we are motivated by love of what is noble, which we feel with our hearts; that is to say, we are motivated by conscience. Rousseau's language is not entirely consistent on this matter. Later he says the following:

What is meant by a virtuous man? He who can conquer his affections; for then he follows his reason, his conscience; he does his duty; he is his own master and nothing can turn him from the right way . . . This [love for Sophie] is your first passion. Perhaps it is the only passion worthy of you. If you can control it like a man it will be the last; you will be master of all the rest, and you will obey nothing but the passion for virtue.[43]

In this case Emile's heart needs to be controlled by conscience, but this does not contradict the general idea that our conscience is a strong motivating force independent of self-interest. At this juncture Emile's tutor hopes to train him to control even his virtuous passion for Sophie in order that he should later have the strength to control all other less virtuous passions.

It seems fair to say that the enduring interest of Rousseau's writing lies in the fact that he attempts to show how the moral promptings of conscience and the impetus of the passions can be brought into harmony with one another in order for individuals to be able to live easily within the constraints of society. Reason is conceived of as the agency by which this harmony is discovered. Rather than opposing nature, reason should serve to discover its true lineaments, and to show how our human nature, properly developed, will make us natural citizens of a just

republic. Within this schema woman is conceived of as having a particular role to play in stimulating man's conscience through his desire to
be loved: 'Women are the natural judges of a man's worth.'[44] And men,
if they are to be lovers of virtue, must be lovers of virtuous women. The
virtuous wife does not rule her husband so much through kindling his
senses as by ruling his heart.[45] The heart is the seat of conscience, not
of the senses: 'A righteous heart is the true temple of the Godhead.'[46]
Women play an ambiguous role in Rousseau's writing because it is the
perversion of self-esteem, and the related desire to be loved, which he
believes lead to self-importance, inequality, corruption and the artifi-
ciality of civilized society. This degeneration is particularly prompted by
immoral women. Women who inflame men's passions and encourage
them to strive for glory and renown have an influence on civic morals
that is as pernicious as the influence of those other, virtuous women,
who kindle higher love in men's hearts, is good. But while woman's role
is ambiguous, it is also crucial. In order to see how crucial, we need to
return to Rousseau's description of the origin of civil society.

As already mentioned, Rousseau takes issue with the rationalism of
Hobbes, and, interpreting the state of nature as a genuine stage in human
development rather than a hypothetical device, points out that creatures
existing prior to society could not have entered into society through
rational consent to a social contract, since language and reason, which
are presupposed by such consent, themselves depend on society. Even
the association of the family is social and cannot exist prior to language.
Humans are, however, naturally capable of feeling the sentiment of pity,
and from this quality flow all the social virtues. This sentiment is strong
in nature but reason, which engenders self-importance (*amour-propre*),
weakens it.[47] Thus the state of nature as Rousseau depicts it is an idyll
of natural independence. Since all are able to fend for themselves and
are inclined to pity the weak, there are no great conflicts. Even the
conflicts which in civilized society arise from love are absent, for the
physical desire for sex is easily satisfied and leads to no conflict, while
'the moral part of love is an artificial sentiment born of usage in society
and cultivated by women with much skill and care in order to establish
their ascendancy and make dominant the sex that ought to obey.'[48]
Without this moral aspect, love would induce few passions. But what
exactly is this moral aspect of love? It comes about when, in love, we
consider one person more acceptable than another. Women promote it
because, since they suffer the inconveniences of pregnancy, it is in their
interest to stimulate men's pity and hence acquire men's aid. But in order
to make a man consider her exclusively as an object worthy of his aid,

a woman must both make herself more attractive than others and adopt a modest attitude towards sex. Once the receipt of her sexual favours is valued, the man's self-interest is transformed into a desire to oblige her. This is surely what is intended by the following:

> Is it not of vital importance that she should learn to touch his heart without showing that she cares for him? It is a pretty story that tale of Galatea with her apple and her clumsy flight. What more is needed? Will she tell the shepherd who pursues her among the willows that she only flees that he may follow? If she did it would be a lie; for she would no longer attract him.[49]

The woman having made herself an object of value, a man's self-esteem will be increased by possessing her. Thus love becomes a central prop to self-esteem, and the withdrawal of love a threat to one's self-esteem. So arises jealousy.[50] It is only after love has acquired this moral aspect through the introduction of exclusiveness, or at least limitation, in the choice of sexual partners that love excites the passions, for it is now able to enhance or threaten our self-esteem.

Like Hobbes, Rousseau implicitly views society as having developed through two stages, the first populated by families which only later come together in the formation of states. But whereas for Hobbes the patriarchal family is the result of woman's rational consent to male domination achieved under duress, for Rousseau the first family is apparently egalitarian, held together by mutual affection and liberty. It is woman who needs the help which conjugal relations provide, so it is woman who is motivated to renounce the original independence of the state of nature, in order to initiate a new stage in which her independence, along with that of man, will be undermined.

To a thinker who has been been alerted, by feminist critique, to the mythical nature of natural independence, a contradiction in Rousseau's thinking becomes apparent at this point. If woman is, as Rousseau suggests, independent in the state of nature, she cannot need man's help, but if she needs man's help, the state of nature is not, after all, an idyll of mutual independence. Rousseau's thinking can, however, be made more consistent if we take his point to be the following: women in the state of nature *are* independent and can acquire enough food for the survival of themselves and their offspring. But since men too can acquire more food than is necessary for their own survival, women and their children will have a greater chance of survival if men have a motive to produce a surplus and to contribute it to the wellbeing of women and their children. Thus women are the ones who are led to desire dependence. Yet, even in this picture, there is a tension between the obvious dependence of children and the supposed independence of natural man. It is the dependence of children which motivates woman to relinquish her independence, and at least half of these children will grow to be men. So the dependence that women seek is in the end forced upon them by the dependence of infants, half of whom are infant men. Mutual interdependence seems a far more accurate characterization of the relationship between human individuals even prior to the existence of large social groups.

The inconsistency in the picture provides an important critique of Rousseau, for at least part of his rationalization of the subordinate position of women in the family appears to be captured in the following thought, which assumes a complete original liberty for men. Women develop the moral aspect of love in order to set up a mutual inter-dependence which it is in their interest to promote. To do this they learn to govern both the sentiments and passions of men. But this would be the enslavement of men, if men were not in their turn to govern women. Men have given up their liberty for woman's sake. Such slavery is, Rousseau contends, particularly obviously the result of marriages in which men marry their social superiors.[51] And it would be general if men were not accorded social superiority. Women can govern men through governing their senses and their hearts without claiming it as a right. Men, because of this, should have their reciprocal right to govern women acknowledged. It is only fair that woman should submit to man's judgement since her power over his heart makes her the mistress of his desire. This reciprocal government is made explicit in the last pages of *Emile*:

> Oh, Sophie, . . . When Emile became your husband, he became your head, it is yours to obey; this is the will of nature. When the wife is like Sophie, it is, however, good for the man to be led by her; that is another of nature's laws, and it is to give you as much authority over his heart, as his sex gives him over your person, that I have made you the arbiter of his pleasures . . . he will give you his confidence, he will listen to your opinion, will consult you in his business, and will decide nothing without you. Thus you may recall him to wisdom, if he strays, and bring him back by a gentle persuasion, you may make yourself lovable in order to be useful, you may employ coquetry on behalf of virtue, and love on behalf of reason.[52]

Since it is women who rob men of their original liberty it is only fair that women too renounce their liberty.[53] But this still cannot be the whole story, for what has happened to the egalitarian family that was held together by ties of mutual affection? Moreover, why is it not possible for men to govern the hearts of women? Women too have natural self-esteem which is enhanced by being loved, and since, according to Rousseau's own story, women gain more from dependence than men do, men have a further power over women through their capacity to withdraw the contribution of their surplus production from a woman's children.

Part of Rousseau's reply to this is implicit in a passage in *Politics and the Arts*; the other part will take us back to considerations of citizenship. The first part is implicit in Rousseau's thoughts on the respective anatomies of men and women:

> What would become of the human species if the order of attack and defence were changed? The assailant would choose by chance times when victory would be impossible; the assailed would be left in peace when he needs to be vanquished, and pursued without interruption when he is too weak to succumb; in a word, since the power and the will, always in discord, would never permit the desires to be mutually shared, love would no longer be the support of nature but its destroyer and plague.[54]

Modesty is the natural weapon of women, and could not be the natural weapon of men, because for men, but not for women, the capacity for coitus is connected with both desire and energy. Modest men would be easiest to vanquish when they were too ill or tired for sexual relations, and when they were strong and ready they would find it too easy to escape. Moreover modesty is not something which could be given up and social life, as Rousseau knew it, still function, for if both the sexes were equally active in seeking sexual satisfaction 'the passions ever languishing in a boring freedom, would never have been excited; the sweetest of all sentiments would hardly have touched the human heart, and its object would have been badly fulfilled.'[55] The first half of the two-stage process which leads through the development of the family to the growth of civil society thus depends on feminine sexual restraint and modesty. Without it individual love could never arise and the moral sentiments which are engendered within the family would never develop. Rousseau was perhaps the first to perceive the connections between sexuality and the development of ethical motivation which were later developed by Freud. His theory is simpler than Freud's, which, as we will see in later chapters, has played an important part in developing feminist attitudes towards sexuality, but like Freud's theory it indicates that sexuality is integral to politics, not just as an area where there can be an exercise of power, but also as a feature of our experience integral to the reproduction of the ethical individual and hence the reproduction of society.[56]

Rousseau suggests that from the first stage of society two paths of social development are possible. One, the actual history which he describes in *A Discourse on Inequality*, involves the accumulation of property, which leads to inequality, which in turn leads to the establishment of law and right for the protection of property, and to the development of political distinctions, the growth of self-importance, and the introduction of corruption, vice and arbitrary power.[57] Alternatively, the development of the moral sentiments which are aroused by love could lead to a social contract like that outlined in *The Social Contract*, in which each gives up his or her liberty to all in order to preserve the liberty of all.[58] In a society like this, 'the love of humanity and one's country' is engendered, and supersedes mere love of the opposite sex as a motive for duty. In *Politics and the Arts* Rousseau argues against the introduction of the (French) theatre into Geneva partly on the grounds that Geneva, which corresponds largely to his ideal of egalitarian republicanism, would be corrupted by it since the theatre is 'given over to gallantry, softness, love, to everything which can effeminate man and mitigate his taste for his real duties'.[59] In Geneva it would be a deterioration of public morals if individuals were to concern themselves with the passions that theatre arouses, though in some societies it would be an improvement if individuals were at least subject to those passions:

> The most vicious of men is he who isolates himself the most, who most concentrates his heart in himself; the best is he who shares his affections equally with all his kind. It is much better to love a mistress than to love oneself alone in all the world. But whoever tenderly loves his parents, his friends, his country and humankind, degrades himself by a dissolute attachment which soon does damage to all the others and is without fail preferred to them. On this principle, I say that there are countries where the morals [manners] are so bad that they would be only too happy to be able to raise themselves back up to the level of love; and there are others where it would be unfortunate to descend to it, and I dare to think mine is in the latter case.[60]

Just as the nature of man allows for societies to progress through the stage of the family, which is grounded in feminine modesty and 'the moral aspect of love', to the stage of civil society, in which wider concerns of public duty and the 'love of humankind' predominate, so too, the individual education of Emile is manipulated so that at an appropriate age, his first social sentiments are stimulated by his love for Sophie. His tutor then insists that he disengage himself from this love, in order to travel and learn about society, so that he should avoid being a slave to his love, and come to develop the judgement necessary for being a citizen and Sophie's rational 'head'. His love for Sophie may motivate him to desire the responsibility of fatherhood and citizenship, but it must also be transcended if he is to fulfil those duties properly.[61]

This brings us to the second part of Rousseau's answer to the question which we posed him earlier: that of why the family, which he describes in *A Discourse on Inequality* as based on mutual liberty and affection, cannot continue to exist in civil society. One might, indeed, ascribe mere blind prejudice to Rousseau on this matter, and this is certainly suggested by his references to women as 'the sex who ought to obey'.[62] A more charitable interpretation would link his reasoning to the conception of the duties of citizenship, as he outlines them in *The Social Contract*. There Rousseau describes the difference between his use of the word 'citizen' and that of other political theorists. Not all the inhabitants of a city or country are citizens; only those who make up the body politic deserve this name. They are citizens in so far as they share in the sovereign power, and subjects in so far as they put themselves under the laws of the state.[63] The social pact which brings into existence the body politic comes about when 'the obstacles to their preservation in a state of nature prove greater than the strength that each man has to preserve himself in that state'.[64] Thus the social pact is a pact of mutual self-defence, and, in a republic, this places on the citizens a duty to prepare themselves for the defence of the state. A republic needs men. In a tyranny the people are subjects, not citizens, and a monarch may make do with a large army of 'women', but a republic must be made up of men who have the power to defend themselves collectively.[65] Rousseau is aware that Plato, who also believed that participation in the government of the community required the physical strength to defend it, had made women Guardians. But in order to achieve this he was prepared to abolish the family, and

> all the tenderest of our natural feelings, which he sacrificed to an artificial sentiment which can only exist by their aid. Will the bonds of convention hold firm without some foundation in nature? Can devotion to the state exist apart from those near and dear to us? Can patriotism thrive except in the soil of that miniature fatherland, the home? Is it not the good son, the good husband, the good father, who makes the good citizen?[66]

Therefore, men are to be educated to be citizens, hardened for warfare, and made conscious of the requirements of universal duty. Women are to be educated for the family and for inspiring love; they need know nothing beyond the particular needs of those for whom it is their duty to care.[67]

Of all the influential male political theorists, Rousseau had the most to say about women and developed a conception of their character and role in society which continues to have a pervasive influence. His claim that it is through the moral influence of women that the morality of society can be restored echoes Christine de Pisan's views that virtuous women can have a powerful influence over the consciences of bad men, and has been taken up by later feminists both during the fight for suffrage and more recently.[68] His association of masculine thought with abstract reasoning, and universal principles and feminine thought with the concrete and particular, is similarly perennial.[69] And his glorification of feminine difference, although it cannot in any way be construed as feminist, constitutes a distorted premonition of recent work by feminists of difference. It also makes those works problematic, by highlighting the fact that the way in which we think about the difference between the sexes is intricately entwined with a tradition of political thought which characterizes active citizenship as masculine, passive subjection and moral and exemplariness as feminine.

In the next chapter we will look more closely at the inconsistencies in Rousseau's thought, as developed by Wollstonecraft, but at this point it is worth pointing out how, from a modern perspective, the whole edifice may appear flawed by a fault which infected de Pisan's thinking. This is Rousseau's underlying faith in the existence of a virtuous human nature, which includes a natural passion for virtue and a rational capacity to recognize what virtue consists in. Without the faith that God has traced the principles of right conduct on our hearts, what justification can we have in believing that human nature is really virtuous? The earliest and perhaps most powerful *reductio* of this contention was offered by the Marquis de Sade. Since God does not exist and our nature is to live at the expense of others, theft and rape are equally natural and permissible. Nature has given men the right to have any woman they desire by giving them the strength to force their desire on women.[70] His characters glorify nature and natural liberty, but it is a liberty to indulge in every vice that the pornographer can imagine. De Sade's *Justine* constitutes a parody of Rousseau's *La Nouvelle Héloïse*. Although its stated aim is to demonstrate the rewards of virtue, in fact the virtue of the heroine has the effect of encouraging the evil of those who desire to possess, humiliate and torture her.[71] In de Sade's world God is dead and nature cruel. Thus the glorification of nature becomes the glorification of the will to dominate, to have one's own lusts fulfilled, and particularly to torture the weak and virtuous.[72]

In so far as the tradition of feminist humanism continues to cling to a belief in the intrinsic goodness of human nature, whether this is taken to be the result of our God-given reason or of conscience, or merely rests on an uncritical faith that nature is good, it inherits this fatal Rousseauist flaw. As we will see in later chapters, this faith continues to infect much feminist thought and in particular that strand which has been influenced by the tradition of sexual liberation. According to this tradition social liberation will be impossible without the liberation of our natural sexuality. One strand of recent anti-humanism, that developed by Foucault in his *History of Sexuality*, questions this naturalistic faith and needs to be given serious consideration.[73] His questioning of the tradition of sexual liberation will be further discussed in the chapter after next. In some ways it seems to coincide with the sentiments of feminists who are perturbed that, far from leading to a liberation of socially positive energies, the loosening of sexual controls which took place during the 1970s, has led to nothing but the growth of a pornography and prostitution industry which celebrates acts and images of sexual domination and mastery. At the same time, Foucault's theoretical position is quite opposed to the sexual prescriptivity of radical feminist critiques of heterosexuality. This conflict suggests that we may need to rethink the relationship of sexuality and liberation, and that certainly, optimism that merely unleashing our natural desires will be beneficial for society is misplaced. In the following chapters I will, however, argue that Foucault's and de Sade's challenges to naturalism can be met, and that one of the most interesting areas for continuing feminist research lies in the attempt to understand how sexuality and ethical motivation are linked, in order to understand how to reproduce societies in which individuals are autonomously motivated to be social and egalitarian rather than, as is now too often the case, to dominate and humiliate others.

5

The Female Citizen

Mary Wollstonecraft was born in 1759, and her feminism arose, at least partly, from personal experience. Her father was a drunkard who had started life with a fair inheritance that dwindled through mismanagement. When a young girl she is alleged to have spent nights sleeping on the floor outside her parents' bedroom so that she could intervene if her father beat her mother. She was left mostly to 'run wild' and through fortuitous circumstances gained the opportunity of educating herself. Her short novel, *Mary*, is largely autobiographical and worth reading for the light it casts on her development. Determined not to fall into her mother's abject dependence on a drunken husband, she tried a number of careers, including running a girl's school and being a governess.[1] Finally she became a writer and translator and part of a circle of English radicals. Among other works she wrote, in 1790, *Vindication of the Rights of Men*, a reply to Burke, which was followed soon after by the *Vindication of the Rights of Woman*, which she dedicated to Talleyrand in the hope that its principles might be incorporated into the French constitution.[2]

This work constitutes a major advance in feminist thought. Although other writers had pointed out the conflict between the claimed equality of all individuals, which was fundamental to the radical new democratic philosophy, and the social subordination of women, Wollstonecraft's tract stands out for the vigour and originality of its arguments. She mounts a sustained attack on Rousseau's attempt to justify the continued subordination of women within the family, revealing its inconsistency in the face of his commitment to an egalitarian ideal of masculine citizenship. There are some difficulties with her arguments which, as they stand, do not always provide a satisfactory refutation of Rousseau's contentions, for they sometimes involve rather uncharitable interpretations of his thought. Nevertheless, they can be developed to provide the groundwork for a compelling refutation of his confinement of women to the private sphere. Wollstonecraft demonstrates that Rousseau's conclusions are inconsistent with his own principles, and she develops a far more cogent characterization of female citizenship than the one he offers. Yet the liberal feminist position which Wollstonecraft was the first to work out in detail has itself received a great deal of criticism from feminists, on the grounds that it extends a philosophical tradition which assumes both an abstract conception of humans as rational individuals and a mind/body split, which are themselves a projection of masculine psychology.[3] It has been claimed that this extension is problematic, for the human whose rights are protected in liberal democratic thought is implicitly a man, and liberal ethics abstracts away from the realities of embodied existence, implicitly assuming the existence of a non-physical self.

One might wonder whether acceptance of a mind/body split is particularly deeply connected with one's gender orientation. Hobbes, after all, was resolutely materialist, while de Pisan was able to exploit the spirituality of the soul in order to defend the idea that women as well as men are made in God's image. Historically, the immateriality of the soul has provided a promising justification for treating women as men's equals. Wollstonecraft's feminist predecessor, François Poullain de le Barre, explicitly adopted Descartes's mind/body split to justify the equality of the sexes.[4] This suggests it is not obvious that such a philosophy is inimical to women's interests. However, I will not defend Wollstonecraft on this ground, for what feminists are objecting to in the mind/body split is not so much a metaphysical doctrine as a lack of recognition of our embodiment, and, we will see, although Wollstonecraft believed in God and life after death, her understanding of the human mind is quite compatible with a conception of ourselves as, essentially, embodied, feeling creatures.

The masculine standpoint which manifests itself in liberalism is often claimed to result from enduring features of male psychology, yet, in order for Wollstonecraft and other liberal feminists to be criticized for having adopted such a standpoint, theories need to be able to be identified as masculine in virtue of their content, rather than merely in virtue of their genesis. In chapters 2 and 3, influenced by the contrast between de Pisan and Hobbes, I suggested a way of understanding the difference in content that is characteristic of masculine and feminine standpoints, which emphasizes that what is at issue is a matter of moral psychology.

But, as it turned out, if we designate theories 'feminine' because they postulate the existence of basic *moral motives*, or sentiments, connected with innate tendencies to love, and we designate theories 'masculine' when they assume that moral motivation is derived from non-moral desires and reason, Rousseau emerges as a 'feminine' theorist. In this chapter I will demonstrate that the same can be said for Wollstonecraft.[5] Wollstonecraft's conception of human nature is much closer to Rousseau's than to Hobbes's. She believes that we are endowed by nature with the capacity to acquire moral sentiments and that the foundation of the social virtues is self-love, or self-respect, which she identifies with the love of justice or morality.[6] And although her views differ somewhat from Rousseau's, for she equates conscience and reason, this 'reason' is no cold or selfish calculation, but a capacity that shows us that true happiness arises from 'the friendship and intimacy which can only be enjoyed by equals'.[7] Her reason:

> has, at last, shown her captivating face, beaming with benevolence; and it will be impossible for the dark hand of despotism again to obscure it's radiance, or the lurking dagger of subordinate tyrants to reach her bosom. The image of God implanted in our nature is now more rapidly expanding; and, as it opens, liberty with maternal wing seems to be soaring to regions far above vulgar annoyance, promising to shelter all mankind.[8]

And this reason is associated with an 'enlightened moral love of mankind'.[9]

According to our first proposal for distinguishing 'masculine' from 'feminine' theories, Rousseau and Wollstonecraft would both count as 'feminine'. But this is only one way of understanding the distinction, so perhaps something else is at stake. Jane Flax's paper on the patriarchal unconscious suggests that what is central to masculinity is the isolation of the masculine subject which comes about because dilemmas of separation and individuation have not been resolved.[10] If the mark of a 'masculine' theory is that it unwarrantedly assumes that individuals enjoy a natural independence in the state of nature, then, as we saw in the last chapter, since there is an inconsistency in Rousseau's story which derives from just such an assumption, we may conclude that this 'masculine' orientation provides an explanation for the inconsistency. On this interpretation of the contrast between 'masculine' and 'feminine' standpoints, Wollstonecraft's liberalism will be similarly 'masculine' if it likewise assumes an untenable human independence or isolation in the state of nature. But, as we will see, Wollstonecraft's philosophy avoids all such assumptions.

Feminist interpreters of the liberal tradition have tended to see Rousseau as a philosopher of difference, who pits culture against nature, man against woman, and reason against passion, thus justifying a social structure in which men are rational agents in the public sphere, while women function as guardians of the natural and emotional private realm. By contrast these interpreters have tended to explain Wollstonecraft as an egalitarian rationalist, whose central thesis is that since men and women are all essentially rational spirits, whose virtues are of the same kind, they ought to be given the same education, rights and liberties.[11] Reading Wollstonecraft in this way encourages the criticism that she has adopted, as a universal human norm, a characterization of what it is to be a person which is already implicitly biased towards a masculine rationalism. Jacobus, for instance, suggests that in the *Vindication of the Rights of Woman*, 'A plainspoken utilitarian speaks not so much *for* women, or *as* a woman but *against* them.' She claims that it is only in her fiction, and precisely at the point where she evokes the terror of madness, that Wollstonecraft 'negates . . . the assumptions of her earlier essay in order to show how, if "sense" excludes women, "sensibility" confines them – yet offers a radical challenge to patriarchy; a challenge that it must repress'. For Jacobus, Wollstonecraft only escapes the prison of a masculine rationality when she expresses 'what it means for women to be on the side of madness as well as silence'.[12] But, just as I have argued in the last chapter that this common characterization of Rousseau is too simple, so I will argue against the corresponding interpretation of Wollstonecraft.[13] This task has been made considerably simpler by the recent publication of Virginia Sapiro's excellent scholarly discussion of Wollstonecraft, *A Vindication of Political Virtue*.[14] To identify Wollstonecraft as a cold rationalist, in the style of Kant, would be to associate her with 'masculine' styles of thought in the first sense distinguished above. But, as I have already noted, there is less difference between Rousseau's and Wollstonecraft's views than this allegation would make out. At one level the *Vindication of the Rights of Woman* is a more consistent working out of Rousseau's ideas, extended to women, than is *Emile*. Wollstonecraft shares Rousseau's love of nature and his interest in the moral sentiments.[15] Her conception of the interplay of social influence, passion, sensibility and reason in the making of a mature moral individual is completely distorted by suggestions that her liberalism is grounded in a conception of human beings as merely or abstractly rational. In fact, as we will see, she develops a concept of liberal autonomy which cannot be faulted, as Rousseau's can, for resting on implausible assumptions concerning human independence in the state of nature.

However, not all of Wollstonecraft's arguments are compelling, as they stand. And a fair criticism of her outlook is that her refutation of Rousseau remains unsatisfactory, because, due to her naiveté in economic matters, her work fails to clarify how women are going to be able to secure the level of economic independence necessary for them to be truly equal partners in marriage, and so does not refute the functionalist elements in Rousseau's writing.[16] There is also an understandable gap in her thought, in so far as she does not explicitly tackle the question of the psychosexual underpinnings of male domination: neither the validity of Rousseau's assumptions about the importance of chaste women to the generation and maintenance of male moral motivation, nor more recent worries that male sexuality is deeply implicated in domination, nor the more general question of female sexuality. Yet this is hardly a damning criticism, since it would be unreasonable to expect Wollstonecraft to have contributed to a debate which has only developed in the twentieth century. Moreover, as we will see below, a careful reading of her texts suggests a more sophisticated position on these matters than is usually attributed to her.

The *Vindication of the Rights of Woman* is largely polemical and was written in great haste. These features obscure the subtleties of the position that Wollstonecraft develops, so it is worth examining her argument in some detail. The result, I believe, will be a recasting of the fundamentals of Wollstonecraft's liberalism, which will bring out its enduring strengths as a basis for an on-going feminism. She begins her critique of Rousseau's philosophy by disagreeing with him over the source of the evil they both recognized in the society in which they lived. It is not the unnaturalness of society which is to blame. What is needed is not a return to nature, for nature, as even Rousseau admitted, knows no morality.[17] Instead of Rousseau's faith that all was good in the past, she adopts a perfectionist stance, which suggests in the background an Irenaean theodicy according to which God has created us, as we are, in order that our passions and the power of reflection should lead us to improve our nature and 'render us capable of enjoying a more godlike portion of happiness'.[18] The evils of society result not from its unnaturalness, but from the inequalities in power and property which are ubiquitous, and which are inimical to the virtue both of those that have power, and of those that do not. For the powerful and wealthy are looked up to, not because they are virtuous, but because of their possessions. They are able to live in idleness, corruption and luxury, with no regard for the poverty of the masses. The powerless, at the same time, are led to fawning, deceit, sycophantism and every sort of vice in their attempt to acquire what the rich have. In a situation in which some have excessive power and others have none, truthfulness, independence, generosity and the pursuit of one's own duties and interests, with due regard to the interests of others, become impossible.[19] Wollstonecraft's general account, in the *Vindication of the Rights of Woman*, of the impossibility of moral development under circumstances of material inequality had already been developed in her *Vindication of the Rights of Men*.[20] In her later book she extends her analysis of the corrupting influence of inequalities of power to explain the situation of women, suggesting that both men and women are corrupted by a situation in which women are slaves, brought up to have no means of supporting themselves except by entering into marriages with men, who consequently have a complete licence to tyrannize over them.[21] Rousseau attributed the corruption of aristocratic society to the disorder of women and the perversions of *amour-propre*. Wollstonecraft insists, by contrast, that it is the inequalities in power entrenched in society which result in the disorders of women.

Since all humans are equally perfectible and have been born to achieve moral autonomy, women as well as men must have the right to develop themselves as moral individuals. And since 'every being may become virtuous by the exercise of its own reason . . . the most perfect education . . . is such an exercise of the understanding as is best calculated to strengthen the body and form the heart.'[22] This observation, Wollstonecraft believes, shows that those who have argued that the sexes ought to aim at different characters in the attainment of virtue have been mistaken. There is but one way, the exercise of reason, which can lead mankind to virtue.[23] However, as it stands, this argument against Rousseau is rather unsatisfactory, for it trades on the ambiguity between virtue and the virtues that we already noticed in the discussion of de Pisan. Wollstonecraft's insistence on the perfectibility of humans is reminiscent of de Pisan's inclusion of women in the City of God. But whereas de Pisan accepted that rational creatures, with different natural capacities, could be equally virtuous while performing different functions for which different virtues were required, Wollstonecraft interprets Rousseau's version of this argument in such a way that, rather than being an argument for the development of different virtues – sympathy over courage, or patience over decisiveness, for instance – it is an argument for the development, in women, of traits which do not plausibly count as virtues at all. Interpreting Rousseau in this way does not do justice to the plausibility of one traditional conception of the differences between the sexes, according to which they can each equally pursue conscious virtue through the development of the different virtues, appropriate to their differing social functions.

There is, however, some justice in Wollstonecraft's interpretation of Rousseau. For instance, in the notorious passage quoted in the last chapter, he says, ' "What will people think" is the grave of a man's virtue and the throne of a woman's.' And he speaks of women being formed to obey men and to suffer injustice all their lives.[24] Such injunctions are surely incompatible with seeing women as having, like men, a duty to strive for moral autonomy and conscious virtue, since they imply that women should obey even the unjust. Nevertheless, he does not consistently deny woman's rational moral autonomy. A few pages after the notorious passage which stirred Wollstonecraft's indignation he makes the following comment:

> Perhaps I have said too much already. To what shall we reduce the education of women if we give them no law but that of conventional prejudice? . . . For all mankind there is a law anterior to public opinion . . . This law is our individual conscience . . . if these two laws clash, the education of women will always be imperfect. Right feeling without respect for public opinion will not give them that delicacy of soul which lends to right conduct the charm of social approval; while respect for public opinion without right feeling will only make false and wicked women who put appearances in the place of virtue.
>
> It is, therefore, important to cultivate a faculty which serves as judge between the two guides, which does not permit conscience to go astray and corrects the errors of prejudice. That faculty is reason. . . .
>
> The reason which teaches a man his duties is not very complex; the reason which teaches a woman hers is even simpler, the obedience and fidelity which she owes to her husband, the tenderness and care due to her children, are such natural and self-evident consequences of her position that she cannot honestly refuse her consent to the inner voice which is her guide, nor fail to discern her duty in her natural inclination.[25]

All of which implies that Rousseau would agree with Wollstonecraft that virtue requires the exercise of reason, but he would insist that, since the knowledge that is required for the exercise of a woman's duties is not very abstract, and since acquiring knowledge is not a virtue when it interferes with the exercise of one's maternal duties, the pursuit of higher learning is not a virtue in women.

Although this first attempt to refute Rousseau's argument might be thought to fail because it is based on a rather uncharitable interpretation of his intentions, later comments by Wollstonecraft suggest an extension of her objection, which has more power. Wollstonecraft rightly observes that Rousseau has made a single moral individual out of the couple. In order to ensure that they complement each other, the two sexes are seen by him as asymmetrical parts of a greater whole. She alludes to his image of woman, the graceful ivy clinging to man the oak, and later quotes at length the following passage:

> The social relations of the sexes are indeed truly admirable: from their union there results a moral person, of which the woman may be termed the eyes, and man the hand, with this dependence on each other, that it is from the man that the woman is to learn what she is to see, and it is of the woman that man is to learn what he ought to do. If woman could recur to the first principles of things as well as man, and man was capacitated to enter into their minutiae as well as woman, always independent of each other, they would live in perpetual discord, and their union could not subsist. But in the present harmony which naturally subsists between them, their different faculties tend to one common end: it is difficult to say which of them conduces most to it: each follows the impulse of the other; each is obedient and both are masters.[26]

To which she responds by pointing out that the image is absurd. It might be acceptable if man did attain 'a degree of perfection of mind when his body arrived at maturity', but as things stand, since many husbands are overgrown children, what will actually result from the limitations placed on the development of a woman's reason will be the blind leading the blind.[27] Moreover, since each half of the relationship needs to act independently, each needs both reason and right feeling, both principle and the perceptual capacities necessary for sensitively applying it. Women who are educated to dependence are nevertheless expected to manage a family, but if we are to conceive them as obeying blindly and suffering injustice, how are they to manage the home? 'As they submit without reason, they will, having no fixed rules to square their conduct by, be kind, or cruel, just as the whim of the moment directs.'[28] Even in the best scenario, where her husband is a good guide, a woman may be left a widow and, if she is incapable of independent action, tragedy is likely to ensue.

Throughout Wollstonecraft's work, the asymmetry between the sexes, which was part of conventional wisdom and which Rousseau had tried to defend, is attacked as unjustified and ultimately motivated by male self-interest, libertinism and, in the case of Rousseau, an excess of sensibility. 'He debauched his imagination and reflecting on the sensations to which fancy gave force, he traced them in the most glowing colours.'[29] Or, as we might more prosaically say, Rousseau's views on this matter are more a projection of his own sexual desire than the product of unclouded judgement. This observation has a deal of plausibility, since, by his own account, Rousseau's thoughts on Sophie were written after his passionate friendship with Mme d'Houdetot, who bore the same name, and whose resistance to his sexual advances lead him to such a fever pitch that he is led to claim that it was only in this relationship that he ever felt love.[30] What is more important, however, is not the motivation for Rousseau's views, but rather that in the end the asymmetry of his treatment of the sexes leads to inconsistencies. The society which Rousseau wants to achieve is a society of independent equals in which all are sufficiently secure in their own self-worth to be able to treat others as persons. But can Emile really be treating Sophie as a person if she overwhelms his senses, or guides his passions, but is incapable of stimulating his mind? Can Sophie really be treating Emile as a person if she sees him as a means to her ends and, making the most of herself as an object of desire, attempts to inflame his senses?

One might object to Wollstonecraft's interpretation of Rousseau by pointing out, as has been argued in the last chapter, that this is not quite what Rousseau intends. Sophie is to be modest and so inflame Emile's heart (the seat of conscience) that his desires will be properly moral, rather than merely inflaming his senses. But, in fact, this is not much better, for it is clear that Rousseau is assuming that the way to a man's heart is via his senses, and, in any case, if Sophie is to calculate the fine line between modest coquetry and lasciviousness, which will effect the difference between respectable marriage and the doom of seduction, she will be relating to Emile not as to a rational equal, but rather as a sexually enslaved source of material support, which needs to be carefully managed if it is to bow beneath her gentle yoke. With regard to this mode of behaviour, Wollstonecraft has the following to say:

> ... it has been shrewdly observed by a German writer, that a pretty woman, as an object of desire, is generally allowed to be so by men of all descriptions; whilst a fine woman, who inspires more sublime emotions by displaying intellectual beauty, may be overlooked or observed with indifference by those men who find their happiness in the gratification of their appetites. I foresee an obvious retort – whilst man remains such an imperfect being as he appears hitherto to have been, he will, more or less, be the slave of his appetites; and those women obtaining most power who gratify a predominant one, the sex is degraded by a physical, if not a moral necessity.

But she rejects the inference that, since men are not reasonable, women should, out of self-interest, act as Rousseau recommends, relying in her rejection on her faith in the possibility of moral autonomy for both sexes.[31] To assume as Rousseau does that a man must be manipulated through his senses is ultimately to be pessimistic about the possibility of male moral autonomy.

The inconsistencies which arise from the differences between the sexes, as Rousseau conceives them, ultimately render his picture of the role that love plays in moral motivation incoherent. It is love of particular virtue in a woman, which is supposed to stimulate the love of universal good in man, but can this really be virtue on woman's part if, as Rousseau also suggests, modesty in women is grounded in prudence (long-term self-interest)? If women are to be truly moral, they must love virtue for its own sake, but there seems to be no room within Rousseau's picture for this to happen. For, if women act out of prudence in manipulating men's desire, and if they encourage 'the moral part of love' out of self-interest, their behaviour in this regard cannot count as exemplary virtue. In order for modesty and maternal devotion to count as moral disposi-tions, it appears that they must be grounded in rational understanding and the general desire to do one's duty. But the education necessary for the discovery of the rational ground of moral behaviour is denied to women. As Wollstonecraft complains, 'Why do men halt between two opinions, and expect impossibilities? Why do they expect virtue from a slave, from a being whom the constitution of civil society has rendered weak, if not vicious?'[32] On the one hand, Rousseau idolizes his virtuous woman and makes her the linchpin of the reproduction of the moral citizen in the ideal society; on the other hand, he denies her the oppor-tunities which are required if her actions are truly to count as virtuous.

The asymmetry between the sexes also effectively undermines Rousseau's starting point: his justification of the ideal of liberty as grounded in the natural independence of humans in the state of nature. If women were naturally independent in the state of nature, why were they motivated to 'enslave' men? The answer lies in the fact that, because of their breasts and because motherhood gives them a natural interest in the wellbeing of particular children, they are by default the primary caretakers of children. Children are thus implicitly recognized as depen-dent, but the dependent are, at least half of them, boys, who are not after all naturally independent. Woman's needs, in Rousseau's picture, turn out to depend on the lack of independence of human children. So it becomes absurd to see those needs as robbing men of their natural independence. What independence men have as adults derives from their having been cared for by women when they were in a state of dependence.

Yet, having effectively shown the inconsistencies in Rousseau's version of liberalism, has Wollstonecraft not undermined the foundations of her own philosophy? If men are not naturally independent, what justification can there be for the assumption that the good society is one in which independence and liberty are preserved? Wollstonecraft's reply to this has already been touched on. She grounds her philosophy not in a belief in the existence of a past state of nature in which everything was good, but in the possibility of a future in which individuals will be good. In such a future people will freely act for the best. In order for such a state to exist, individuals must be morally autonomous; they must be free to act on the basis of their own principles. Still, one might wonder whether this is an advance. Those who are less convinced of the existence of God, or less sanguine with regard to the inevitable perfectibility of humans, will want some justification for the fundamental liberal principle according to which individual moral autonomy, guided by reason, remains a human ideal. And this demand is the more urgent, if one suspects that humans' much-vaunted reason is, often enough, a mere arbitrary authority put at the disposal of those who wish to maintain themselves in power.

In support of Wollstonecraft's vision we can, nevertheless, make two important observations. First, as has already been pointed out, the liberal ideal can be seen to follow from the basic intuition that all humans are equally valuable, and it is clear from the following passage that this is one of Wollstonecraft's major assumptions: 'It is necessary emphatically to repeat that there are rights which men inherit at their birth, as rational creatures, who were raised above brute creation by their improvable faculties; and that, in receiving these, not from their forefathers, but from God, prescription can never undermine natural rights.'[33] The liberal concludes, from this, that one only accords equal value to individuals, who are in many respects different, by allowing them the freedom to act according to their different tastes and values. But in order to draw this conclusion, one needs to have some faith in the basic rationality and goodwill of at least the vast majority of individuals. Otherwise, what guarantee is there that freedom will not lead to a free-for-all, in which individuals act to the detriment of themselves and others; in which selfish tastes, which lead to the neglect of the dependent, imprudent tastes for self-indulgence, and aggressive tastes for sexual domination, will vie on equal terms with altruism, prudence and sexual reciprocity? Wollstonecraft had this faith, but it was grounded in a belief in God and the perfectibility of mankind. Could she have founded it on some more secure ground? Perhaps not; at some point political theory must rest on some basic intuitions, and Wollstone-craft's is that the majority of people, given the freedom to choose for themselves, and freed from the constraints which are imposed by poverty and gross social inequality, will recognize that the good life con-sists in freely choosing to live in accordance with moral principles that one has adopted because they are rational, and to live with one's fellow humans in a way in which one believes that one can justify to oneself as an exemplar of rational humanity, with human needs for fellowship, affection and forgiveness.[34] If we have no faith that social progress is possible through free choice, and that 'acquaintance with the nature of man and virtue, with just sentiments on the attributes, would be suffi-cient ... to lead some to virtue', then attempts at social reform must either be seen as futile, or take a paternalistic and totalitarian form.[35] Wollstonecraft was uncertain whether the majority of people could be led to virtue except through religious belief, but if such belief cannot be founded in reason, as she thought it could be, then we will have to rely on the possibility of human self-comprehension as grounding a belief in the possibility of a more just society. Since the alternative to liberalism, totalitarianism, is obviously bad, this gives a second reason for retaining a secularized version of Wollstonecraft's faith.

It may be useful to distinguish, at this point, a number of elements within the notion of autonomy, which are to some extent run together in Rousseau's writing. On the one hand, there is physical or material independence; on the other, there is moral autonomy. In between there is a notion of psychic independence. It is tempting to interpret Rousseau's glorification of independent man as resting on the assumption that humans are by nature physically independent and that society ought to be organized so as to preserve this autonomy. Yet, to the extent that this is what Rousseau believed, he is inconsistent, for as we have seen, Rousseau's own text implicitly refutes any such assumption. Humans are particularly dependent creatures. But Rousseau can be read another way. According to this reading, what is of fundamental importance for human wellbeing is moral independence.[36] Total physical independence is impossible, once we live in society, but it is important to retain it, to as great a degree as possible, in order to preserve one's moral autonomy. If one depends on the goodwill of others for one's livelihood, one is forced to act and speak as they require, and moral independence is lost. Psychic independence, on the other hand, is more ambiguous. Those who are totally psychically independent are not yet moral individuals; they are pre-social and care for no one but themselves. This is illustrated by Rousseau's early play, *Narcisse, ou l'Amant de Lui-Même*, discussed by Joel Schwartz.[37] But psychic dependence, like physical dependence, can be a threat to moral independence. It is for this reason that Emile must leave his Sophie, in order to gain some distance from his desire and regain his moral independence in his new state of psychic and social dependence. It is the emphasis on the importance of moral independence which Wollstonecraft inherits from Rousseau. It should be noted that this does not imply any commitment to an implausible belief in actual physical independence. In fact, she is clearly aware that humans are not created equal and that the weak, in the state of nature, will depend on the strong. The end of government is to mitigate this natural physical inequality in order to enable individuals to fulfil their moral potential.[38] Psychic dependence, however, poses conundrums for Wollstonecraft, who, like Rousseau, sees it as both desirable and problematic. But before discussing this complex issue, it is worth returning to Wollstonecraft's remaining objections to Rousseau.

As was pointed out in the last chapter, Rousseau can be interpreted as claiming that an egalitarian family is incompatible with the institution of a republic, because the citizens of a republic must be citizen soldiers who can unite together to defend their common interests. In response to this Wollstonecraft says:

> if defensive war, the only justifiable war in the present advanced state of society, . . . were alone to be adopted as just and glorious, the true heroism of antiquity might again animate female bosoms. But fair and softly, gentle reader, male or female, do not alarm thyself, . . . I am not going to advise them to turn their distaff into a musket, though I sincerely wish to see the bayonet converted into a pruning hook.[39]

Her point is that, in the general run of life, just occasions for going to war are few and far between. A society truly interested in only defending itself would not need to promote military arts to any great degree. She goes on to observe that, even in a society in which men had, as part of their duties as citizens, to leave the family to train or prepare for war, the wife would in any case be equally an active citizen 'intent to manage her family, educate her children, and assist her neighbours'.[40]

As well as indicating the deep inconsistencies in Rousseau's picture, Wollstonecraft also demonstrates that Rousseau's method of educating daughters is designed to fail in its intended aim:

> I now appeal . . . to the good sense of mankind, whether, if the object of education be to prepare women to become chaste wives and sensible mothers, the method so plausibly recommended in the foregoing sketch

be the one best calculated to produce those ends? Will it be allowed that
the surest way to make a wife chaste is to teach her to practice the wanton
arts of a mistress?[41]

Those who have been taught to think of themselves as objects of desire
rather than as reasonable companions will make bad wives and mothers,
since, after a time, possession will dampen a husband's desire and women
will look elsewhere to satisfy their need to be desired. Moreover, men
will be less happy in marriage than they might otherwise be:

> The man who can be contented to live with a pretty, useful companion,
> without a mind, has lost in voluptuous gratifications a taste for more
> refined enjoyments; he has never felt the calm satisfaction that refreshes
> the parched heart like the silent dew of heaven – of being beloved by one
> who could understand him ... 'The charm of life', says a grave philo-
> sophical reasoner, is, 'sympathy; nothing pleases us more than to observe
> in other men a fellow-feeling with all the emotions of our own breast'.[42]

Wollstonecraft points out further that writers like Rousseau and Dr For-
dyce are simply wrong about the amount of influence that a virtuous
woman can have over a man's conscience. More often than not men
leave narrow-minded virtuous wives at home and go abroad to seek
more exciting company.[43]

Taken together, these observations constitute a compelling rebuttal of
Rousseau's attempt to reconcile the subordination of women within marriage and republican egalitarianism. But, from the point of view of some
influential strands in contemporary feminism, one might object that in
so far as Wollstonecraft qualifies her assertion that women's 'first duty
is to themselves as rational creatures' with the acceptance that 'the next,
in point of importance, as citizens, is that, which includes so many, of
a mother', and in so far as she shares Rousseau's end of educating women
to play the part of chaste wives, she has failed to come to grips with
the real nature of woman's oppression, the repression of their sexuality
in the service of patriarchal marriage.[44] Wollstonecraft and Rousseau
agree on one thing: a woman's maternal role is a very important one.
A woman ought to suckle her own children and care for them. Rousseau,
however, justifies this conclusion on the basis of its naturalness; Wollstonecraft on the basis of its reasonableness. This emphasis on the duties
of mothers may seem misplaced, but once it is understood in the light
of the situation that existed in their time, it has considerable relevance
to our contemporary circumstances. In the eighteenth century, aristocratic women very generally resorted to the use of wet nurses, so

as not to be inconvenienced in their social life by the demands of their babies. Since this was the fashionable thing for the wealthy to do, the practice was spreading to the middle classes, while many working-class women had no option but to use wet nurses, or to send their infants to foundling homes, since they had no means of subsistence apart from employment in jobs incompatible with caring for children. The infant mortality rate among children cared for by these wet nurses was staggering. French figures suggest it was between 30 and 50 per cent and that the children were often appallingly neglected. Infants suckled by their own mothers, on the other hand, had a less than 20 per cent chance of dying.[45] So the duty of mothers to look after their own children was a moral issue of some importance. The neglect of their children in the pursuit of pleasure was just one of the characteristics of moral corruptness that democrats like Rousseau and Wollstonecraft could point to in the aristocracy. And the neglect and abuse of children, with the resulting reproduction of neglect and abuse, is of continuing concern. Wollstonecraft, like Rousseau, accepted that the just society requires the production of moral individuals. She believed, in addition, that the moral sentiments are generated out of the affections of family life. She was in favour of day schools, rather than boarding schools, because in day schools 'children have the opportunity of conversing with children, without interfering with domestic affections, the foundation of virtue.'[46] So the duties of mothers have considerable importance not only for the sake of children but also as an avenue through which women can develop themselves as reasonable moral individuals.[47] As an aspect of the shared parental responsibility which is necessary for the reproduction of a just society, the duties of mothers are part of the duties of citizenship.

Wollstonecraft agrees with Rousseau on the importance of the duties of motherhood, but, at least in her earlier writing, she has quite different views as to the role of love in the family. In the *Vindication of the Rights of Woman*, sexual love is seen as an unstable foundation for anything as important as family life.[48] Sexual passion soon fades, and if a woman is motivated by a desire to be desired, her husband's waning interest is sure to lead her to infidelities. Instead, marriage should be based on friendship between equals. A genuine regard for the genuine good qualities of one's spouse should found a union between autonomous individuals united in their sense of duty towards their children. This position seems more logical than Rousseau's. For, if vanity and a concern for public opinion are inimical to justice, as Rousseau suggests, they should not be the basis of an important social institution like the

family. At the same time, Wollstonecraft's early comments on the importance of sexuality underestimate human needs. Her last, unfinished novel
shows a more acute awareness of the emotional needs which are associated with sexuality and the conflict these set up with ideals of full moral
autonomy. We will return to the question of the place of the passions
in Wollstonecraft's conception of humanity below. But first it is worth
discussing an objection to her liberal outlook which is more easily dealt
with.

As has already been mentioned, Wollstonecraft leaves it unclear how
the family situation that she envisages is to be brought about. She
requires, for instance, that wives should be economically independent.[49]
Clearly this is necessary for them to be able relate to their husbands as
equals and in order for them to have the capacity to leave a tyrannical
husband. With the benefit of hindsight one might wonder whether
education and legal rights are sufficient to guarantee economic independence, of any meaningful sort, to women with young children, particularly if one retains, as Wollstonecraft appears to, a traditional picture
of the duties of motherhood, which far outrun the duties of fatherhood.
Diana Coole asserts: 'Wollstonecraft does not seem to realize that the
sexual division of labour which she advocates must reproduce the
patriarchal family, since cultural equivalence cannot cancel out economic dependence.'[50] And this constitutes a standard socialist objection to
Wollstonecraft's liberal feminism. However, the tenor of Wollstonecraft's thought, which holds up the ideal of marriage as an equal relation
of affection and respect between morally autonomous persons, suggests
that she would welcome the more recent developments of liberal feminist
thought, which include in the duties of egalitarian parenthood an obligation on the behalf of fathers to care for their children, which is similar
to that borne by mothers.[51]

It is often assumed that the political programme which can be justified
on the basis of liberal feminism is exhausted once women have the vote
and there is genuine equality of opportunity. But while women continue
to contribute more than men to the maintenance of the family, and do
unpaid work within the private sphere, equality of opportunity is
unlikely to lead to anything like equality of outcomes. If there is competition for positions of power and prestige, those who are free of the
demands of childcare will, all other things being equal, be in a better
position to succeed, and, as is now the case, the vast majority of these
positions will be held by men whose wives are prepared to carry the main
burden of childcare, or by childless women or men. Frustrated with the
slow rate of change in the position of women in actual liberal societies,

some feminists have argued that feminism must ultimately undermine the liberal capitalist state.[52] But this assumes that inequities in the distribution of power between the sexes are necessarily linked with the inequities in the distribution of private property accepted by liberal capitalism. It assumes also that the avenues for gaining power within a socialist state will not equally disadvantage women, and that the structures of the liberal states that now exist are in fact structures which exemplify liberal principles, consistently applied. This last is certainly not the case if one's conception of what the liberal state ought to be is that indicated by Wollstonecraft in the following passage: 'Nature having made men unequal, by giving stronger bodily and mental powers to one than to another, the end of government ought to be, to destroy this inequality by protecting the weak.'[53] If the liberal state has a duty to protect the weak, and if woman's important duties in relation to children can be expected to put them at some disadvantage in a free competition for places within the structures of the state apparatus, the conclusion that should be drawn is that women, as a group, should have their own guaranteed representatives. This was, in fact, Wollstonecraft's conclusion.[54] It may well be, as I once argued elsewhere, that the only way of guaranteeing that women are represented within the state apparatus in numbers sufficient to ensure that their interests are protected is to insist that 50 per cent of the seats in the legislature are filled by women.[55] In that earlier paper I suggested that this might be done by dividing the electorate so that women voted for women. This suggestion has some drawbacks, since women lose their capacity to influence the election of men. Another possibility would be for pairs, consisting of one man and one woman, to be pre-selected by parties, and for voters to vote for pairs, who would then be treated as individuals in the parliament. In any case, the details of such a proposal are not important here. The fundamental point is that the actual achievements of liberalism to date should not be thought to accomplish liberal feminist aspirations.[56] Wollstonecraft's general observation that moral autonomy is impossible in the face of substantial differences in power implies that a liberal state committed to equal moral autonomy will need mechanisms to guarantee that differences in power are minimized.

But even such amendments to Wollstonecraft's liberalism might not be thought to go far enough. Cora Kaplan claims that:

> It is unfortunate that Wollstonecraft chose to fight Rousseau on his own terms, accepting his paradigm of a debased, eroticised femininity as fact rather than ideological fiction . . . mid-century women writers and

feminists looking for ways to legitimize their feminism and their sexuality, as well as their desire to write them both out together, found small comfort in *A Vindication* where the creative and the affective self are split up and separated.[57]

There are two elements in Kaplan's criticism of Wollstonecraft. One concentrates on the apparent prudery of many of Wollstonecraft's remarks, the other on the alleged split, in her writing, between the affective and creative self, the creative self being identified with the rational spirit, the affective self with a debased sexuality. Kaplan's worry is part of a more general objection which might be put as follows: the distrust of sexuality which Wollstonecraft displays is evidence that she has taken over a masculine conception of the rational individual and an opposition between mind and body, reason and passion that is central to the male point of view. As we saw, in Mary Jacobus's reading of Wollstonecraft, this thought is transformed into the assertion that, in so far as Wollstonecraft writes as a reasonable and utilitarian thinker, she writes against woman. It is only in her evocation of madness that she expresses her feminine voice.[58]

In this chapter, I will attempt to discuss only the second element of this general worry: the claim that the individual subject of Wollstonecraft's liberalism is a pure rational spirit split off from its affective self.[59] A full discussion of the incoherence of a philosophy which endorses both sexual restraint and feminism will have to wait for the now much-heralded next chapter. We have already seen that there are reasons for being suspicious of a hasty identification of the feminine voice with a language opposed to rationality. A discussion of Wollstonecraft's views on the relationship between reason and passion will confirm this suspicion, for it will demonstrate that Wollstonecraft is among those who believe that rationality and passion are complementary elements within the human psyche, both of which are necessary in the formation of a moral individual. Even Wollstonecraft's prudery is not so much a rejection of sexuality *per se* as a rejection of debased sexual relations, in which women expect to be treated as mere objects of sexual desire, and men use women as the means for satisfying their sexual urges without considering them as persons, as is made clear by the following:

'The sentiment, that a woman may allow all innocent freedoms, provided her virtue is secure, is both grossly indelicate and dangerous, and has proved fatal to many of your sex.' With this opinion I perfectly coincide. A man, or a woman, of any feeling, must always wish to convince a beloved object that it is the caresses of the individual, not the sex, that are received and returned with pleasure; and that the heart, rather than the senses, is moved. Without this natural delicacy, love becomes a selfish personal gratification that soon degrades the character.[60]

Wollstonecraft's concern here is to reject any tendency in men and women to treat each other as sex objects, rather than as individuals for whom affection, esteem and self-esteem are intimately related.

Far from splitting the affective from the rational aspects of the moral individual, Wollstonecraft was particularly concerned in her treatises on education with the development of the right moral sentiments, which she suggests, echoing Rousseau, are innate.[61] Her *Original Stories from Real Life* are largely concerned with the task of developing the appropriate motivation in a pair of children whose moral education has been neglected. They are shown the destructiveness of anger, are taught to feel the pleasure which arises from the capacity to give to the needy, and learn that virtue is the truest source of pleasure.[62] One of her most forth-right expressions of her commitment to the idea that the passions and reason are interconnected comes in the following passage:

> I must therefore venture to doubt whether what has been thought an axiom in morals may not have been a dogmatical assertion made by men who have coolly seen mankind through the medium of books, and say, in direct contradiction to them, that the regulation of the passions is not always wisdom. On the contrary, it would seem, that one reason why men have superior judgement, and more fortitude than women, is undoubtedly this, that they give a freer scope to the grand passions, and by more frequently going astray enlarge their minds ... But if, in the dawn of life we could soberly survey the scenes before as in perspective ... how could the passions gain sufficient strength to unfold the faculties? ...
>
> And love! ... To see a mortal adorn an object with imaginary charms, and then fall down and worship the idol which he had himself set up – how ridiculous! ... Would not all the purposes of life have been much better fulfilled if he had only felt what has been termed physical love? And would not the sight of the object, not seen through the medium of the imagination, soon reduce the passion to an appetite if reflection, the noble distinction of man, did not give it force, and make it an instrument to raise him above this earthly dross, by teaching him to love the centre of all perfection, whose wisdom appears clearer and clearer in the works of nature in proportion as reason is illuminated and exalted by contemplation, and by acquiring that love of order which the struggles of passion produce? ...
>
> Besides, it is not possible to give a young person a just view of life; he must have struggled with his own passions before he can estimate the force of the temptation which betrayed his brother into vice ... The world cannot be seen by an unmoved spectator; we must mix in the throng and feel as men feel, before we can judge of their feelings ... prudence early in life is but the cautious graft of ignorant self-love.[63]

Here there is no splitting of the affective from the rational self. Rather, these passages show that Wollstonecraft believed that we need to feel before we can think. We cannot derive true knowledge or understanding of the world, its dangers and temptations, from reading books or being taught moral axioms. Ethical understanding is achieved partly through making mistakes and indulging the passions which 'unfold the faculties'. Love is in a sense an illusion; we confer ideal qualities on mere mortals, in a manner that can appear quite ridiculous; but reflecting on this passion will lead us to see that it is these ideal qualities that we love. And in order to understand our fellow humans rationally, to know how to forgive and when to censure, we must have felt all the passions that a human feels. It is only by reflecting on our emotions that we are led to ethical principles and in particular to a rational assessment of which sentiments ought to be encouraged and which curtailed.[64]

Wollstonecraft was no stranger to the desire to be loved and the conflict that this desire sets up within an individual who aspires at the same time to independence.[65] Her novel, *Maria, or the Wrongs of Woman* deals with the story of Maria, a sensitive woman led by Rousseau's *La Nouvelle Héloïse* to aspire to love, who finds herself separated from her child and flung into a mad-house by her avaricious husband.[66] Despite the treatment she has received at the hands of men, she continues to yearn for love and to meet a man with 'genuine sensibility'. Mary Poovey, in her account of Wollstonecraft's thought, suggests that like Maria, Mary is incapable of extricating herself from the 'sentimental idealism' and 'romantic expectations' which led her to want to be loved as she was capable of loving.[67] Poovey believes that, ultimately, Wollstonecraft's feminism failed in its radicalism because she fell prey to the ideology of feminine feeling and propriety.[68] It is part of the aim of this book to throw some light on the question of whether we should consider this tendency in her work as the manifestation of a genuine feminine voice or as the adoption of a bourgeois ideology. The issue at stake will be made somewhat clearer in the next three chapters. In the last chapter I will argue for the cogency of the kind of feminist humanism implied in Wollstonecraft's writing. Of particular importance is her perception that a liberalism which fails to take into account the place of love and affection in the reproduction of the moral individual is incomplete. Here, we need only note that Poovey's account of Wollstonecraft's writing confirms that she was no cold rationalist, but believed that reason, feeling and imagination were all integral elements of the moral personality. Wollstonecraft did not have time, in her short life, to leave us a well-worked-out treatise on this subject, so her views have to be pieced together from fragments and hints. This task has been greatly aided by Sapiro's careful reading of her texts.

Of particular importance in Wollstonecraft's understanding of the 'reasoned, passionate self' is the role played by imagination.[69] In a letter to Imlay she chides him for not sufficiently respecting the imagination and suggests that:

> ... it is the mother of sentiment, the great distinction of our nature, the only purifier of the passions – animals have a portion of reason, and equal if not more exquisite senses; but no trace of imagination, or her offspring taste, appears in any of their actions. The impulse of the senses, passions if you will, and the conclusions of reason, draw men together; but imagination is the true fire, stolen from heaven, to animate this cold creature of clay, producing all those fine sympathies that lead to rapture, rendering men social by expanding their hearts, instead of leaving them leisure to calculate how many comforts society affords.[70]

The imagination is here seen as producing sympathy and rendering men social; it is the 'mother of sentiment' and in particular of the kind of fellow feeling which makes us moral and social beings. Elsewhere Wollstonecraft claims that 'True sensibility, the sensibility which is the auxiliary of virtue, and the soul of genius, is in society so occupied with the feelings of others, as scarcely to regard its own sensations.'[71] Imagination is the prerequisite for such true sensibility, for it is imagination which enables us to feel as others must feel in the situations that they are in, even when we ourselves are very differently placed.

It is clear that this is no cold Kantian rationalism. And Wollstonecraft explicitly disagrees with Kant:

> Mr Kant has observed, that the understanding is sublime, the imagination beautiful – yet it is evident, that poets, and men who undoubtedly possess the liveliest imagination, are most touched by the sublime, while men who have cold, enquiring minds, have not this exquisite feeling in any great degree, and indeed seem to lose it as they cultivate their reason.[72]

It is imagination rather than reason which is sublime and associated with genius and exquisite sensibility. When reason alone produces works of art, or when they are produced by reason in imitation of other works, rather than from the immediate reflection of reason on its own sensations, enlivened by imagination, we have cold works, 'shrivelled by rules'.[73] In her letters from Sweden she makes it clear, reflecting on aesthetic experience, that reason, feeling and imagination are in no way in opposition, but rather interact in complex ways to take us beyond the mere finite existence available in perception:

In these respects my very reason obliges me to permit my feelings to be my criterion. Whatever excites emotion has charms for me; though I insist that the cultivation of the mind, by warming, nay almost creating the imagination, produces taste, and an immense variety of sensations and emotions, partaking of the exquisite pleasure inspired by beauty and sublimity. As I know of no end to them, the word infinite, so often misapplied, might, on this occasion be introduced with something like propriety.[74]

The mind and the passions have, on this view of things, a very complex interaction. Imagination is produced by the mind, but is not the same as cold calculation; rather, it produces feeling and is strongest in those passionate individuals 'most touched by the sublime'. The passions thus produced 'unfold the mind'. Wollstonecraft is here indicating a conception of human reason in which the capacity for imagination, and its consequent stimulation of sympathetic fellow feeling, are central to human rationality and ethical development. In the last chapter of this book, I will take up some of the threads suggested by these quotations. But for the time being it will be sufficient to note that the charge that Wollstonecraft has severed the affective from the rational self is totally without foundation.

6

Socialism, Sex and Savage Society

Between Wollstonecraft's *Vindication of the Rights of Woman* and the gaining of female suffrage there was only minor development within mainstream feminist thought. There is no marked progress in philosophical content between Wollstonecraft's text and John Stuart Mill's *Subjection of Women* (a work greatly influenced by his wife, Harriet Taylor). Indeed, there is some loss, in so far as the moral psychology which was hinted at in the earlier work has disappeared, as has the recognition that men and women are sexual beings, and both works suffer from the lacuna which we saw in the last chapter: the difficulty that in a society in which power and financial independence are to be acquired through relatively free competition, women will be disadvantaged competitors if they continue to play their traditional role as childcarers. If women are to have sufficient economic independence to be able to achieve full moral autonomy, it seems that economic reward and political power cannot simply be tied to success in the market, but must rather be related to need and desert. This line of reasoning results in the conclusion that socialism is a necessary prerequisite for women to escape their oppression. An argument to this conclusion was first offered by William Thompson in *Appeal of One Half of the Human Race*.[1] The connection between feminism and socialism also emerges out of the feminist critique of Rousseau's conception of humans as essentially independent. If, by contrast, humans are essentially dependent creatures, whose very existence depends on the willingness of others to provide the basis for their existence, it is natural to generalize this and to think of society's role as that of providing for the needs of all its members. Together these two thoughts suggest that feminism both requires and implies socialism.[2]

The connection between socialism and feminism is most famously associated with Engels, whose *The Origin of the Family, Private Property and the State* has been taken to imply that the advent of socialism and the abolition of private property will suffice to free women from their oppression. Engels's work was largely a rewriting of Lewis Henry Morgan's *Ancient Society*, which developed an evolutionary account of the development of society; according to this, women occupied an important place in primitive societies, which was eroded by the rise of private property and a transition from matrilineal to patrilineal kinship systems. Morgan postulated three epochs of society: savagery, barbarism and civilization, which correspond roughly to hunter-gatherer societies, early agricultural societies organized along lines of kinship (clan or gentile organization), and later societies in which agriculture has been supplemented by commodity production and trade, and in which gentile organization is replaced by the nuclear patriarchal family and the state. He also claimed that the family had evolved from an early stage of promiscuity, that is a stage in which there were no sexual taboos, to the 'consanguine family', in which all members of a generation were husband and wife, but there was an intergenerational incest taboo, through the *'punaluan'* family in which the incest taboo is extended to brothers and sisters (and all maternal cousins are counted as brother and sister), to the 'pairing family' and the ill-named 'monogamy'. The differences between these last two amount, roughly, to the fact that in the first there exists a recognition of the matrilineal clan, and marriage can be easily dissolved by either man or wife, while in the second kinship is purely patrilineal, marriage is largely indissoluble and fidelity, for the wife, is strictly enforced. It is 'monogamy *for the woman only'* (and would more appropriately be called monandry).[3] According to Engels, 'Morgan has quite independently discovered the Marxian materialist conception of history.'[4] And he used Morgan's evidence and theories, supplemented by those of Bachofen, to establish the claim that 'the world historical defeat of the female sex' had occurred with the rise of private property, the need for men to secure their wives' fidelity for the sake of inheritance, and the consequent replacement of matrilineal by patrilineal lines of descent.[5] Thus it could be assumed that the abolition of private property would lead to the emancipation of women. For in a society in which women were no longer confined to the role of producers of heirs, they would no longer be forced to submit themselves to the legal prostitution of marriage, and would be able to give themselves to a man from motives of love alone.[6] The assumption that sexual repression is the result of the rise of private property, and that woman's oppression consists in the control of her sexuality, can therefore be traced back to Engels, and became, during the 1960s and 1970s, a fundamental presupposition of feminist thought. This, perhaps inappropriately named, 'second wave' of feminism was hugely influenced by Simone de Beauvoir's *The Second Sex*, which largely accepted Engels's earlier work, and, as a result, much feminism developed as a branch of socialist political theory, with a somewhat incongruous existentialist overlay. De Beauvoir herself was originally rather suspicious of the feminist movement, since, as she herself states, she believed that the real cause of woman's oppression was capitalism, and hence the important fight was the one for its overthrow.[7] But despite her personal ambivalence, her influence on feminist thought has been profound. This is no doubt partly because her views were largely complementary to those of the sexual liberationists who came to prominence in the first half of the twentieth century. Thus, in her seminal manifesto *The Dialectic of Sex*, Shulamith Firestone was able both to dedicate her work to de Beauvoir and to rely, for her views concerning the feminist future, on the theory of sexual liberation.[8]

Within the classical statement of the relationship of sexual relations and socialism originating with Engels, and developed by Bebel, the particular question of the emancipation of women becomes subsumed within the larger struggle for communism.[9] But circumstances were to lead to the development of versions of Marxism which made the abolition of the family and the freeing of sexual relations appear to be the precondition for the development of the longed-for communist utopia, in which free individuals would act each for all and all for each. Central to this evolution within Marxism was the independent development of Freudian psychoanalysis. A heady mixture of Marxism and psychoanalysis thus came to provide the background presuppositions of much twentieth-century feminist thought. But, before discussing the conjunction of these two influences, and the emergence of the philosophy of sexual liberation, we need to reach further back to the origins of Marxism in Hegel's thought, if we are to understand the various influences at work in the contemporary feminist suspicion of rationality and humanism, and its interconnections with views about sexuality and the family.

The degeneration of the French Revolution into the reign of terror shattered Wollstonecraft's easy belief in the perfectibility of man and had a similar effect on another young radical who had likewise looked forward to the dawning of a golden age.[10] Hegel reacted to the disappointment of his optimistic radical hopes not, as Wollstonecraft did, by pessimistically postulating the necessity of evil, but by effectively denying the conflict between the ideal world of utopian dreamers and the real world of irrational conflict, fear, extremism and brutality. The failure of the French Revolution was taken by him not to demonstrate the illusory nature of the Enlightenment's faith in reason and the progress of humanity, but to show that rational freedom could only be achieved in a state organized on rational principles. He developed an elegant, though incredible, philosophical system within which the conflicts of past history were interpreted as necessary stages in the development of the world (itself conceived of as a mind coming to self-consciousness) through a dialectical process, at each stage of which a contradiction was resolved through 'synthesis' or 'sublation'. Hegel's system is 'idealist' in the sense that the ultimate nature of reality is thought of as *'Geist* – that is, as immaterial – but this is an objective idealism; the nature of reality is quite independent of individual ideas of it. At each stage of the development of *Geist* there is a conception of the 'objective' material world which we take to be different from and opposed to our ideas of the material world, but this 'material' world is ultimately recognized as being identical with the ideal, for it is nothing but the projection of consciousness at its stage of development. This philosophy was taken over by Marx, who 'turned it on its head' and interpreted the dialectic of history not as the process of development of *Geist*, but as a material process. Thus, whereas for Hegel, at each stage of history, 'material reality' is just a projection of the contemporary mind, for Marx, the ideas or beliefs of a particular period are just a projection of the contemporary processes of material production. Out of this background was born the concept of 'ideology'. At each stage in the material dialectic (leading as in Hegel's scheme inevitably and by its internal logic to a reconciliation of all oppositions), there is a class opposition in which one class – that which controls the means of production, distribution and exchange – exploits the other class or classes. This social situation appears natural, because the beliefs of the individuals involved are the result of their relationship with the material world. Such a set of beliefs, appearing to capture the truth, thus serves to rationalize a social situation of domination and submission; but since social relations are not natural relations, it does not capture the truth but is an ideology.[11]

Within early Marxist thought the concept of ideology did not play a very significant role. Since the deterministic processes of the conflict of classes were expected to lead to the communist revolution, the ultimate *telos* of history depended not on the ideas in the minds of men, but on the inevitable working through of the development of material production. However, during the 1920s and 1930s, at a point in time when it appeared that capitalism was collapsing, many members of the German working class turned to fascism, rather than embracing the communist revolution. The explanation for this appeared, to many Marxists, to be that capitalist ideology was more deep-seated than had appeared. Wilhelm Reich observed at this period:

> Until now, social ideology was envisioned only as a sum of ideas forming 'in the heads of men' about the economic process. But after the victory of political reaction in Germany's gravest crisis and the experience of the irrational behaviour of the masses, ideology can no longer be regarded as a mere reflection of economic conditions. *As soon as an ideology has taken hold of and moulded human structure, it becomes a material social power.* There is no socioeconomic process of historical significance which is not anchored in the psychic structure of the masses and activated in the form of mass behaviour.[12]

Combined with Freud's development of psychoanalysis, which was based on the twin principles that individual character developed out of the psychodynamics of the family, and that conscious motivation is merely the visible tip of human motivation, which is more often guided by the unconscious residue of our sexual development, the foregoing led Reich to develop a theory of the place of the family in the reproduction of the ideology of class society which has remained profoundly influential, despite the rejection of most of Reich's other views. According to this theory, 'compulsive marriage ... constitutes the backbone of the authoritarian ideological factory, the patriarchal family – that being its political function in a reactionary society.... the social purpose of the demand for asceticism in youth and for sexual suppression in early childhood is, therefore, the insuring of man's capacity for lifelong compulsory marriage.'[13] Juliet Mitchell, who is otherwise critical of Reich, nevertheless uncritically retains this fundamental Reichian assumption.[14]

Freud's early work on hysteria had led him to postulate the existence of the unconscious as a repository of repressed infantile sexual drives. According to Freud, only a very small part of an individual's real motivation is accessible to consciousness, even the ego is partly unconscious, and the real springs and forces which motivate us are the repressed drives, concealed in the unconscious, which manifest themselves only in dreams, jokes, slips of the tongue and neurotic symptoms. This repression is necessary in order for individuals to comply with the demands of the 'reality principle' and to take their places as full, morally motivated members of society. The super-ego, or conscience, which motivates individuals to comply with the constraints of living within a culture, is the result, in men, of the resolution of the Oedipus complex, in the face of the fear of castration, which is engendered in them by their fathers' power and prohibition. This resolution involves the renunciation of incestuous desire for the mother and identification with the role of the father. The situation is slightly different for women, who cannot fear castration but rather come to resent the fact that they are already 'castrated', thus being led to transfer their sexual desire from the mother to the father. According to Freud, an advantage of this theory is that it 'explains' why the super-ego is never so inexorable in women.[15] Freud in his later writings postulated that the fear and guilt which motivate the boy during the Oedipal period cannot simply be the consequence of his own individual experience, and he therefore hypothesized a primal origin of society in an act of parricide. In *Totem and Taboo* he develops a theory of the origin of culture which equates it with an original act of parricide, carried out by a band of brothers, who have been excluded from sexual access to the females of the primal horde by an all-powerful patriarch.[16] Thus for Freud, civilization requires sexual repression, and the neuroses and sexual maladies which occur as the result of deviations within the process of repression are an inevitable price to be paid for cultural progress.

Wilhelm Reich was one of Freud's younger colleagues, who, while accepting Freud's theory of the existence of an innate sexual drive, and the existence of repression which leads to neuroses and sexual discontent, rejected Freud's theory of the universality of the Oedipus complex and the necessity of sexual repression. Instead of Freud's hypothesis of the origin of society in an act of parricide, he adopted Engels's account of the evolution of society from the primitive horde through matriarchy to patriarchy. Using Bronislaw Malinowski's observations of life in the Trobriand Islands to back up the Morgan/Engels account of the origins of social life, Reich argued that individual character under patriarchy is distorted by sexual repression, leading to patterns of authoritarianism and submissiveness. He concluded that the toleration of infantile and adolescent sexuality is a necessary prerequisite for the development in individuals of a democratic, non-authoritarian character, capable of participating fully in an egalitarian and democratic state. For, according to him, 'suppression of the love life of children and adolescents is the central mechanism for producing enslaved subordinates and economic serfs.'[17]

Reich's views came to diverge from those of most Freudians in a number of ways. One centred on his emphasis on the mechanistic aspects of Freud's theory, in contrast to an emphasis on the symbolic and psychological aspects, which have remained central to mainstream psychoanalysis. In his early work Freud often spoke of the libido in terms that suggested a flow of energy, which could be dammed or diverted or provide the impetus behind the normal heterosexual patterns of erotic attachment. It was this aspect of Freud's work which most impressed Reich, and which led him ultimately to the 'banal' view that 'there is only one thing wrong with neurotic patients: *the lack of full and repeated sexual satisfaction.*'[18] Ultimately, the banality of this view constitutes one of its greatest weaknesses. Reich observed that among the patients who visited his clinic, neurotic individuals universally suffered from disordered sex lives. This correlation lead him to the hypothesis that it was the lack of sexual relief which caused the psychological difficulties and character disturbances from which his patients were suffering. Thus Reich was one of the originators of the twentieth-century belief in a good sex-life as universal panacea. But one could equally well conclude, from his evidence, that character disorders and psychological difficulties cause sexual disorders, or that they are interrelated in complex ways. One of the consequences of Reich's simplistic orientation has been an interpretation of sexual liberation which ignores the interpersonal and emotional aspects of sexual life, and reduces it to a mechanistic business of tension and release.

Reich's most sustained argument for the connection between sexual liberation and the development of an egalitarian and non-authoritarian character occurs in *The Invasion of Compulsory Sex-morality*, where he bases his argument largely on the anthropological data from the Trobriands, reported by Malinowski in *The Sexual Life of Savages in North-western Melanesia*. Malinowski described the Trobriand society as one in which there was matrilineal descent and inheritance, women took a leading part in economic and ceremonial activities, it was generally believed that children are formed by the mother only, and infantile and adolescent sexual behaviour was tolerated to a considerable degree.[19] Although fidelity within marriage was generally expected, anecdotes imply that it was not always practised, and marriage was easily dissoluble by either the wife or husband.[20] Indeed, since a woman's economic position was dependent on her own labour and the contributions of her brothers, and since her husband benefited from these contributions, there was no economic disincentive for divorce on her behalf, while there was a considerable disincentive for her husband to divorce her. Malinowski's description of the Trobriands has much in common with Morgan's description of societies which have developed 'pairing marriage', although Malinowski made scathing comments in relation to the Morgan/Engels evolutionary theory.[21] Despite this, Reich uses his material to back up that view, concluding that:

> Social development from primeval clan society to the present-day national state shows two interrelated processes. On the one hand there is the development from primeval economic work-democracy to the capitalist state ... On the other hand there is the development from natural, sex-economic freedom* and the clan consanguine family to the ideology of extramarital asceticism and lifelong compulsory monogamous marriage; and consequently, increasing restriction, repression, and distortion of genital sexuality.
>
> * This is exactly the opposite of sexual libertinism due to orgiastic impotence ...
>
> The natural morality of the primitive matriarchal peoples, living in sexual freedom based on gratification, was infinitely superior to the morality of our age. This is particularly apparent in the absence of anti-social sexual behaviour (rape, sexual murders, etc.) ...
>   This process of sexual suppression is older than the 'class conflict' between man and woman and is the cause of this antagonism.[22]

Reich assumes a natural, heterosexual and promiscuous, genital orientation which is progressively repressed and diverted into sexual aggression, homosexuality, perversion and neurosis as the economic aspects of marriage become paramount and lead to the imposition of sexual restraints.

However, Reich's use of Malinowski to show that sexual repression is not necessary for the functioning of society is somewhat disingenuous. In his own discussion of Freud and the Oedipus complex, Malinowski clearly shows that there *is* sexual repression in the Trobriands, but argues that it takes a different form to that prevalent in western patriarchal societies. Instead of fear and veneration of the father there is fear and veneration of the maternal uncle; instead of a repressed incestuous desire for the mother there is a repressed incestuous desire for the sister.[23] Moreover, Malinowski's observations clearly show the existence of authoritarian behaviour, violence and conflict in the Trobriands. Rather than treating her husband as an authority, a woman crouches before her brother 'like a commoner to a chief'.[24] And while there is premarital sexual freedom, there are stringent restraints on sexuality after marriage, beauty is equated with relatively pale skin colour and associated with lack of sexual desire, sexual abstinence is expected from parents after the birth of a child until it is weaned, and accusations of promiscuity in women are capable of engendering a degree of shame sufficient to motivate suicide.[25] While he is aware of these deviations from his ideal of a sexually liberated society, Reich puts them down to the fact that Trobriand society has developed some way from a purely promiscuous state to one in which economic considerations have entered into sexuality, thus corrupting it. He says the following:

> We shall show, by means of Malinowski's own reports, that the 'unrestrained' biologically regulated life of the Trobrianders is, nevertheless, at odds with their institutions of marriage and the family. And if we have to take a stand for the 'unrestrained', with no neuroses or perversions, or for marriage and the family, with perversions and neuroses and sexual misery, there is nothing left for us but to decide in favour of one or the other.[26]

Thus he goes beyond any evidence provided by Malinowski, in order to derive the existence of a previous, more perfectly liberated state of humanity, in which sexual promiscuity was completely unrestrained by marriage or any form of sexual restriction. Malinowski's own attitude to such a deduction is perhaps worth noting. Morgan's evidence for the prehistorical existence of complete promiscuity and group marriage consists in features of nomenclature. This requires the hypothesis that names remain constant as family structure changes or, as Engels reports:

> While the family undergoes living changes, the system of consanguinity ossifies; while the system survives by force of custom, the family outgrows it. But just as Cuvier could deduce from the marsupial bone of an animal skeleton found near Paris that it belonged to a marsupial animal . . . so with the same certainty we can deduce from the historical survival of a system of consanguinity that an extinct form of the family once existed which corresponded to it.[27]

To which Malinowski replies: 'Cuvier was able to reconstruct his antediluvian monster from a tiny bone only because he knew the correlation of the bone to the rest of the skeleton. It is in the relation between a detail of structure to the whole that its meaning and its reconstructive virtue lies.'[28] He goes on to point out that the status of the deductions is quite different, since while there are living examples of marsupials, no actual society has ever been observed in which group marriage or universal promiscuity is practised.

Despite the fact that they do not justify Reich's conclusions, Malinowski's observations do have important implications, which will be drawn out in the last chapter of this book; for they appear to show, as Malinowski himself argued, that the Oedipus complex as it occurs in western patriarchal societies cannot be, as Freud assumed, necessary for the development of moral motivation. Trobriand Islanders are just as motivated by thoughts of honour and self-esteem, by the desire to do good by their own lights, by shame and public opinion, as are westerners. This fact suggests three possible options: either Malinowski is wrong and the Oedipus complex does exist in Trobriand society, or in the Trobriands the super-ego is formed through the authority of the maternal uncle, or Freud is completely mistaken in his account of the genesis of moral motivation. Ernest Jones attempted to defend the first of these possibilities.[29] Malinowski, in reply, points out that it is simply illicit to discover traces of the Oedipus complex in a society where none of its manifestations are to be found.[30] He goes on to observe that orthodox Freudians accept that the Oedipus complex is the source of culture and suggests that this explains Jones's attitude, but, as Malinowski demonstrates, Freud's story as it is outlined in *Totem and Taboo* is circular and grounded in the quite implausible assumption that culture was initiated by a single act. If the brothers, who it is claimed committed parricide, are to feel guilt about that parricide they must already have a conscience, but a conscience is 'a most unnatural mental trait imposed upon man by culture'.[31] Freud is in fact aware of this difficulty and tries to get around it by postulating that the brothers feel remorse because they had ambivalently loved and feared the father.[32] However, the hypothesis that there is love between the sons and a patriarch whose role is to service their various mothers is quite implausible. Malinowski's own view may be captured in the second possibility, as is indicated by his comment that, 'mother- right . . . "splits the Oedipus complex", dividing the authority between two males.'[33] But the fact that children brought up by sole mothers show no particular tendencies towards moral degeneration suggests that male authority figures may be less relevant to the development of moral motivation than Freud assumes, though this is an issue which cannot be decided here. The main point, that there is sexual repression in Trobriand society, and apparently no culture without *some* sexual repression, is all that is needed to show that Reich's proposal – that complete sexual liberty will automatically lead to the development of a new 'healthy' character, naturally disposed to adopt the egalitarian conventions of a new 'work-democracy' – is not justified by the evidence.

Behind Willhelm Reich's conclusions one can detect a naive Rousseauist faith in the goodness of human sexual nature. He assumes, first, that there is a natural sexuality which is genital and heterosexual, and that leaving our sexual drives to develop freely and making sure they are fully satisfied will result in personalities that are no longer unhappy, neurotic or authoritarian. Moreover, he assumes that no more is required for the development of the moral individuals who will people the communist state than a reliance on the fundamental goodness of our basic instincts. Marcuse argues in *Eros and Civilisation* that this ignores the data which Freud had amassed of the anti-social nature of many of our fundamental drives: the incestuous desires of the little girl and boy, the aggression generated by the frustration of those desires, the basic selfishness of the pleasure principle and the existence of the death drive.[34] Without some basic repression, these anti-social impulses would lead to anarchy. Marcuse therefore distinguishes between basic repression, that which is necessary for the development of social responsibility, and surplus repression, the extreme interdiction on libidinal pleasure which results in the authoritarian personality. That there is such a distinction to be made is borne out by Malinowski's tentative comments on the differences between the Trobriand Islanders and their more sexually repressive neighbours.[35] However, while the distinction between necessary and surplus repression may be useful, Marcuse subtly changes the orientation of sexual liberation without any clear justification. Whereas Reich possessed some anthropological evidence for the existence of societies whose members manifest a relatively unrepressed, genital heterosexuality, concomitant with an absence of homosexuality, neurosis, rape and sexual murder (though not with an entire absence of violence by men towards women), and so had some evidence for the existence of a natural genital orientation and the benefits which follow from its expression, Marcuse follows Freud in assuming that we are naturally 'polymorphously perverse', but cites no evidence for the assumption that the expression of this perversity and 'eroticisation of the whole body' would imply any of the material aspects of liberation. Nor is there any evidence that societies which indulge in more 'perverse' pleasures are particularly egalitarian. The famous example of ancient Greece might suggest the opposite.[36] Indeed, in the wake of Marcuse's theorizing, some interpreters have accepted even the perversities of de Sade as expressions of a liberated sexuality.[37] Yet it seems absurd to think of the liberation of sadistic desires as in any way correlated with a general social or political liberation. Furthermore, Marcuse's theory does not overcome the criticism which he levelled at Reich. He too adopts an over-optimistic assessment of humanity's fundamental nature. While he, unlike Reich, recognizes the need for some sexual repression if a child is to develop from self-centred pleasure-seeker into a moral agent, whose love of self has been transformed into love of the other, he postulates that there is a natural tendency for this development to take place within the context of a non-authoritarian repression. His optimism about the possibility of the congruence of instinctual freedom and reason seems to be just that – optimism. Is there any empirical data to suggest that it is warranted? This question needs to be dealt with in greater detail than can be attempted here. It is of fundamental importance, however, if feminists are to resolve the thorny issue of the place of sexuality in sexual oppression. As we will see below, the implicit answer offered by contemporary radical feminists to this question is 'no'. Yet this response also seems precipitous, since serious research into the relationship between sexual repression and authoritarianism seems hardly to have got off the ground.

During the 1960s and for the early part of the 1970s women's liberation was closely allied to sexual liberation. In *The Dialectic of Sex* Shulamith Firestone gave a scathing account of possessive love, and argued:

> if we grant that the sexual drive is at birth diffuse and undifferentiated from the total personality (Freud's polymorphous perversity) and, as we have seen, becomes differentiated only in response to the incest taboo; and that further, the incest taboo is now necessary only in order to preserve the family; then if we did away with the family we would in effect be doing away with the repressions that mold sexuality into specific formations.

She concluded: 'In our new society, humanity could finally revert to its natural polymorphous sexuality – all forms of sexuality would be allowed and indulged.'[36] In adopting this conclusion she was clearly following Marcuse, but, as we have seen, he offered no evidence that indulging our 'natural' polymorphous sexuality would have any tendency to be accompanied by a non-oppressive, egalitarian character. De Sade's philosophical pornography needs to be remembered at this point. De Sade paints human sexual nature as essentially involving the desire to dominate, be filthy, kill, humiliate and generally do evil. According to him the release of the instincts is the release of all that is anti-social from the constraints of a despised good, which, it is important to note, he identifies with the mother. This is a point to which we will return later. But first I want to identify an assumption common to both those working within the Rousseauist tradition and the Sadian challenge to that tradition. This is the assumption that there *is* a human sexual nature which exists independently of the way in which the sexual individual is constructed out of his or her interaction with the environment. It was arguably Freud's great contribution to our understanding of sexuality that he recognized that a mature adult's sexual dispositions are not innate, but are rather acquired through the interaction of some primary but diffuse drives with the actual, lived experience of the child. What is primary, according to Freud, determines neither any specific outcome nor the particular character of an individual's psychosexuality, and although the route to maturity does characteristically pass through certain well-defined stages, the result of each of these may be as much a matter of the character of chance incidents, which happen to take on particular significance because of their association with other incidents, as with any underlying pattern. The evidence of anthropology confirms that although Freud may not have always got the details of the process correct, sexual character is partly the result of societal and familial forces, and develops differently in different societies according to the way it is conceptualized, its role in economic life, specific taboos and child-rearing custom.

Freud's work thus comes to have a special relevance for feminism, for if psychosexuality is not simply natural but in some sense social, then it is reasonable to hope that we might come to understand how the psychology of masculine dominance and feminine submission reproduces itself, and, even more optimistically, we might come to understand how to escape such reproduction. But what of de Sade's alternative assumption, that our sexual nature is evil and essentially linked with the desire to kill and dominate? Oddly enough, there is now a considerable body of feminist opinion which apparently coincides with him, at least over the character of male sexuality. Andrea Dworkin makes this explicit. De Sade conceives of the sexual act as a relationship of domination and violence; for him masculine freedom is 'the right to compel submission' and the ultimate sexual act is murder. According to Dworkin, 'Sade's work embodies the common values and desires of men.'[39] In him 'the authentic equation is revealed: the power of the pornographer is the power of the rapist batterer is the power of the man.'[40] Mary Daly also emphasizes the sadistic side of male sexuality, and apparently takes there to be an essential, timeless difference between male and female sexual natures, such that the first requires domination, violence and the suppression of women, while the second is fruitful, life-affirming and non-violent.[41] Daly, like de Sade, accepts that masculine sexual nature is essentially cruel and domineering. She differs from him only in disagreeing over female sexuality, which she sees as potentially positive, nurturing and creative, at least when woman–directed. Such forms of radical feminism are based on a myth of natural difference, as unlikely to be true as are the obverse myths of the patriarchal tradition, according to which women are evil, sensual and the source of all corruption. But the theme expressed in Dworkin's assertion does not have to be associated with biological essentialism, and Dworkin, as well as Catharine MacKinnon, has distanced herself from the essentialist elements in Daly's work and explicitly emphasized the point that sexuality is socially constructed, while retaining a conception of heterosexuality according to which it is eroticized domination and violation.[42]

Adrienne Rich, Andrea Dworkin, Catharine MacKinnon and Sheila Jeffreys combine the explicit claim that male sexuality is socially constructed with a critique of heterosexuality, as the political institution through which male dominance is organized and maintained.[43] This position is forcefully represented by three of them in the following quotations:

> the institution of heterosexuality itself [is] a beachhead of male dominance.[44]

> Sexuality, then, is a form of power. Gender, as socially constructed, embodies it, not the reverse. Women and men are divided by gender, made into the sexes as we know them, by the social requirements of heterosexuality, which institutionalises male dominance and female submission. If this is true, sexuality is the linchpin of gender inequality.[45]

> Heterosexual desire is . . . sexual desire that eroticises power differences . . . In heterosexual desire our subordination becomes sexy for us and for men.[46]

To this is added the belief that the way in which women are constructed as sexual objects within patriarchy is perpetuated by modes of discourse, particularly pornography. Thus the fight against pornography becomes central to feminism. For pornography is the most obvious realm of discourse devoted to women and men as sexual beings, and women are often represented in pornography as submissive objects of a masculine sexuality which expresses itself through violence and rape.

As already discussed, within the Marxist tradition of epistemology, knowledge is thought of as having a history, which is conceived of as the history of the development of an ideology which unfolds with the changing structure of class relations. Late twentieth-century feminism, having largely developed out of the new-left Marxist tradition, has taken over this Marxist concept of ideology. Extended to feminism, this leads to the idea that all forms of knowledge, so far, having been constructed by men under conditions of patriarchal domination, are forms of discourse which serve to construct women as inferior sexual objects, men as superior rational subjects. This extension of Marxist method is particularly clearly articulated by Catharine MacKinnon.[47] She differentiates her position sharply from those socialist feminists who continue to ally themselves with the politics of sexual liberation, but shares with orthodox Marxists a reliance on the concept of ideology and a suspicion of the idea that any particular behaviour is 'natural'.[48] In this regard she is, superficially, more consistently Marxist than was Reich, for his assumption that there is a 'natural' sexuality conflicts with the Marxist idea that what is taken to be human 'nature' is, at each epoch, an ideological construction, determined by the underlying material conditions. Marxism teaches us to be wary of claims of naturalness, which, it suggests, are often attempts to depict changeable social relations as natural relations. Extending this thought, Sheila Jeffreys accuses the sexual liberationists of attempting to perpetuate patriarchy, which was under threat due to the advances of a nineteenth-century feminist movement that was largely suspicious of male sexuality, by promoting the ideology of the naturalness of sex and sexual enjoyment.[49] She argues that 'An analysis of sex therapy in the late 1950s illustrates the function of sexual intercourse in enforcing male power and shows clearly the male-supremist philosophy which lay behind the practitioners of sex therapy at that time.'[50] And though the 'proof' of her claim that the function of sexual intercourse is the enforcing of male power resides in the observation that, for sex therapists, healthy sex is genital heterosexual sex, and as a proof this is somewhat circular, the challenge which she and the other radical feminists pose for any easy assumption that sexual liberation is in women's interests needs to be taken seriously.

It is hardly possible to imagine a more extreme divergence over matters of sexuality and its place in the feminist revolution than that between writers like de Beauvoir, Firestone and the early Greer, who follow the Marxist tradition and associate the rise of sexual repression with the rise of capitalist patriarchy, and the new, radical anti-pornography campaigners, for whom sexual liberation is merely the latest phase of patriarchal oppression.[51] Nevertheless, there are some common assumptions. One is that sexual relations are political relations, and, more strongly, that changes in erotic behaviour are, by themselves, integral to human liberation. The next is that it is useful to retain a Marxist epistemology and in particular the notion of ideology. A related belief is that sexual behaviour is 'socially constructed': by which is meant that the behaviour is determined by the ideology which upholds the contemporary class structure and in turn serves to perpetuate that class structure. In the remainder of this chapter I will argue that the dispute over sexual liberation cannot be resolved within the framework provided by these common assumptions.

A first indication of this is the way in which both the sexual liberationist camp and those who are against sexual liberation make selective judgements concerning the 'social construction' of sexuality. As Jeffreys is aware, sexual liberationists tended to see women's disinterest in sexual intercourse and tendency towards 'frigidity' as 'socially constructed', the result of patriarchal conditioning.[52] On the other hand, masculine desires for uninvolved, casual sex were deemed natural. By contrast, Jeffreys implies that masculine desires for casual sex and erotic domination are socially constructed, as are female heterosexual desires, while frigidity or lesbianism are woman's natural sexual orientation and constitute the path to liberation.[53] Similarly, Andrea Dworkin implies that penetrative heterosexual intercourse is essentially violation, because it is invasive of women's bodies.[54] She assumes this even though her official position is that sexuality is socially constructed, which would suggest that, if sexuality is experienced as violation, this is because of the way it has been socially constructed, as the liberationists assumed. How can one resolve this dispute within the framework set up by Marxist epistemology? Naive responses on each side would be to point out that the needs of reproduction make it unlikely that women have no natural tendency towards heterosexuality, and, alternatively, that the experience of many societies suggests that most humans can exist with fairly restricted sexual experience. But, if all our beliefs are 'ideological', these naive responses can both be rejected as themselves deriving from heterosexist ideology. In fact within the theory of ideology not only is it the case that sexual response is 'socially constructed', but all these different theories of sexuality will also be socially constructed, as are the behaviours which the naive theories attempt to justify. Yet these different behaviours and theories exist in the one society. The society, then, cannot be quite as effective in its capacity to mould human character to its needs as talk of social construction suggests, for it seems that in our case, it has been socially constructing masculine and feminine sexuality in quite incompatible modes. We should conclude that claims to the effect that certain ways of experiencing sexuality are socially constructed amount to little more than expressions of the theorist's disapproval of the particular sexual behaviour, unless they are accompanied by an independent account of the way in which this way of constructing sexuality serves the interests of the group in power. For the sexual liberationists prudery, frigidity and possessiveness are socially constructed; according to the radical anti-pornographers masculine promiscuity and perceived need for sexual release are socially constructed. In reality, all sexual response is, presumably, the result partly of social pressure and partly of biological features. Variations in hormone levels, genital shape and size and other bodily characteristics, all contribute to mature sexuality, as do the individual features of upbringing, education and chance incident.[55] Below I will use Foucault's development of Nietzsche's epistemology to bring out the bankruptcy of the general notion of ideology, but first, it is worthwhile examining the other assumption common to both these strains of thought: that sexuality is of itself political.

It has been an assumption of this book that sexual relations are political relations. However, what has been designated by 'sexual relations' is in fact made up of a combination of elements, some to do with the organization of kinship and reproduction, some to do with economic relations, and some to do with erotic life. In every society, sexual relations in this broad sense are political relations, and in most societies political relations, in general, are intimately connected with the politics of sex. In Trobriand society, one's social status is determined by clan status and so by one's mother's family. Women are economically independent of their husbands and so have an independence, relative to their husbands, which Malinowski found striking in comparison to the situation he had left in Europe. Since property only comes to men through marriage, the only way in which men can acquire more property than average, and thus rise to the status of chief, is by having many wives.[56] And, as both Malinowski and Reich note, this feature of the society introduces features which conflict with the general matrilineal principle, introducing 'political' cross-cousin marriages to enable chiefs to pass on their power to their sons.[57] The relative economic independence of women in this society manifests itself in their relative erotic independence. All the evidence is that this is the conclusion we should draw, for it is in their relationship to their brothers, on whom they are economically dependent, that Trobriand Island women show a deference similar to that shown by western women to their husbands. Both the sexual liberationists and their radical feminist opponents are inclined to treat erotic relations in isolation, as though, by themselves, they are political. But sexual promiscuity can, surely, be either an expression of free choice, or a case of being dominated by someone on whom one is economically or emotionally dependent, depending on features of the case, as can be entering into a homosexual relationship (or for that matter, remaining chaste). In societies like the Trobriands, and in almost every society before the rise of modern capitalist and socialist economies, wealth and power were inextricably linked to traditional family connections to land and other resources. In late twentieth-century capitalism, wealth and other forms of power are probably less closely tied to sexual and family relations than at any other stage of human history. Given that this is the case, there is no obvious reason to assume that changes in erotic behaviour will automatically lead to changes in the distribution of wealth and power between the sexes. It is particularly doubtful that the abolition of heterosexuality would necessarily enhance women's social and economic power.[58] There is more reason to suppose that, so long as all individuals have sufficient economic independence to maintain a genuine moral and personal autonomy, they will be free to discover, for themselves, the nature of the good life, and this may or may not involve heterosexual, homosexual, lesbian and even sado-masochistic practices. This is the assumption that lies behind liberal humanist attitudes to sexuality, and it is the logical extension of John Stuart Mill's famous argument in *On Liberty* to the effect that there ought to be as great a personal freedom as possible, compatible with the prevention of harm to others.[59] The fact that sexual relations are often linked with the reproduction of society has the potential to raise questions concerning this principle, but it may well be less confusing to tie the responsibilities which flow from relations to children directly to procreation rather than to sex. Contraception has loosened the connection between sex and procreation and this has lead to confusion in the matter of sexual morality, for taboos that have grown up for the sake of protecting child-bearing women and reproducing the next generation are thought of as applying to sex *per se*.

It is important to note that this liberal attitude is quite different to that of the sexual libertarians whose theories were grounded in those of Reich and Marcuse, according to which sexual possessiveness and the introduction of taboos are the origin of all possessiveness, class division and authoritarianism. The liberal makes a clear distinction between those practices which harm others and those which do not. Thus rape, the sexual abuse of children, and any sado-masochistic practices which are not voluntarily entered into by individuals who are in a position to judge their own best interests clearly fall outside the range of practices acceptable to a liberal. Moreover, a case may be able to be made out, from liberal premises, for the banning of those kinds of pornographic literature which represent women (or men) as less than human creatures, who may be bound, abused, humiliated or killed.[60] Indeed, the existence of sado-masochism itself presents something of an embarrassment to liberals, for it suggests that actual human beings are far from the rational creatures whose concept of the good life is compatible with the good of others that, in some sense, a liberal must assume if he or she is to have faith that liberty can result in the maximization of genuine happiness. Real people have almost always been brought up in situations of inequality, and often of brutality and neglect. So real desires are likely to conflict markedly with those which are compatible with truly egalitarian interpersonal relationships. Thus, the case of sado-masochism might incline even a liberal to consider some erotic relations political, if only in the sense that the existence of erotic relations of that kind is an indication that the society falls short of the liberal ideal. But this would leave open the question of how best to respond to the existence of such relations. It may well be that the toleration of such blemishes is one of the prices that a liberal will have to be prepared to pay for allowing real people to live in a society in which the institutions have at least partly been formed in the light of an ideal of individual equality, which, paradoxically, entails the equal toleration of conceptions of the good life when, as a matter of fact, some of these conceptions conflict at a personal level with the full realization of the ideal of equality.

It is, however, in a narrow sense of sexual relations – that is, erotic relations – that sexual liberationists and the radical feminists who oppose heterosexuality consider sexual relations political. The crudest form of sexual liberationism might be characterized by the slogan 'Universal sex is universal love.' The selfishness and disregard for the interests of others, or their concerns as persons, which is often characteristic of such practices as 'swinging' and extreme promiscuity shows the emptiness of this thought. Love requires that one is prepared to modify one's behaviour in order to promote the wellbeing and happiness of the loved one. In by far the majority of cases of sexual love, where the beloved loves in return, this will involve making him or her the exclusive object of your sexual interest. For being sexually desired by, and sexually satisfied by, the person you love makes, for most people, an important contribution to happiness and wellbeing. At the same time, the falsity of this crude theory does not invalidate a more moderate hypothesis which was integral to sexual liberation. This hypothesis was suggested by Malinowski's observations, by Margaret Mead's rather similar observations in Samoa and by practices in a number of other societies.[61] It is that a tolerant attitude towards infantile sexuality and a period of adolescent promiscuity is more likely to be conducive to a satisfying married relationship and overall happiness than are the sexual repression of infants and virgin marriage. To confirm this hypothesis thoroughly one would need to do considerable empirical work. But, whether or not it is true, it could only sustain the claim that erotic relations are, of themselves, political relations if it could also be shown that a close connection exists between, on the one hand, the proportion of the adult population who have emotionally and sexually satisfactory heterosexual relationships, and, on the other hand, other political indicators such as the wealth, education and power of women. It could turn out, in opposition to Reich, that a satisfactory sex-life compensates people for other disadvantages, thus making them happier to put up with injustices in the public realm than they would otherwise be.

For the radical feminists, the connection between erotic life and politics is far closer than this. Heterosexuality is claimed to be a 'political institution' which eroticizes power differences and is equated with sado-masochism.[62] Sheila Jeffreys goes so far as to suggest that whenever male homosexuals or lesbians indulge in sado-masochistic practices they are being 'heterosexist'.[63] This is surely special pleading. Since many heterosexuals are not sado-masochistic in their love life, and some homosexuals are, it would be more interesting, from the point of view of achieving an understanding of sado-masochism, to look at other similarities between those who do and those who do not find that they need such practices for sexual satisfaction. More importantly, at this juncture Jeffreys seems to forget her official view that sexuality is socially constructed. If it *is* socially constructed, the most one could claim would be that, within a certain society, one in which men and women are unequal in power, heterosexuality serves to eroticize this power difference. If this *were* the case, part of the task of changing the power imbalance might be to eroticize egalitarian heterosexual relations. This was always part of the positive side of feminist sexual liberation. Women were to be able to express their own sexual longings, to take the initiative in sexual matters, to say 'no' or 'yes' according to their sexual likings, and not according to constraints imposed by economic dependence or the need to appear chaste. This positive side of sexual liberation should not be forgotten, for it has given many women the confidence to insist on their right to sexual satisfaction and led to the development of an ideal of heterosexual life, as the mutual giving and receiving of pleasure, which, although not universal, is at least as prevalent as the attitude that women's bodies are mere vehicles for the release of masculine aggression.[64] The conclusion which Jeffreys draws, that only chastity or lesbian existence are unproblematic expressions of feminism, would perhaps be justified if male sexuality were immutable, but if it is not, then the best strategy for feminists to adopt is the one most likely to lead to a change in masculine eroticism. It is difficult to see how turning one's back on men, denying the possibility of offering even the most sympathetic and loving of them sexual intercourse, is going to be the best strategy for encouraging changed behaviour. It is true that chastity and lesbianism need to remain recognized options, available to any woman whose preferences, or actual dealings with men, are such that she is led to conclude that life without an intimate relationship with a man is better than life with one.[65] But, at the same time, within a particular society, the extent to which free women, who have genuine alternatives, find that they are able to live happily with men should be a measure of the degree to which men have renounced their patriarchal heritage and are able to forge egalitarian and mutually satisfying relationships with women.

In *Pornography and Silence*, Susan Griffin suggests that the loathing that Hitler expressed for the Jew and the loathing that the pornographer expresses for women are partly self-loathing.[66] In chapter 7 we will look at some psychoanalytic theories in an attempt to provide a basis for understanding how such attitudes are generated and how they might be avoided. Psychoanalytic hypotheses need to be explored with care if we are to understand the genesis, in some male individuals, of a need to dominate women, which has its most extreme expression in the sex-murderer and sadist. But if psychoanalysts are at all correct in their suggestion that self-loathing is the internalization of dislike, or hate, directed towards the self, it is hard to see how the institutionalization of the dislike of men, implicit in the goals of lesbian separatism, could lead to an improvement in male attitudes. Andrea Dworkin begins her book *Intercourse* with a description of Tolstoy's *Kreuzer Sonata* in which the wife-murdering husband expresses his loathing for himself as a sexual being and projects this loathing onto the woman who stirs his sexual desire.[67] One cannot help finding in this story, in which sex is explicitly conceived as an animal urge which degrades the spiritual man, a vindication of Reich's intuition that sex-murder and antagonism towards women are the result of prudish and punitive attitudes towards infantile sexuality, which generate in the male a hatred of his body and of sexual desire. Dworkin does not ask how the attitudes which Tolstoy expresses in this story come to be socially constructed, perhaps because this question inevitably leads towards questions of child-rearing, parental responsibility, mothering and fathering; questions which lurk obscurely in the shadows of her discourse, which completely divorces erotic life from the reproduction of society. Perhaps Dworkin is endorsing Tolstoy when she reports his musing, that only chastity is honourable, and that if it leads to the extinction of the race, this is simply the price of honour. If so, those who see political theory as aiming for a sustainable model of the good society need not take her vision seriously. When Dworkin speculates, in a later paper, that intercourse is intrinsically a violation of woman's private space,[68] she forgets that here too we have a way of looking at the matter which is deeply implicated in a web of social significations, not least among which are those that underlie capitalism. We should remember here Locke's dictum that we have property in our bodies, and the whole nexus of concepts which are tied together in English and even more clearly in French through the word *propre* (clean); proper names, propriety, property and proper. Rousseau thought that it was just with the rise of feminine modesty, and the placing of a price on the entry to woman's private parts, that both property and *amour-propre* came into existence. Those who are chaste never give themselves. Those who are lesbian only give themselves to women. And while women may well complain that many men, through their brutality, have forfeited any right to receive women's generosity, it would be a bleak world indeed in which no gifts were exchanged between the sexes. Dworkin forgets too that there are other, more positive significations to intercourse; the welcoming of the 'other' into the self, a return to the home, the sense of wonder that might be experienced in a relationship between two irreducible selves, the mingling of fluids and the gift of pro-creation. These thoughts have become themes in Irigaray's recent work, which has turned from a deconstruction of the masculine imaginary towards an attempt to reconceptualize the fecundity of sexual relations between the two sexes.[69]

According to Freud, the element of sex which is natural is merely an energetic potential which may be directed into heterosexuality, homo-sexuality, fetishism or neurosis, or sublimated into the self-restraint necessary for the pursuit of higher cultural activities. The actual shape of this energetic potential of the id is determined by factors of social and individual environment. So social intervention ought to be possible in order to shape the development of psychosexuality in such a way as to promote that range of behaviours, whatever they are, most conducive to overall social harmony, in the material conditions that actually exist. In order to take this path one needs to be able to distinguish the limits placed by physical circumstance and human biology on what is socially possible, and to weed out mere 'ideology' concerning human needs and nature from the truth. However, the possibility that this picture holds out for human liberation is challenged by Foucault, on the basis of an argument which ultimately shows the internal inconsistency of theories of ideology. Foucault's early writing took off from an interest in the ideological function of science, but at the same time it challenged the usefulness of the notion of ideology.[70] One way of putting the difficulty which underlies this challenge is that ideology is always opposed to truth, yet the epistemology which grounds the notion does not justify a belief in our access to any non-ideological truth. As we have seen, both sexual liberationists and those who are against heterosexuality criticize the beliefs that they oppose as 'ideological', while accepting other beliefs, that have been generated within exactly the same society, as true. But if beliefs were merely the reflection of the economic and material infrastructure, there would be no reason to deem any of them any more true or false than any other; the most that one could perhaps say would be that where a society generates conflicting beliefs, these represent the interests of different classes. Marx privileges the point of view of the working class while accepting that an undistorted view of reality will only really be available after the abolition of class domination. Some feminists have similarly claimed that, as the oppressed, women's standpoint is better than men's, but this is problematic since women differ from each other in their judgements. Catharine MacKinnon shows some awareness of this problem. Her solution is to give up on the object/subject split and to claim that the demand for objectivity is itself part of the ideological practice of sexual objectification. She does not explain how this will contribute to reasoned debate on this issue.[71] In other places she displays not the slightest doubt that she has access to the truth about pornography, and that liberal feminists display 'thundering ignorance'.[72] This attitude politicizes debate, making knowledge a matter of muscle rather than honest inquiry. Since even in a society in which men do not oppress women there may well be differences between the sexes, we do not have any simple method of judging a priori what counts as a society that lacks sexual oppression. The loudest or most popular voice will not necessarily be right on these matters. We need some more objective means of judging what differentiates legitimate group difference from oppression.[73]

The same point can be made in a different way using rather different vocabulary. Feminists have often followed Hegel in criticizing the liberal tradition for its abstract notion of freedom and an 'abstract individualism' which takes desires as given.[74] Within Kant's ethics, reason is always thought of as opposed to desire, yet without some desires, it appears that Kant's categorical imperative 'act only so that the maxim of your action can be willed as a universal law' is an empty formula incapable of leading to any particular action, or more precisely, capable of being met by any consistent system of rules.[75] Hegel developed this criticism in order to ground his conclusion that it was only in an organic community organized on rational lines that the desires of the members of the community would be in harmony with the demands of the universal law. But the limitations of his own description of 'the rational community' (which turns out to coincide with the nineteenth-century, patriarchal Prussian state) should make us suspicious of claims to be able to recognize which desires are in accord with reason. And our discussion of the dispute between sexual liberationists and their feminist opponents brings home the difficulty. If we are to criticize 'abstract individualism' for its incapacity to recognize that some desires are irrational, and have been generated by circumstances of oppression which they help to perpetuate, we need some criterion for differentiating rational, acceptable desires, which may or may not be natural, from those among their socially constructed counterparts which help to perpetuate oppression.

Foucault, following Nietzsche rather than Marx, is more consistent. For him there are only 'games of truth' which interact with power relations, and there is no body or sexuality or desire which is not socially constructed.[76] His early work *Madness and Civilization* explored the inter-relationship between knowledge and power by giving a precise genealogy of the interconnected emergence of the science of psychiatry and the psychiatric practices of normalization and institutionalization.[77] In that work he appeared to be giving an account of the science of psychiatry as an institutional power which represses madness: 'reason's subjugation of non-reason'. Since that period he has also become suspicious of the notion of repression. At a deep level this later suspicion is related to his earlier criticism of ideology. In order for practices to be seen as repressive, one needs some concept of our true nature, what we would be were it not for the distorting influences of society. In the first volume of *The History of Sexuality* Foucault argues against the idea that power is exercised through repression, and replaces it with a notion of power as the positive construction of sexed subjects. During the Victorian era a proliferation of discourses devoted to sexuality increased society's control over people, not by repression, but by active prescription.[78] Taken seriously, this undercuts the strategy of both the sexual liberationists and their opponents, for it makes it impossible to distinguish true from ideological conceptions of sexuality. At the same time, given Foucault's acceptance of an essentially Nietzschean epistemology, it is difficult to see how these negative observations are capable of being supplemented by a positive account of liberation.[79] The most he can offer is a liberation which consists in an aesthetics of the self which goes beyond the limits of the games of truth handed down to us by history.[80]

So far in this chapter we have attempted to follow the tangled threads of the influence of Marxist epistemology and psychoanalysis on feminism. Our exploration took off from writers like Poovey and Kaplan, whose criticism of Wollstonecraft was, in essence, that her prudishness and sense of propriety made her incapable of offering women a genuine sexual liberation. This assumes a socialist explanation of the place of sexual repression in the reproduction of capitalism. Wollstonecraft's admonitions against the debased sexuality of those women who, seeing marriage as a trade, were content to concentrate their lives on making themselves the most marketable commodities, were seen as suspect and read as an attack on sexuality *per se*. Wollstonecraft, however, judged that such women fall short in the light of a conception of human nature according to which human dignity requires a reasonable moral autonomy, within which sexuality makes a significant but not essential contribution. What is suspect in women who participate in such sexual behaviour is that their attitudes are grounded in an outlook that views men merely as means to the end of securing a comfortable life, and not as ends in themselves, whose desire is to have their own self-esteem validated by the esteem of another whose human values they respect.[81] Thus, they degrade themselves by allowing themselves to be experienced as mere objects of desire, rather than affirming themselves as subjects of desire, whose desire is to be desired *by* a subject worthy of respect *as* a subject worthy of respect. Wollstonecraft's critique of debased sexuality is humanistic, for it assumes a conception of what it is to be a human which takes us to be self-conscious, ethical subjects. Such a conception implies not that we are disembodied or dispassionate, but only that our consciousness of ourselves as embodied and passionate needs to be incorporated into our consciousness of ourselves as rational and ethical. Those who, by implication, criticize this form of humanism for, at the one extreme, taking a socially constructed sexual modesty as part of our nature or, at the other extreme, taking a socially constructed heterosexual desire as part of our nature, are not able consistently to take us beyond humanism. Rather they implicitly enter into a debate within humanism as to our 'true' nature. For in criticizing the way sexuality is constructed, they cannot help falling back on the assumption that there is a truth concerning the harmfulness of this construction for our real interests. Yet the epistemology which they accept gives no coherent account of how our true interests are to be judged. Is there any way to answer this question? The strand of anti-humanism epitomized by Foucault argues not. And similar assumptions, deeply embedded in the socialist/existentialist legacy passed down to feminism by de Beauvoir, suggest that answering this question is deeply problematic. The only solution to the problem is to clear away the distortions imposed by the concept of ideology in order to reinstate a careful and empirically based discussion of our genuine best interests.

As we will see in the next chapter, there are a number of deeply conflicting strands within de Beauvoir's thought which need to be straightened out if we are to see our way to grounding a reasonable discussion of these matters. I will argue that the most fruitful strand in de Beauvoir's thought is one which suggests accepting the actual historical writings of women as providing a basis for developing such an understanding. This strategy also provides us with the opportunity of articulating a distinctive feminist humanism. Ultimately, the essentials of Wollstonecraft's position stand the test of time. Great differences in power corrupt human relations, and the central demand of feminism remains the demand for equality in power. Most members of our liberal society recognize that individuals ought to have equal rights to exercise the power to govern the society, and that there are no differences in value between men and women, yet effective power is still denied women. This is evidence that women continue to be discriminated against. Eradicating this discrimination needs to go forward within a framework which recognizes our existence as emotional, feeling beings whose development as moral individuals depends on the fulfilment by others of duties to love. The reproduction of the just society is grounded in personal relations, as Rousseau saw. But if this reproduction is not to continue to depend on the exclusion of women from positions of power, the structure of political representation needs to be changed. And in the end, if personal relations between the sexes are to be relations between equals, there needs to be genuine equality in power between the sexes.

7

Flight from the Other

De Beauvoir's *The Second Sex* has provided late twentieth-century
feminism with many of its fundamental assumptions. Among them are
the following: that for man, woman is Other, an object, an immanent
thing against which he poses himself as subject; that woman has, historically, been Other even for herself; and that she has 'no past, no history,
no religion' of her own.[1] If one adds to this the idea that the subject is
constructed through language and that language comes down to us
through history, which, while not explicit in de Beauvoir, has been
widely accepted by feminists influenced by structuralism, it is but a small
step to the conclusion that in order to articulate our own subjectivity
we need to transgress the limits of all past language and all past constitu-
tions of the subject.[2] Thus de Beauvoir paves the way for those post-
structuralist feminisms which identify the articulation of a genuine
feminine voice, or an *écriture féminine*, with deconstruction and the
rejection of past metaphysical conceptions of the subject as a rational
and unified ego, who is capable of knowing about an objective external
world. At the same time, her work has been subjected to considerable
criticism from the point of view of feminists of difference. At one level
the criticism has been that, while she should be appreciated for the practical pursuit of social justice which she inspired, her pursuit of equality
is suspect, as is her assumption that there exists a unified subject, and
her adoption of a tone of hierarchical authority.[3] Another problem
raised is that her analysis of woman's position assumes an existentialist
conception of the human condition, which in Sartre's writing is articulated in strikingly misogynist language, and which, at a deep level, glori-
fies a notion of transcendence which is conceptualized as opposed to the
bodily, immanent and feminine.[4] According to existentialism, to be

human is to be a transcendent ego, a for-itself which is essentially free and which creates itself in opposition to the immanent in-itself. The in-itself can threaten the for-itself, and in one notorious passage, Sartre describes this as the threat of engulfment by the feminine viscosity of the for-itself.[5]

In this chapter I will argue that, if these criticisms are cogent (and up to a point they are) the assumptions that feminists have taken over from de Beauvoir are unjustified. But, once these assumptions are rejected, there is little reason to believe that feminist theory and deconstruction have a common aim in the overthrow of western metaphysics and all past conceptions of the subject. Although feminists need to be alert to the implicit sexism of much past philosophy, there is no reason why one should not find in past women's writing authentic women's voices. There is an instability in de Beauvoir's position which derives from her attempt to combine existentialism with the Marxist epistemology that was problematized in the last chapter. Her development of the idea that woman is Other extends Hegel's understanding of the master/slave dialectic to include the relationship between men and women, explaining woman's acceptance of her subordination as the acceptance of the view of herself projected by the master. At the same time she advocates the pursuit of transcendence, which has always been conceptualized in opposition to the bodily. So her own positive philosophy can be criticized as itself a version of the master's ideology. Within the framework of Marxist epistemology it becomes impossible to resolve the resulting epistemological paradox. This leaves us no option but to return to humanist epistemology, which attempts to use reasoned argument and careful, scholarly and empirical research, in order to decide such vexed questions as the nature of the society which best serves women's interests.

In the introduction to *The Second Sex* de Beauvoir sets out to analyse the situation of women. She begins by disassociating her own view both from biological essentialism, according to which to be a woman is to instantiate a timeless feminine essence, and from a nominalism which would make 'woman' a mere arbitrary designation and deny the existence of sexual difference. To deny that there are women would be 'a flight into inauthenticity' and 'no woman could, without bad faith, pretend to situate herself outside her sex.'[6] Like Jews or Blacks women exist, and exist as the group that men have set up as their Other. But this hardly explains the situation of women for, within the structuralist framework that de Beauvoir here assumes, and which she inherits from Lévi-Strauss, Granet, Dumezil and Sartre (each in his own way the heir of Hegel), each group asserts itself by setting itself up as the One in opposition to the

Other. How is it that women have never opposed men's definition of them? The answer that de Beauvoir gives to this question is fourfold. Women are dispersed among men of different cultures, races and classes; this means that they do not have the concrete means to consider themselves as a class.[7] Moreover, women need men, just as men need women; 'she is the Other in a totality of which the two elements are necessary to one another.'[8] Furthermore, the temptation to flee one's position as free and responsible is widespread; women thus find it easy to comply with their position as Other.[9] And this attitude is reinforced in women because 'in maternity woman remained closely bound to her body, like an animal', while men came to transcend mere species life through risking their lives.[10] In this analysis there are strong echoes of Sartre's discussion of bad faith, and a hint that woman's subjection is the result of 'a moral fault', as well as talk of woman's complicity in man's setting himself up as sovereign.

If this were the totality of de Beauvoir's analysis, the criticism that the reliance on existentialist ethics and Sartre's voluntarism makes *The Second Sex* an inadequate account of women's oppression would surely be correct.[11] But emphasizing this element misses a crucial step in de Beauvoir's argument. Having observed that men and women need each other, de Beauvoir wonders why this reciprocal need has not provided the ground of woman's liberation and a relationship of mutuality between the sexes. She observes that between the master and slave there is also, in reality, a reciprocal need, but this is not internalized by the master. He has the power to satisfy his needs without this satisfaction being mediated by a recognition of his dependence. On the other hand the slave, experiencing dependence, fear and hope, internalizes his need for the master, and this consciousness of dependence (which is ultimately a false consciousness since it is blind to the master's reciprocal need for the slave) is one reason why the liberation of the oppressed is frequently so slow. Similarly, woman internalizes her need for man, for his protection and his earning power, while he sets himself up as free and independent.[12] Although she does not use the term, de Beauvoir's point could be framed in terms of the notion of ideology. The mutual interdependence of the sexes is masked by an ideology in which man posits himself as the essential, transcendent One, and woman as the inessential, immanent Other, and this ideology is internalized by women, who are compelled 'to assume the status of the Other'.[13] Read this way, de Beauvoir's text is an account of the ideology of patriarchy within which men, as masters, posit themselves as essential and women, as slaves, accept from the masters a conception of themselves as inessential, as objects rather than subjects. It is this reading of de Beauvoir which has, I believe, had the greatest influence on subsequent feminist thought, though it is not a reading which is always made explicit.

This illuminates an important tension in the analysis of the situation of women, as characterized in de Beauvoir's text, which has generated a range of contemporary criticisms. It is clear that de Beauvoir's positive aspiration for woman is that she should cease to conceive of herself through the distortions of a masculine vision which has posed her as Other, and that she should aspire to a transcendence as free and self-determining as that of men. But, by the logic of her own analogy of the master and the slave, the conception of the self as unconstrained transcendental ego, which has come down to us in the philosophy of the masters, is as much an ideological construct as is the conception of woman as Other. There are no absolutely unconstrained transcendental egos, and the project of attempting to live by this model is that of taking up an ideological conception of the self developed by men as masters.[14] The dilemma to which this gives rise is eloquently expressed by Irigaray, when she asserts that in taking up any theory of the subject a woman is either 'subjecting herself to objectivization in discourse – by being "female"' or else 're-objectivizing her own self whenever she claims to identify herself "as" a masculine subject'. [15] Having rejected both horns of the dilemma posed by de Beauvoir's dualistic characterization of subjects as either transcendent or immanent, Irigaray's early writing apparently has nowhere to go in the search for an authentic feminine subjectivity but beyond all past theories, logics, languages; perhaps forwards into a language not yet able to be articulated or, alternatively, backwards to a pre-Oedipal, pre-symbolic self. Either way there are difficulties.[16] But there is no need to follow Irigaray down this path, for I hope to demonstrate that de Beauvoir's analysis of the situation of woman in terms of the idea that a patriarchal ideology has been internalized by woman, which constructs her as Other and has led to her docile acceptance of millennia of oppression, collapses under its own weight. De Beauvoir's solution to the dilemma posed is 'for women to reject these flights from reality and seek self-fulfilment in transcendence', yet her own understanding of transcendence, and her own characterization of past women, make this search more difficult and paradoxical than it need be.[17]

The bare outlines of my argument are as follows. De Beauvoir sets out to explain, from the point of view of existentialism, how it is that women have accepted their oppression with so little manifest resistance. She criticizes the explanations of women's situation offered by biologists, psychoanalists and historical materialists because, although each of these points of view contains useful insights, in the first two cases women's situation is described as natural and inevitable, leaving no room for women to change their situation, and in the third, although 'the theory of historical materialism has brought to light some most important truths',[18] ultimately historical materialism takes for granted facts which need to be explained; in particular the connection between the rise of private property and woman's enslavement.[19] It is existentialism which is able to fill the explanatory gap: 'If the human consciousness had not included the original category of the Other and an original aspiration to dominate the Other, the invention of the bronze tool would not have caused the oppression of woman.'[20] Yet, by filling the gap in this way, de Beauvoir seems to rob women of the basis for developing the feminine transcendence to which she believes we should aspire. For de Beauvoir adopts from historical materialism the assumption that humans are historical beings who create themselves through praxis. Since woman is, like man, a historical being and 'not a completed reality but rather a becoming', her transcendence involves taking up a conscious attitude to her history, transforming it, interpreting it and taking responsibility for it. Yet at the same time, in so far as she explains woman's lack of resistance in terms of her having accepted the position of Other, de Beauvoir robs woman of her history. Everything we have thought, written, said or done in the past becomes suspect. And de Beauvoir's analysis of historical women becomes irritatingly carping: hardly any woman has achieved true greatness, no woman has lived in complete authenticity. It is this aspect of her writing which can make it appear that a feminine transcendence must involve the complete dislocation of all values, signs, ways of conceptualizing our place in the world, that have come down to us in a philosophical tradition dominated by men. At the same time, we have no identity apart from our history. By writing us out of history as subjects, de Beauvoir leaves us with two options. We either return to essentialism and the attempt to forge our identity from some ahistorical given – maternity for instance, or perhaps the female body – and/or we reject the project of becoming transcendent subjects as itself grounded in a patriarchal philosophy which has created a myth of the subject by denying women and bodily existence. In the work of Irigaray, for instance, both these tendencies can be perceived in a confusing tension which has left her interpreters deeply puzzled.

Among English-speaking feminists the first option is probably more prevalent. The second is taken up by those who see feminism as fundamentally allied with deconstruction. A third option is to rediscover ourselves in history as subjects with a historical subjectivity which can provide the basis for the creation of a future, grounded in an attitude to the past. But to do this we need to reject de Beauvoir's crucial hypothesis; that is, that the explanation of our subjection lies in a consciousness of ourselves created by men and internalized as patriarchal ideology. My strategy for achieving this will be somewhat *ad hominem*. It will be to argue that, on the one hand, there is as much reason to deem the theories on which de Beauvoir bases her belief that woman has been Other to be patriarchal ideology as there is, on the other, to assume that woman's view of herself is the internalization of a masculine world view. But if the view of women that de Beauvoir accepts is itself ideological, we need to start elsewhere in our attempt to create ourselves as historical beings. A good enough place to start is with women's own writings and own conceptions of the good life. These do not provide an undistorted, objective record of the world. They are merely the best records we have of our historical self-understanding. They provide us with the basis for our becoming self-conscious *qua* women, and they provide the data for a feminist humanism in which we accept, in line with one important insight in de Beauvoir's thought, that there is neither a timeless feminine essence, nor a merely arbitrary class of humans who happen to be designated 'women', but a group with a history, a changing relationship to biology and something to say to all of humanity, both women and men.

De Beauvoir's text is fissured by a great contradiction. On the one hand she adopts a humanist Marxism which sees history as a human creation, through which human self-consciousness has grown out of our transformation of the material world. This is particularly clear in *The Ethics of Ambiguity*.[21] On the other hand, she accepts an anti-humanist explanation of woman's consciousness as the imposition on women of a way of seeing the world determined by men. What prevents this contradiction from collapsing is her use of the masculine history and anthropology which was dominant when she wrote. It had already written women, as creators of culture, out of history, and turned them into objects of exchange between men. From this point of view, women become part of the immanent world against which men create themselves. But the partiality shown to men in this picture needs only to be pointed out to be rejected. If humans create themselves through transforming the material world in which they find themselves, women too, in transforming the material world through work, create themselves. If women create themselves in the image of 'woman', passed down to them by a history and class structure over which they, as individuals, have

no control, the same must be true of men, who are constrained to be
'men'. It is partly because she does not see motherhood as work or
creativity that de Beauvoir fails to recognize the first of these possibilities. But in accepting that women could have been caused by men to
fail to recognize their essential freedom, she undermines one's faith in
genuine choices. Her text therefore points in at least two alternative
directions: towards a consistent humanism or a consistent anti-
humanism.[22] In arguing for the adoption of the first of these options I
will discuss the structuralist anthropology of Lévi-Strauss, in the light
of recent work by feminist anthropologists on woman's place in society,
in order to clear the way for the development, in the next chapter, of
an account of a distinctively feminist humanism.

Inspired by the Marxist reduction of social relations to material relations, Lévi-Strauss reduced kinship relations to relations of material
exchange, interpreting them as essentially the exchange of women between men.[23] In this theory women are objects, property or tokens,
which circulate among men. Like shells, money or gifts of food, they are
objects used to seal relationships between social subjects, men. If this
theory is correct then women can have no language, no culture, no
history of their own. The history of culture up to this time has been the
history of relations between men, what Irigaray calls, a hom(m)osexual
monopoly. Irigaray draws the conclusion that 'heterosexuality has been
up to now just an alibi for the smooth workings of man's relationship
with himself, of relations among men' and 'what the anthropologist calls
the passage from nature to culture thus amounts to the institution of the
reign of hom(m)o-sexuality.'[24] De Beauvoir, before Irigaray, accepted
Lévi-Strauss's characterization of kinship relations, and for this reason
interpreted the oppression of women as more ancient than the rise of
private property. Within this framework she was left to explain woman's
acceptance of her object status. She did so by putting existentialism to
work, and particularly Sartre's contention that the for-itself has a
tendency to flee its freedom and to identify itself with the in-itself.

But recently, feminist anthropologists have begun to question Lévi-
Strauss's assumptions which write women as subjects out of culture. And
in many ways these assumptions always sat rather awkwardly with de
Beauvoir's existentialism. According to existentialism our freedom is a
metaphysical condition, grounded in our consciousness of objects which
are always other than consciousness. This metaphysical freedom is the
same in men and women. De Beauvoir attempts to show how it is that,
while being transcendent in this sense, women have failed to create
themselves as transcendent beings. But, because she places such a high

value on liberty and on the idea of transcending life through heroically facing death, she arguably presupposes that only masculine modes of being deserve to be valued.[25] Women have no history, or rather, they have little history, in the sense that they have themselves written little history, and have been written out of the history written by men. In particular, there is no history of women's ideas, no framework of great women thinkers in relation to whose thought women can situate themselves. Yet women have been participants in culture throughout history and in this sense they do have a history.[26] The short shrift given by de Beauvoir to actual historical women, who are almost all deemed by her to have failed to achieve full transcendence, cuts off the most promising route for the construction of a feminist identity which is not essentialist. For, whatever women may make themselves in the future, they will differ from men in their relationship to the history of the culture they inhabit. Inevitably, as cultural creatures, we construct ourselves in the light of the past as it is available to us. As already mentioned, historical identity provides the basis for articulating the difference between the sexes without resorting to either an unchanging biology or apocalyptic pronouncements of the coming of new thoughts or an unconscious yet to be heard. Moreover, it does so in a way which does not efface the differences between women. For women from different races and cultures will stand in different relationships to the past. To find our identity in our history is not unthinkingly to endorse our historical ways of being, but it is to find an identity, as a sex, which is both clearly ours, and so the basis for a feminist solidarity, and also mutable, and so the basis for feminist difference with regard to its projection into the future. Having seen women through the eyes of the masculine anthropologist, as objects rather than subjects, de Beauvoir thus seems to foreclose, from the outset, the most fruitful path to a feminine transcendence. At most she offers the hope that woman's lived history is still to come.

Feminist anthropology suggests a different interpretation of kinship relations and a different understanding of feminine consciousness to that offered by de Beauvoir, according to which we have only seen ourselves as the Other of man. In establishing this I will rely on the work of Dianne Bell, though similar evidence has been amassed by others.[27] Bell, who has worked extensively with the Warlpiri, Kaytej and Alyawarra aboriginals of Warrabri in central Australia, argues that the anthropological perception of the women of these tribes, as excluded from the ritual, social and political life of the tribe, is an artefact of the male domination of anthropology. Her evidence suggests that in the largely sex-segregated society of the aboriginals, the women's group is

economically independent, and has its own rituals and an important role
to play in other central tribal rituals such as initiation.[28] At one level,
her research confirms Lévi-Strauss's claim that 'exogamy provides the
only means of maintaining the group as a group, of avoiding the indefi-
nite fission and segmentation which the practice of consanguineous marriages would bring about.'[29] But it suggests that women, as well as men,
consciously work for the maintenance of these structures of reciprocity
in their dreamings, dancings and negotiation of marriages. The aboriginals of Warrabri identify themselves by their matrilineage and by their
patrilineage, giving rise to a complex division of the tribe into groups
that stand in intricate relations of reciprocity and avoidance to each
other.[30] The women see their role, that of keeping these 'families
straight' through the establishment of appropriate marriages and the
performance of necessary rituals, as being as important to the religious
and cultural integrity of the tribe as are the men's contributions. They
appear to be 'joint owners and managers of country and ritual along with
their male kin'.[31] The joint responsibilities of men and women can be
illustrated through the example of the male initiation ceremony. Some
elements of this are the men's independent concern – the choice of
the circumcisor, for instance – while others, such as the choice of the
initiate's mother-in-law, are the independent responsibility of the
women.[32] Although the boys to be initiated are ritually captured by
the men from the women's camp, the agreement of the mother that her
son is ready to take on his adult status is secured in the months before
the ceremony. And the dancing of the women involves their participation in the transfer of power to the young initiates.

It would be a mistake to depict this society as one without conflict
or strain in sexual relations. Conflict there clearly is. And the myths that
Dianne Bell relates show that in this society too, there is the threat of
sexual violence, and there are stories of men who will, if thwarted, use
violence to gain sexual access to women, while at the same time wanting
to be loved and admired by them.[33] What is significant is that the
women are not blind to this conflict, they conceptualize it in their own
way, they do not conceive of themselves as men conceive them, and they
have mechanisms, in particular the women's camp, which provide support for individual women against individual men. In this society, where
culture is passed on by word of mouth, where social roles are learned
by participation, and where the relationship to land is integrally connected with economic survival, there seems little reason to deem culture
an artefact of male consciousness, unless one implicitly assumes that

warfare and hunting are intrinsically more essential to culture than ritual and reciprocity.[34]

However, while in the case of the Warrabri aboriginals the apparent exclusion of women from the creation of culture may be an artefact of masculine anthropology, there are many societies in which the acts of reciprocity between clan groups apparently exist only as the exchange of women, who are controlled by men, and valued largely for their capacity to produce sons. It might be argued that in these cultures, and they are numerous, women have become objects and not subjects of culture. But this idea of subjectivity needs unpacking. Even under the most oppressive circumstances, women have an attitude to their situation which is different from that of objects. Rather than seeing women's position as one of complete annihilation as subjects, it seems more accurate to see it as a constrained, oppressed subjectivity which, nevertheless, works with the means available to establish its cultural values. To do otherwise is to assume that the only authentic human subjectivity is one which refuses to see itself as constrained, and which aspires to the isolation of Adam, thinking of itself as an isolated ego.[35] Women have little reason to conceptualize their own condition in terms of mastery and free creation, but this way of understanding the human condition is itself illusory. So there is no reason to assume that a constrained consciousness cannot be authentic. In an important discussion of women's oppression, Nicole-Claude Mathieu argues that even in societies far more repressive to women than the Australian aboriginal societies studied by Bell, and more openly patriarchal, it is a mistake to think that the explanation of women's subordination is that women have internalized an identity offered them by men.[36] Women's oppression is in a sense over-determined. There is little need to propose that woman is Other even for herself, given the plausibility of the Hobbesian explanation of woman's oppression discussed in chapter 2. There I argued that a consideration of the implicit account of woman's subordination to be found in Hobbes's work forces us to identify two kinds of consent: consent under duress, and that which would be given were the circumstances free from duress. I argued that only the second kind of consent can be used as a criterion of the justice, or moral acceptability, of a contract. Nicole-Claude Mathieu makes something like the same point by distinguishing yielding from consenting. The fact that one yields to a social situation in which one's position is one of oppression is quite different from giving one's free consent. Nor is there a need to accuse women of having fallen into immanence, or having seen themselves as Other, if their consciousness of themselves is as of agents creating a culture under circumstances dominated by powers that are beyond their control. In language which is very reminiscent of Hobbes, Mathieu points out that the oppressed person wants to survive and that submission is the means of survival.[37] Her attack on the idea that 'the stronger force is not the violence of the dominators but the consent of the dominated to their domination' is extremely powerful.[38] Individuals are dominated when they yield to a situation in the face of economic or social violence which they are unable to combat. They do not consent merely because they share the ideology of the oppressor, although the existence of ideological beliefs, like the inherent inferiority of women, may assist the maintenance of oppression.

As I argued in the preceding chapter, the appeal to ideology to explain actions which we judge to be inimical to the real interests of an individual becomes vacuous when there is disagreement between theorists over these real interests. Many of Mathieu's observations suggest, moreover, that appeal to the internalization of the ideology of the oppressor is idle. However, Mathieu's final conclusion differs markedly from the one that I believe we should draw. She accepts that women have no culture, and ultimately rejects the idea that the oppressed consent, because she assumes that consent must be conscious, while there exists in fact, among the oppressed, a denial of their oppression.[39] But this claim that domination is not even conceptualized by the oppressed, and so cannot be consented to, is undermined by the evidence that she herself cites that women in patriarchal societies are well aware of the power of men. Rather, I think that one should conclude, on the basis of the evidence that she provides, that there are goals which women value more highly than the freedom they would have to fight for, at such great expense, against an opposition which has so many advantages, with some basis in nature, and which have been increased by cultural practice.

In many ways Christine de Pisan's writing affords a valuable insight into women's understanding of their own contribution to culture. Interestingly, there are continuities between her thought, the perceptions of the aboriginal women studied by Bell, and more recent conservative women such as Caroline Chisholm, who extol women's civilizing role.[40] Central to these women's preoccupations is the control of sexuality and a related desire to maintain the structures of reciprocity between people which prevent societies from collapsing into warring bands. It is hardly surprising that these issues have been central among women's preoccupations. In every society women are faced with three reproductive prospects; celibacy, forced sex under conditions over which they have no control, or negotiated sex (I omit lesbianism since, of itself, this is not traditionally a *reproductive* choice). Celibacy is an option which is available for some women in some societies, but it is hardly a viable option for the majority of women in societies whose women wish to reproduce themselves. Moreover, celibacy will only be guaranteed if the women of the society are able to prevent men from resorting to rape. Rape, or seduction in situations in which women have no power to enforce any material contribution by men to the wellbeing of their off-spring, is clearly not in women's interest. So, working from a position of vulnerability, women have everything to gain from encouraging patterns of reciprocal obligation between men and women, tied to access to sexual rights. Men see these restrictions as constraints on their liberty, and feminists are surely partly right to see, in the movement for sexual liberation, the expression of a common masculine dream of unlimited sexual access to women without reciprocal obligations. But it goes too far to say that heterosexuality is necessarily oppressive. For heterosexuality provides a bridge between the sexes which gives them a joint investment in the future of society. It is also an open question to what extent, given safe contraception, it is in women's interests to express themselves sexually in ways that were once imprudent. In extolling liberty, de Beauvoir fails to recognize that in traditional societies there is little to be gained by women in removing the social restraints and taboos which surround sex and associate it with complex patterns of social obligation, which ultimately ensure that some of the surplus production of men is transferred to the women and children. What means are available to women if their aim is the creation of a culture in which men's powers are harnessed to the needs of women and their children? One obvious strength which women have in regard to men derives from their position as mothers of sons and their ability to use the ties of affection that exist between mother and son to encourage responsible sexual behaviour. But if this only led to brothers' responsibilities to sisters, the population would fissure into families headed by women. In order for a community to emerge, sons and/or daughters need to be exchanged between families or clans. It is thus that the relatively egalitarian system of reciprocal exchanges described by Bell might be thought to have grown up. It is a mistake to think that society has always developed as it has simply through its imposition on women by men. Rather, it often embodies a compromise between men's desire for sexual access to women and women's desire to limit and control that access in order to maximize male contributions to children's survival. But this compromise has within it tensions which have, in many circumstances, led to the erosion of women's power to control the terms of the compromise.

Men's allegiance is divided between the individual family to which they belong and the same-sexed group of men. Women's allegiance is equally divided. Yet there are important asymmetries between the sexes which enable some men to strengthen the position of their families over the group in general. We have already noted the asymmetry due to child-bearing. Another lies in a man's capacity to increase the number of his children indefinitely through having many wives. It is not particularly in woman's interest to acquire more than one husband, for her ability to reproduce offspring is fairly limited. It is generally only in very poor communities, in which survival is difficult, that polyandry occurs, and it does nothing to extend the sphere of a woman's political influence, since it cannot significantly increase her kin. But polygamy and the acquisition of slave-wives from other tribes are common features of the development of cultures on the move from a low level of wealth accumulation to the sophisticated structures of trade and state that currently exist. Once a system of property rights and allegiance based on family membership is established, the men of a group can advantage themselves and increase the numbers of their offspring by acquiring many wives, either as a right recognized within the society, or by conquest of another society. As was noted in the last chapter, both Malinowski and Reich comment on the polygamy of the Trobriand chiefs, and its tendency to conflict with the general pattern of exchange between clans. And the potential which polygamy offers men to extend their political influence over a wide segment of the community constitutes an asymmetry between the sexes which has not been widely discussed. Ties of reciprocity become distorted when they are used by powerful polygamous chiefs to promote the interests of one clan over those of another. But it may be that external pressures encourage members of the community to accept such 'big men'. They provide a focus of leadership in times of attack and have a surplus large enough to mount friendly or warlike expeditions into distant territory. Once such a power structure is in place there is little women can do to right the balance. Women's interests become further divided, since the division of power between men in the society makes it prudent for women to compete for the favours of the most powerful men.

Where polygamy exists in conjunction with the capture of women from other societies, the influx of low-status women might seem, in the short term, to enhance the position of the warrior's own wives and mothers, because slave-wives are captured and given as servants to the women of the conqueror's group. Yet it can be demonstrated that it subtly undermines women's power.[41] For the captured women have every reason to attempt to wrest favours from their master at the expense of his existing wives. If a more servile devotion or greater sexual attractiveness are means to this end, they are likely to be employed. A common theme of myths and fairy tales is the story of the patient girl who through self-sacrifice and devotion wins the favours of a prince or chief, where other, less patient, more selfish 'sisters' have failed. The Biblical book of Esther is a good example of a story of this kind. It begins with the banishment of a too-proud wife who is replaced by the humble and beautiful daughter of an oppressed group, whose servile patience results in her people being saved. These tales are no doubt partly legacies of a tradition which has attempted to teach women submission through promising rewards. Yet they also incorporate an element which is true to women's situation. If one is not powerful enough to coerce others to provide one with benefits, then one is forced to use other means in order to control the powerful others; to move their hearts, stimulate their sympathy or deserve their gratitude. Once women's solidarity with women is rendered ineffective, through the introduction of vast differences in property and power among men, individual women are forced to rely on such strategies to motivate men to promote their interests. Perhaps, too, women have an unreasonably high faith in the efficacy of such means because, in their own dealings with children, and men, they tend to be easily moved to care for the powerless.

The exchange of women knits together elements of a potentially warring community. And the women who are exchanged have as great an interest in peace as do other members of their community. The patience, intelligence and diplomacy which this role requires can reach heroic proportions, as they do in the Biblical story of Esther. It is these qualities which Christine de Pisan sees as necessary to the medieval princess, whose marriage constitutes an alliance between potentially warring countries. And this function, fulfilled consciously by women in societies where the threat of war between opposing groups of men is always present, should not be overlooked. The production of offspring who have allegiances to both the mother's and the father's line acts as a deterrent to war, since both sides will, to an extent, be killing their own, but this is not the only reason why the exchange of women is more efficacious in building alliances than is the exchange of other gifts. The women exchanged are not mere objects. They can do their job well or ill, and in performing it well they benefit themselves, preserving peace and ensuring a safe environment for their children's survival. While modern society has given up the practice of exchanging women in order to bring together potentially conflicting groups in a web of reciprocal relationships, the obverse tendency still exists. Where groups are more or less openly at war with each other, intermarriage is still either explicitly or implicitly prohibited.

In adopting this analysis I am going some way in the direction of agreeing with Rousseau that women have historically had a particular interest in the control of sexuality. This agreement involves rejecting the Marxist claim that the sexual restrictions which uphold the family are merely imposed by men on women. Unlike Rousseau, however, I do not take this as constituting an unqualified endorsement of sexual fidelity in the service of the family. Nevertheless, the question has to be asked what forms of sexuality it is in women's interests to promote; and, in the end, for those women who are interested in bearing children, there may be an advantage in promoting an ideal of sexual love which emphasizes responsibility for, and commitment to, the wellbeing of the other over a long period of time. Sex as sensual self-indulgence is fun at the time, but does nothing to shore up mutual parental responsibilities. It is difficult to see how women could maintain a double standard, preserving rights of free sexual expression for themselves but not for the fathers of their children. Which suggests, at least for those women who are interested in maintaining men's contribution to the reproduction of society, an inevitable commitment to ideals of loving sexual responsibility for parents.[42]

Rousseau implicitly recognized that the actual historical state is made up of men who come together for the joint protection of their property. In discussing his work I argued that it was this protective and warlike function of the state which led him to think of women as ultimately subject and not sovereign within the democratic republic.[43] The sovereignty of a group of men depends ultimately on their capacity to defend what is theirs – land, women, children and chattels – against other men. As was argued in chapter 3, the historical state is not based on a rational social contract entered into by equals; if it were, women would be among the contractors. It is a structure upheld by force which maintains the power of one group over others. In aristocratic societies this structure is compatible with a measure of power wielded by women, as the deputies of their menfolk. But in democratic societies the levelling of men leads to a levelling of women, and men's historical control over the apparatus of the state led, in the nineteenth century, to a situation in which women were more clearly excluded from political power, under democracy, than they had been under aristocratic forms of government. Winning the vote has only slightly mitigated this situation and the state continues to be a largely male-dominated organization. In order for women to be fully incorporated into it, it needs to transform itself from a thinly disguised war machine, committed to establishing the hegemony of one group of men against other national groups, into the necessary minimum means of upholding a genuine social contract between equals.

It was previously suggested, in the discussion of de Pisan's philosophy of ethical responsibility and submission, that, practised from a position of lack of power, women's concern with love, and with the obligations to individuals that love fosters and entails, does nothing to remedy oppression. Perhaps no one is more aware of this than de Beauvoir, whose comments on love are precursors of Firestone's even more vitriolic attack on romantic love. Love is for women, according to de Beauvoir, 'a supreme attempt to overcome, while assuming it, the dependence to which she is condemned'.[44] De Beauvoir accepts in her account of love a claim, made by Nietzsche and Byron, according to which for women love is a devotion in which she gives up her soul and body, whereas for men love is just an occupation which involves at most desiring a devotion of this kind. According to her the woman in love 'chooses to desire her enslavement so ardently that it will seem to her the expression of her liberty; she will try to rise above her situation as an inessential object by fully accepting it.'[45] Yet she obscures a number of issues by concentrating, in her discussion of the woman in love, on this one kind of love, a love which is essentially a desire to be loved and to take the place of the child in relation to the lover. This kind of love, as de Beauvoir perceptively comments, is an attempt to get back the mother as much as the father (and perhaps more so).[46] It is an attempt to seek validation through being recognized by someone strong and comforting. Yet this is not the only kind of love that women have expressed. Wollstonecraft, for instance, clearly both desired to be loved and also feared the vulnerability which loving brought with it. Her love was not a desire to submerge herself in her lover. It was, rather, the desire for the mutual give and take between equals prepared to admit that they were equally desirous of the other's approval and equally desirous to care for each other. This structure of mutuality is, in fact, far closer to de Beauvoir's own picture of a healthy love than to the abject self-effacement which she implies women have sought. Love as the 'mutual recognition of two liberties', which de Beauvoir finds articulated in George Gusdorf, might equally have been discovered by her in Wollstonecraft's letters to Godwin. Even Christine de Pisan understands by true love a kind of mutual recognition, though her true lovers recognize not so much the liberties of others as the way they are constrained by social obligation. Love as mutual recognition deserves to be credited as an ancient feminine ideal, and one in which the strands of reason and feeling are combined in a delicate harmony. For the feeling which makes us desire to love and be loved finds its expression in the rational recognition that the other is a rational and valuable individual, both dauntingly different from, and deeply similar to, the self. It is this capacity for care and respect across boundaries of clan and sexual difference that aboriginal women foster in a system of exchanges which does not negate difference but which knits them into a cohesive whole. It is in the service of a similar bridging of difference that de Pisan advises her young princess to be dutiful, wise and mild.

The love that a woman gives as a mother has a different character. But it too needs to be taken into account if one is to discuss what love has meant to women. It is given from a position of relative strength and rests in the recognition of the need of the other for reassurance and validation. Often enough, in real relationships, women who are able to love as mothers will also take this attitude towards their lovers, while at the same time desiring to be loved as a child is loved. Ideally a man will provide for a woman the same kind of invocation of a secure and valued existence as she provides for him. But this is very different from the one-sided devotion which de Beauvoir describes as love. The attitudes that de Beauvoir decries are as much the result of the inequalities in the social situation within which love is being played out as difficulties with love itself. She partly recognizes this, since she comments that it is 'the difference in their situations that is reflected in the difference men and women show in their conceptions of love'.[47] Yet she fails to distinguish economic and social dependence adequately from psychic dependence. This means that, rather than simply being critical of some forms of love, her works suggest a fear of any kind of psychic interdependence and vulnerability. It is true that without mutual economic independence, love is likely to degenerate into a glorified submission which merely palliates an already subjected situation. Yet, in a world where we were all totally psychically independent, love would be redundant. It is the very dependence of others, our importance to them, their need for our material and psychological aid, which inspires us to love. Equally, we depend on others for confirmation of our worth and for the pleasure that we feel in finding that our existence gives others pleasure. It is the position of social inequality from within which these values are pursued that leads to their degeneration.

If this is correct, then the conclusion we should draw is that if women are to pursue the interests they have traditionally pursued, as well as all those others which have been opened up to them by low infant mortality, contraception and abortion, without the traditional commitments perpetuating their disadvantage, what is required is the institution of political structures which ensure their representation. In the society of the aboriginal the women as a group can negotiate with the men as a group. In a society which is as divided along lines of class, race, ethnicity and ideology as are modern democracies, there is little reason to think that the women of a society will be any more united than are the men. The society is too large and diverse for representatives of the two sexes to argue out differences face to face. No single individual can represent women, since women are as divided over the fundamental questions concerning society as are men. Nevertheless, one simple measure which would assure the equal representation of women's and men's interests would be the equal representation discussed in chapter 5. Some feminists have argued that what is required is the disappearance of gender roles.[48] Others have argued for an escape by women from male society and a flight from heterosexuality.[49] Others again have suggested the re-evaluation of the maternal and the image of mother and daughter.[50] Still another has suggested compulsory equal representation in all areas of authority.[51] All of these suggestions are prescriptive, implicitly presupposing that the writer can judge for the mass of women how they should best live their lives. In fact, the search for the good life is an ongoing enterprise which has to be taken up by each generation of women, for themselves, in the light of the material conditions that then exist, and the understanding of the world that has been passed down to them. The most plausible defence of the liberal state resides in the idea that the structures set up provide a framework within which different conceptions of the good life can compete fairly in the determination of the governing of the state. The historical liberal state has, however, been built on the foundation of the patriarchal family. Women's emancipation is particularly difficult because this family has some features traditionally valued by many women, which we should not lose sight of. In particular it preserves individual identity based on affective ties with place and kin. And, although it has traditionally constrained women, it has also constrained men and provided a framework within which they have undertaken obligations towards their children. At the same time, its traditional structure, plus the procedure of open competition for positions of power, continues to militate against the full integration of women into the state. A parliament equally composed of men and women would remedy this immediately, making the debate between women over the nature of the good life part of the on-going public discussion of the development of the state, and leaving actual outcomes to be determined by this. The responsibility for governing which women would then see as theirs would stimulate them to contribute more fully to the making and dissemination of policy. And the presence of so many women in the state would ensure that they were representative of many different women's interests.

8

Reason, Femininity, Love and Morality

So far I have argued that the tradition of feminist humanism differs in emphasis from the tradition of masculine humanism, and that it does not succumb to the criticisms which feminists have levelled against humanism in general. In the last chapter, I established that de Beauvoir's implicit use of the idea of patriarchal ideology as a critical tool ultimately undermined the positive message in her own project. The pursuit of transcendence by women requires us to take up values as women. But if we accept that all culture up to now is the creation of men, that laws, language, values and reason are simply artefacts of the masculine mind, it comes to appear that femininity must be a rupture, an excess, below, above or beyond language and culture. This has led to an uneasy alliance between feminism and post-modernism, for it seems both are committed to a critique of all past metaphysics and the 'end of philosophy'. Yet how can women create language and themselves *ab initio*?

The view that we need to do this rests partly on confusing written masculine history and the actual past, so that we come to equate our past selves with men's images of us. It also rests on an untenable conception of the way humans acquire an identity. The radical individualism which is part of existentialism, and which remains implicit in the idea that we can create ourselves totally anew, sits uneasily with the recognition that one's identity necessarily comes largely from outside, from the society in which one lives and the ways of interpreting the world which are available in the language that one speaks. Moreover, the view that woman is Other, even for herself, encourages a kind of collective bad faith. It encourages the view that, as women, we have no responsibility for what we are. Although she herself made no such claim, de Beauvoir subtly encourages women to transfer the blame for their condition from biology onto men, who are conceived of as equally beyond women's control. A more positive basis for developing our future transcendence is to recognize that we have been conscious participants in the social construction of the past. If femininity is not a biological essence, but a historical creation, then transcendence will involve the conscious interpretation of the available history by taking up an attitude to it and seeing ourselves and our consciousness as differentiated and developing. We implicitly denigrate past women if we assume that they were incapable of forging any values for themselves, and hastily dismiss the consciousness of previous women as defective. De Beauvoir's analysis has partly encouraged her descendants to disregard the rich legacy of writing left by actual women. Much of that legacy resides in women's understanding of the place of care and love in the maintenance of culture, and in an acceptance of the subordination of individual desire to social duty. To reject all this as foisted on us by men is to accept men's myth of their own transcendence, their creation of culture, their autonomy. All men start off as boys, none is in control of the influences which form them, and many are deeply affected by women, as well as by men. The legacy of women's writing on love and morality suggests a greater historical awareness by women of women's impact on society, and her place in the reproduction of culture, than was acknowledged by the male authorities on whom de Beauvoir relied. In this chapter I will draw out the implications for our thinking about the moral individual of the conception of humanity that is implicit in this tradition. This is a conception of a reasoned, passionate and embodied being, who strives to live in a world in which feelings are in harmony with justice. It implies a feminist ethic which takes seriously the humanist acceptance of an underlying human nature, and the possibility of the discovery of some truth, while at the same time incorporating the perception that we are embodied, emotional beings.

Recently, care and love have returned to feminist thought in a more positive guise than that depicted by de Beauvoir, and it has been suggested that it is rather the abstract ideal of a universal and autonomous comradeship which is inescapably patriarchal. The tradition influenced by Gilligan, Noddings and Ruddick rehabilitates the feminine, and some writers have warned against identifying a feminist ethic with a feminine ethic.[1] This worry can, I think, be allayed by observing that by itself an ethic of care is not necessarily feminist, but it becomes feminist when incorporated into a theory of the good of society which attempts to bring about the good of women as well as the good of men. This rehabilitation of love, care and other traditional feminine values has come from a number of directions. One has been the rise of what Sandra Harding has called 'feminist standpoint epistemologies' which have developed a new account of the implications of Freud's psychoanalysis and Marxism for feminism.[2] Another derives from Gilligan's empirical work on differences between the moral responses of boys and girls.[3] Both of these strands are more or less influenced by versions of psychoanalysis, particularly the work of Melanie Klein and the more recent applications of object relations theory by Nancy Chodorow.[4] Another influence has been Jean Baker Miller's new psychology.[5] There are significant differences in emphasis among different writers in this movement, but there are broad commonalities. One is the frequent use of some version of Freudian psychoanalysis in order, first, to justify the idea that men and women have different subjectivities, grounded in their differing psychosexual developments, and, second, to explain some of the features of these differing subjectivities. Another is a critical attitude towards features of thought which are associated with the masculine standpoint and a positive attitude towards ways of thinking which are identified with the feminine.[6]

I have argued that the thesis developed by these writers is borne out by an examination of central historical feminist writers, and that rather than rejecting the views of these egalitarian feminists because of their liberalism or humanism, we should use their thoughts as the basis for developing our on-going feminine voice. Yet there are a number of criticisms which can be levelled at standpoint epistemology, particularly when it relies on Freud's theories for its characterization of the masculine and feminine points of view, and it is worthwhile airing these, in order to set up a defensible version of the claim that there are different masculine and feminine voices, and to rescue this idea from the relativism into which it often descends.[7] One difficulty is that Freudian psychoanalysis is itself open to the charge of being a masculine ideology.[8] In so far as the conception of masculine and feminine gender identities is traced back to Freud, this should make us suspicious of the way they are characterized. Secondly, it is assumed that if it can be shown that a way of looking at the world is characteristic of a male gender orientation, this is sufficient to show that it is defective. This can perhaps be justified, if it is assumed that we have been living within a patriarchy, that men make up the ruling class, and that the beliefs of the ruling class will embody a distorted ideological vision of reality, but, as I argued in the previous chapters, the extension of the notion of ideology to the feminist case is particularly problematic. We need some independent means of sorting ideological from non-ideological beliefs. Once we have given up the blanket assessment of all past theories as patriarchal ideology, we need to be able to give reasons for believing that the point of view, if there is one, which is generated by a masculine psychosexual orientation is defective. If psychoanalysis tells us that men see the world one way and women see it another way, this may just be a fact that we have to learn to live with. Whether or not the difference amounts to a defect on men's part will depend on the relevant features of the case.

This point can be brought out through an analogy with colour vision.[9] We know that colour blindness only affects men. One can imagine a world in which all men suffered from red/green colour blindness. In such a situation women would not only see the world differently, they would see the world better. They would be capable of making useful visual discriminations which men could not make. Once this population had discovered this fact about itself, it would be absurd for it not to take women to be the experts in cases of colour discrimination. There are objectively useful features of the world which they have access to and men do not. But not every case is like this. There is, apparently, a genetic difference between people which makes it the case that some judge a shade between green and blue to be blue/green whereas others judge it to be green/blue. Suppose we imagine a world in which this difference is completely sex-linked, so that all men judge one way, all women judge the other. In this case it would be arbitrary to value men's judgements over women's or vice versa. The shade just is blue/green relative to some observers, green/blue relative to others. So establishing that men and women occupy different epistemological or ethical standpoints is not yet to have determined how these standpoints stand to each other normatively. We need to discover whether the difference is like that between the red/green colour blind and those with normal colour vision or whether it is like the difference between seeing blue/green and seeing green/blue.

In order to draw out the complexity of the intertwined threads in the debate over masculine and feminine orientations, I will concentrate on Carol Gilligan's influential work on the distinction between an ethic of justice and an ethic of care. Gilligan based her original claim that women and men speak with different ethical voices on data collected by women working on Kohlberg's model of moral development.[10] Kohlberg had hypothesized that there are six distinct stages of moral development, similar to Piaget's stages of cognitive development, and he devised a set of ethical dilemmas in order to test the level of development reached in particular populations. It is perhaps worth noting that, from a philosophical point of view, some odd biases are built into Kohlberg's project from the beginning. He rates Kantian ethical reasoning as at a higher stage than utilitarianism, thus making it a matter of moral psychology that disputes in this area are to be settled in favour of Kantians. He also fails to distinguish theories concerning the epistemological ground of ethical judgements, theories about what makes an act morally right, from theories about the motivational ground of ethical action, theories about why individuals act morally. These difficulties need not concern us for the moment, but they are important, for if I am right, part of the content of women's different ethical voice results from the fact that women are centrally concerned with the impact of their actions on the moral motivation of others, rather than with articulation of the most rationally grounded system of rules. Gilligan's hypothesis took off from the fact that the empirical ranking of children into stages of ethical development consistently classed western girls lower than western boys.[11] Gilligan hypothesized that this was not because of an ethical inadequacy on the part of girls, but because the way in which ethical judgements were ranked was already biased in favour of males. She developed an alternative picture according to which female ethical development proceeds by stages quite different to those Kohlberg had described.

There is a great deal of ambiguity in the proposal made in Gilligan's early work. Her claim is that men and women take different ethical stances: women adopt an ethic of care, in which the primary concern is care for others and 'responsibility in relationships'; men adopt an ethic of justice, which is oriented towards 'the fair weighing and balancing of claims' and dealing fairly with others.[12] These different stances are taken to be connected with wider differences in the psychosexual development of boys and girls, but just how this meshes with Kohlberg's theories is unclear. What exactly is the nature of the difference that is operating? Kohlberg was early inclined to see the difference between men and women as functional, as Rousseau might have.[13] Women, since they have their social role in the private sphere of the family, have different ethical duties to men and it is appropriate that they should concentrate on the individual and psychological aspects of ethical dilemmas. Men play their role in the public sphere of impartial justice and their mode of judgement is equally functional. If the data is interpreted this way, one might object to Kohlberg's unjustified ranking of these different modes of judgement and conclude that all is well with the world. Women are well adapted to motherhood, men are well adapted to the public sphere, and, when it comes to ethical dilemmas, Gilligan's data could be used to back up the conclusion that they should keep to their areas of expertise. However, most commentators on Gilligan's observations want to draw more radical conclusions than these.

The enormous response in the literature to Gilligan's claim suggests that it captured a widespread intuition that men and women perceive ethical matters differently. Moreover, many women would claim men see them defectively. But what is the difference? At what level does it operate? What is the relationship between the two perspectives? Is it just that at some fundamental level men and women differ in what they value? Is there a meta-ethical dispute? The two different modes of moral discourse appear, according to Gilligan, in conjunction with two different ways of experiencing the self, the first of which involves distancing, impartiality and objectivity, the second involves specific contexts of interdependence and responses to needs.[14] This is sometimes taken to imply that men are naturally, but mistakenly, objectivists, while women are naturally, and correctly, relativists. But this claim itself involves a commitment to objectivism at some level (that is, the level of descriptive psychology) and so appears self-refuting. In some places Gilligan associates the two different ways of experiencing the self with the contrast between justice and love. In others she accuses the male tradition of having itself engendered the distinctions between judgement and feeling, rationality and emotion, egoism and altruism, and so of having developed oppositions where there is in fact complementarity.[15]

It is the thesis of this book that a way of understanding the female ethic which is grounded in this latter thought is the most productive. It enables us to conceptualize a feminine ethic which is not opposed to rationality. This will provide a normative ethical conception against which those masculine ethics which tend to make reason and emotion incompatible can be criticized. A characteristic feature of most of the developments of Gilligan's thinking is that they have accepted the opposition between reason and emotion, justice and care, disinterestedness and love, objectivity and connectedness. Different writers, inspired by the thought of a feminine ethic, have associated it with emotion, care, love and connectedness, to the detriment of justice and reason.[16] But this approach leaves one with insoluble difficulties as to the relationship between the two points of view. Reason and justice cannot simply be dismissed. Do we then have, as suggested above, the traditional picture of different moralities for different spheres; a public sphere of impartiality, justice and universal values, and a private sphere of partiality, love and agent-relative value? Or are there simply incompatible ways of looking at the world? Gilligan suggests in a number of places that the differing perspectives are like the two interpretations of the ambiguous figure which can be seen as either a vase or a face (she might equally have mentioned the duck-rabbit).[17] With such figures one can switch from one interpretation to the other, but not hold them both in mind at the same time. But the analogy is not very helpful. It suggests that the choice between the two interpretations is arbitrary. More helpful is the suggestion that moral maturity involves being able to use both perspectives.[18] But this still gives us little guidance as to how they relate to each other and in what circumstances one or other perspective is to be preferred.

So far in this book I have developed the hypothesis that one way of developing the contrast between an ethic of justice and an ethic of care is to see them as grounded in different conceptions of moral psychology. I argued that the most cogent reworking of feminist objections to Hobbes made the rejection of the Hobbesian moral psychology the central issue. For Hobbes there is no autonomous ethical motivation. In so far as human beings acquire a desire to be virtuous, this is the product of rational calculation and their more primary desire to preserve their life and increase their material wellbeing. The rejection of Hobbes's picture is not unique to feminists; it has been common to a number of thinkers who have objected that the Hobbesian individual cannot count as genuinely moral. Many such writers have preferred a picture more like that offered by Plato. The Platonic model of the moral individual recognizes three distinct ingredients within an ethical personality; there are ordinary, non-ethical desires, plus a desire to be good (in virtue of doing good or perhaps less demandingly in virtue of avoiding evil), and a capacity to judge what is good and how it might be achieved (reason). Within this model there is a great affinity assumed between the desire to do good and reason. Indeed, if reason is itself thought of as a kind of motive – the desire for truth, and the good is thought of as a kind of truth – the two tend to collapse into each other. Then it will appear that reason can motivate us to do good, and this gives us a picture in which moral conflict is thought of as a conflict between reason and passion. But, as we saw in the discussion of Rousseau, 'passion' is ambiguous in this tradition and should not be thought of as essentially opposed to reason. It is only the non-moral passions which will at times manifest themselves as in conflict with a reason that serves the good.

There is also in this tradition a close affinity between the desire to do good and love; in fact this desire is often understood as a kind of love. Hume did great damage to this picture with his contention that reason could not be a motive. In consequence he levelled all motives to natural sentiments. He tried to show that, nevertheless, there are moral sentiments, which happen to be those which have a certain form of social efficacy. So he makes sentiment central in ethics, but he does so in a way which ultimately divorces ethics from reason.[19] In saying this I am to an extent disagreeing with Annette Baier, who suggests that Hume's moral thought corresponds to the feminine voice because of his emphasis on sympathy and the development of character.[20] The difficulty that I have with identifying the feminine voice with Hume's views is that it leaves us on one side of the divide between reason and emotion, siding apparently with subjectivism, and unable to show coherently why some sentiments are of greater value than others. Nevertheless, it has been argued that a distinction between reasonable, ethical sentiments and unreasonable passions emerges within Hume's developed view.[21] This makes his ultimate picture not too different from Plato's, and in so far as this is the case my divergence from Baier's position may not be too great.

Kant attempted to restore the rationality of ethics. But he did so not by rehabilitating the idea that there is genuine moral motivation, but by turning morality into a matter of reason alone. For Kant, to act out of moral duty is to act from the intellectual apprehension that one's action is required by the truth of the categorical imperative. He develops the intuition, shared by many writers, that an action can only be ethical if it involves the use of reason, and transforms it into the claim that being guided by reason is sufficient for an action to be ethical. Recent critiques suggest that the pure rational ego of the Kantian tradition is an ethical nightmare in which ethics is divorced from the emotional and sexual realities of human existence. This indicates a widespread intuition that Plato must have been partly right and that the ethical personality involves an element which deserves to be considered a necessary condition for the ethical life, and which operates at the affective and motivational level.[22] Kant's characterization of the ethical realm has also been used as a paradigm of the 'maleness' of philosophy.[23] And if I am right, and at least an important part of what is being objected to in the feminist rejection of rational egoism is the reduction of ethical life to pure instrumental rationality, he is rightly typified in this way. Wollstonecraft is notably present among the feminists who have objected to Kant's characterization of the ethical. Her objection was clearly not that he connected morality with reason. She too thought that rationality was a necessary prerequisite for ethical judgement. Rather, she objected that he failed to see the role played by the imagination and the passions in the development of reason. Central to her thoughts on the relationship between reason and passion is the role of imagination. Her comments suggest that in order to judge wisely in matters of ethics, we need to be able to imagine what it would be like to be placed as others are, or have been. But if we have never been in situations in which we have felt such passions, our imagination will be limited and we will be likely to judge amiss. She suggests that often what one is required to know, when it comes to matters of ethics, is how it feels for an individual (who may be different from one in many ways) to be in that situation. One cannot know the feelings of others without having felt oneself. Thus sentiment and imagination are not inessential auxiliaries to our ethical life. They are necessary prerequisites for moral sensibility.

Interestingly, other female philosophers, who have influenced some writers intent on articulating a distinctive feminine voice, have placed considerable emphasis on the role of love and imagination in ethical judgement. Among these is Iris Murdoch, whose thoughts on this subject are alluded to by Sarah Ruddick in her attempt to characterize maternal thinking.[24] Murdoch connects love with knowledge, saying 'Love is knowledge of the individual', and connects this insight with a Christian and Platonic tradition.[25] She also connects knowledge with imagination, suggesting that it is imagination which helps us to see the other individual justly and gain the knowledge which shows us what morally must be done. Imagination and emotion have not been greatly discussed in contemporary ethical theory, but they occupy an interesting position between mere sensation and reason.[26] To imagine how it would be to be placed as the other is placed is not just to imagine what would be true, if one were placed thus, but partly to feel as the other would feel. But imagination, if it is to be intelligent, has also to take into account that the other's feelings, in any situation, may not be the same as one's own. In such exercises of imagination, thought and feeling are intimately intertwined, in a manner that belies the picture of the human psyche as either a disembodied calculating machine, or as an impulse-driven preference-maximizer. Reasonableness involves caring sufficiently to imagine justly; and having imagined a situation as it really is, it involves, as well, feeling appropriately.

Although Murdoch's thoughts on the centrality of love and imagination to the recognition of moral truth were primarily directed against Stuart Hampshire's *Thought and Action*, and against existentialism, she suggests that they apply equally to the influential reformulation of Kant's categorical imperative developed by Hare.[27] Hare introduces the idea that prescriptivism and the principle of universalizability are constitutive of ethical discourse, arguing that if we are not prepared to universalize the principles which guide our action, then those principles are not plausibly ethical principles. He attempts, further, to do more than merely lay down necessary conditions for some discourse to be considered moral discourse, and suggests that we can derive substantive ethical principles from universalizability. In this he is usually thought to have failed, and his failure can be used to illustrate the claim that reason may be necessary for morality, but is not sufficient. One famous problem for Hare's attempt to ground ethical principles in reason is the existence of fanatics. The fanatic is a person who is prepared to universalize, but is so committed to some particular ideal that he or she asserts, for instance, that were he or she a Jew, to take one example, or a bourgeois, to take another, he or she would still think it appropriate that Jews or members of the bourgeoisie should be exterminated. A natural response to such cases is to claim that fanatics are suffering from a failure of imagination; a kind of blindness or numbness which prevents them from recognizing how it would feel to be in the other's shoes. Hare quotes Wollstonecraft's friend and acquaintance William Blake:

> Can I see another's woe
> And not be in sorrow too?
> Can I see another's grief
> And not seek for kind relief?

Hare points out that, as the example of torturers and sadists shows, the answer to this is, for many people, 'yes'. Fanatics seem to be in a similar position, and to be suffering from a kind of failure of perception, caused by the strength of their commitment to their own set of values. It is just because such people are, as we say, 'desensitized' that we believe them to be morally defective. Hare argues that it is a virtue of his account that it is not necessary for his argument to go through that we require people to feel the pain of another as their own pain. Sympathy is not necessary for moral judgement. It is sufficient that 'I cannot know the extent and quality of others' sufferings and, in general, motivations and preferences without having equal motivations with regard to what should happen to me, were I in their place, with their motivations and preferences.'[28] But this attempt to ground ethics without relying on natural sympathy fails. For the fact that one cannot know the extent of another's sufferings without having strong motivations concerning avoiding such suffering oneself need not transform into a motivation to avoid such suffering in the other. It is when a clear perception of the other's pain is felt as the shadow of that pain in oneself, and one feels abhorrence at this evil, that one is motivated to prevent the other's pain. The fanatic can universalize and yet not be moved by another's pain because her or his sympathy for 'mere' suffering has been deadened. No amount of reason will supply this lack in the fanatic's moral capacity. On the view being proposed, and implicit in the feminist critique of a pure ethic of justice, it is simply because fanatics fail to feel for others that they can universalize, in the sense of admitting that they would not like it were they in their victim's shoes, and yet claim that were they in that person's shoes they would still approve of the kind of treatment being inflicted on them. The failure is one of perception and sympathy, and it cannot be mended by reason.

This shows that feeling as well as reason is a necessary part of moral judgement. But how do these observations tie in with the characterization of the contrast between masculine and feminine outlooks which has been developed so far? So far I have developed three thoughts. One is that a sympathetic imagination is a necessary prerequisite for the capacity to judge how it would feel to be in another's shoes, and a necessary element in an ethical personality. Another is that we do have some motivations which are intrinsically ethical. A third is that women tend to speak in a 'different voice', which feminists would like to demonstrate provides a critical perspective on the standard ethic of justice. In what follows I will attempt to connect these three thoughts. Sympathy, imagination and appropriate emotional response are, I have argued, necessary prerequisites for ethical judgement. But to judge ethically one needs also to desire to judge ethically, and thus one needs moral motivation. As I have argued earlier, part of the feminine emphasis on the place of love in our moral life relates to the reproduction and sustaining of the morally motivated person who desires to exercise her or his imagination in pursuit of the good. And women, Gilligan's empirical research suggests, are more inclined to have passed on this capacity successfully to other women. Thus the goal of feminist humanism becomes that of understanding how to help men develop their humanity, and in particular those ethical capacities associated with care.

Like Rousseau, Freud was interested in the genesis of ethical character. His views are particularly important here since modern advocates of a difference in the ethical outlooks of the two sexes have often turned to psychoanalysis for evidence of the competing self-conceptions which are taken to be connected with the differing moral psychologies. But when we turn to Freud the situation starts to look rather complex, and not only because of Freud's patriarchal investments. In so far as Freud has theories which are of relevance to moral psychology, they are most obviously thought of as theories about the development of moral motivation. On the face of it, a theory of the source of moral motivation is very different from a conception of the ground of moral truth like that offered by Kant and Hobbes, Hume or Rousseau. As Philippa Foot argued, it is simply not obvious that any body of ethical injunctions has motivating force.[29] Hobbes believed that reason could transform the natural motivation of self-preservation into ethical motivation, but, as we have already seen, his reasoning is flawed. Kant, on the other hand, seems to have assumed that a recognition of the rationality of the categorical imperative would be sufficient to motivate an individual to obedience. This too seems implausible. If we abstract from the ethical realm, it seems quite possible for an individual to recognize that a course of action is rational and yet not be motivated to follow it. Irrational desires are problematic but not absurd. If Freud is correct, we are often motivated by aims which our conscious selves deem irrational, and in many circumstances we fail to be moved by our perception of the most rational course of action. Moreover, once the point is made, one does not need any great faith in the generality of Freud's propositions to accept it. In ethics as in other areas, the recognition that a principle is rational is, by itself, insufficient to motivate one to abide by it. Even an accurate imagination, though it might produce some impulses towards morality, need not over-ride a desire to do something irrational and bad. It is quite possible to imagine angry and self-destructive characters who accept that they would hate to be tortured and even that their actions are likely to end in their own demise but who commit themselves, in defiance, to expressing their destructive anger. It is also easy to conceive of a sado-masochist who imagines quite clearly the pain being inflicted on another and who never-theless still desires to inflict it. One needs something more than the reasonableness or even the objective worth of principles for ethical action to result. A desire to be rational or good would suffice, as might the belief that one's own best interests will be served by obeying ethical principles, plus a desire for one's own best interest. Following this line of thought, it is natural to treat the justification of ethical principles and an account of the genesis of the motivation to do what is prescribed as two complementary and independent aspects of ethical theory; the first being partly meta-ethical and partly normative, the second belonging to moral psychology and particularly to the psychology of moral development.

In the literature, these two aspects of ethical theory are inclined to merge. An instructive case of this occurs at the beginning of Gilligan's paper on the female voice. There she quotes a famous passage from Freud in which he comments that the super-ego is never so inexorable in women as in men.[30] This he takes as implicit confirmation of his theory that the development of moral motivation takes place through the processes of the Oedipus complex. The Oedipus complex is the result, in girls, of penis envy and their recognition that they are castrated. In boys it is fear of castration which provides the motivation for the resolution of the Oedipus complex. Boys are compelled by a clear and positive fear to give up their desire for their mother and to suppress their rivalry with their father, replacing it by an identification with his power and his law. Girls, by contrast, have 'nothing to lose' by remaining attached to their fathers, in the 'Oedipal' relationship which develops once the recognition of their castrated status leads them to give up the mother, who is the first object of their affection. Freud recommends his theory because it explains women's well-known lack of a sense of justice, and their tendency to be influenced in their judgements by feelings of affection or hostility. Gilligan, in quoting Freud, appears to be accepting that the phenomenon he alludes to can be taken as evidence for the existence of different but equally good moral voices; but if Freud is right, this cannot be the case. Freud's super-ego is the equivalent of the traditional conscience. So, in attributing a weakness in super-ego to women, he is not attributing a feature which is compatible with the conclusion that women pursue a different but equally good set of normative principles. According to Freud, women are simply lacking in moral motivation.

When it is put this way it becomes obvious just how implausible the Freudian claim is. Nothing in women's behaviour suggests a lack in ethical motivation. In fact just the opposite is the case. It is women who are law-abiding, obedient, peaceable and concerned about their reputations. It is men who are alternately rebellious law-breakers, scoffing at women's ethical qualms, and, in other situations, ruthless upholders of their law, deriding women's faint-heartedness and preparedness to give way on matters of 'principle'. But, according to Freud, it is men who are ethical and who have created culture, which has been transmitted to women by cross-inheritance.[31]

As we saw in chapter 6, Freud extends his account of the individual Oedipus complex and gives an account of the origin of society and morality as arising from an original act of parricide. This account has been endorsed by at least one feminist.[32] Yet it seems clear that if any theory deserves to be called patriarchal ideology, this Freudian account of the masculine origin of culture, in the primal parricide of the horde, deserves the name. There is no empirical evidence for the truth of this myth. Moreover, it simply distorts the facts. In societies around the world it is women who do the bulk of the work, reliably creating and recreating the material forms of their culture; cooking their traditional foods, conveying their traditional morality, creating their traditional clothes, and coaxing and cajoling their menfolk into contributing in some measure to the labour of love which maintains culture, food, shelter, cleanliness and home. Women do not need to be paid or honoured in order to be motivated to do what needs to be done for the reproduction of society. They do it reliably, conscientiously and without fuss, in villages and cities throughout the world. So the facts are startlingly different from those that Freud assumes. If we are to have a theory of moral motivation, it should be one which explains women's greater devotion to the needs of others. The Oedipus complex and the development of the super-ego fail dismally in this regard, explaining a 'fact' which has no factual status.

The earlier discussion developed reasons for thinking that Freud's extension of the Oedipus complex to account for the origin of social life and the incest taboo was implausible. While all societies, in order to function, place constraints on sexual behaviour which are closely connected to a system of rights and obligations to provide for other members of the group, there is no reason to think that the internalization of these ethical constraints must be generated by a powerful father figure who generates in his son a fear of castration. Many societies instil in their populations a desire to do the right thing, to avoid shame and deserve honour, without either severe taboos on infantile sexuality or the presence of a powerful paterfamilias. We need, then, a different account of the genesis of moral motivation if we are interested in the differences between the sexes which operate at this level. And we need to show how differences at the motivational level can translate into differences at the level of ethical judgement.

Christine de Pisan and Rousseau have already provided us with some hints on the subject. De Pisan was aware, as educationalists now assert is the case, that children are more likely to be motivated to act as one believes they ought if they are motivated by a love which inclines them to want to please. She was also aware that this love is generated by consistency, generosity and affection. Rousseau made the transformation of self-love into the love of others the central task of his moral education. Freud begins his description of the formation of the super-ego in *The Ego and the Id* by acknowledging that a lost love object is often introjected and forms the basis for a narcissistic attitude. This would connect the giving up of the mother as first love object with the development of a self-love that internalizes the mother's edicts. In fact Freud wonders whether this 'is not the universal road to sublimation'. But he then takes another tack, assuming, with the introduction of the story of the

development of the super-ego through the Oedipus complex and castration anxiety, that the major motivating force for virtue is fear.[33] We
have seen that this story is simply untrue to the facts. But there is another
story about the generation of moral motivation implicit in the feminist
psychoanalysts' story about the development of the feminine self.

The words 'conscience' and 'consciousness' are etymologically very
close. They are still the same word in French and were so in English in
Hobbes's day. So in what follows I will retell Chodorow's account of the
development of the feminine sense of self, the feminine consciousness,
as a story about the feminine conscience, the feminine moral motivation.
This ties in, in Gilligan's words, conceptions of self and morality. We
have already seen, in the writing of de Pisan and Rousseau, evidence of
a tradition which makes women, and particularly mothers, central to the
development of moral motivation. In my previous discussion of
Rousseau, I was concerned to show how his account of women's role in
the development of men's moral sentiments was, as Wollstonecraft had
pointed out, contradictory, for it required that women should be virtuous without giving them the means to attain virtue. But omitting what
is extraneous in Rousseau's thought, his philosophy provides an insight
into the role that women can play in generating in men the desire for
virtue. Women mother, and this gives them a unique position in the
genesis of the complex ties between sexuality, self-esteem and ethical
orientation which go to make up the mature individual. Some evidence
for this is provided by Rousseau's account of how Mademoiselle Lamber-
cier's smack, when he was eight years old, plus the horror of sexuality
which was instilled in him from an early age, resulted in his associating
the satisfaction of his desires with physical correction at the hands of a
woman, so that 'To fall at the feet of an imperious mistress, obey her
mandates, or implore pardon, were for me exquisite enjoyments; and the
more my blood was inflamed by the efforts of a lively imagination, the
more I acquired the appearance of a whining lover.'[34] But what is of
interest to me in this chapter is why it is that this early relationship with
the mother leads too often in men to fear and loathing of women, to
sadism and misogyny, and to the general desire to do evil.

De Sade's life and writing provide an important case study for
generating reflections on these matters. Feminists have asserted that sexuality is socially constructed. Yet they have shown little curiosity with
regard to the question of how de Sade's sexuality was constructed as it
was, and how his experience led to an extreme conceptualization of sex
as domination and revenge on women. For de Sade it is the mother who
stands for prudish and moralistic constraints. Initiation into libertinage

requires the rejection, rape and humiliation of the mother. Interpreted metaphorically this association too suggests the recognition that it is the mother who stands at the centre of the development of moral motivation, and it is the tendency to internalize the desire to retain the mother's love which transforms into the desire to be moral; that is to say, the desire to act in ways which continue to deserve this love. We might wonder whether it was because he was rejected by his mother at an early age that de Sade rejects in his turn the moralistic voice of the mother, punishing her with a sexuality that smacks of infantile rage at her rejection.[35] But perhaps this is not the correct analysis of the construction of de Sade's attitudes, for he also expresses considerable love for his mother, and seems to identify her with Petrarch's Laura.[36] An accurate account would require careful research into the production of the kind of dominating, anti-maternal sexuality that he manifests. But if sexualities and moralities are socially constructed, we need to understand how different sexualities are generated. The fact that it is women who seem to be most strongly morally motivated, and that this motivation is thought to derive from their being allowed to identify with the mother, suggests that nurturing boys in a similar manner may be part of the means to constructing a masculine sense of self which is closer to the feminine paradigm.

In our discussion of Rousseau, de Sade was introduced as a foil. His insistence on the naturalness of all sexual desires, of the desire to murder and to have one's own way, acted as a reminder that Rousseau's faith in the goodness of nature was naive. But I have also suggested that humanism rests on a faith that we have a nature, and that we have sufficient reason to be able to understand how to come to live well in the light of this nature. This faith might equally be thought to be undermined by de Sade. Yet it need not be. What is problematic about all simple appeals to nature is that they attribute to humans a nature which is determinately either good or bad. What is right about social constructionism is that what is natural in humans is at most a potential. Our nature constrains what can possibly count as the good life for us. But the desires that we have as adults are by no means fixed at birth. Rather, the desires that we will come to have as adults are the result of a process of interaction, of extraordinary complexity, with our family and society. Our nature is not fixed, but we all come into the world with a more or less similar set of dispositions to develop in certain ways given certain treatment. The society which produced de Sade was one of corruption, hypocrisy and arbitrary power, not too different in these respects from the society which exists today. One can attempt to change such societies by violent revolution, but the lessons of history suggest that once violence is resorted to, those who are most corrupt, ruthless and arbitrary are most likely to win power. The only option left, then, is to try to transform society by the slow method of transforming citizens. To this end we need women and men who take seriously their duties to participate in the construction of ethical individuals, and those of us who choose to have children need to understand much better than we do now how the oppressive masculinity of the rapist batterer is socially constructed.

Taking this line of inquiry risks censure from those feminists who believe that culture has been completely constructed by men, and who suspect that any attempt to explain women's role in the social construction of masculinity is a misguided attempt to blame the powerless. But women are not any longer entirely powerless. And, despite the inequalities which still manifestly exist, those of us who are middle-class members of the intellectual establishment cannot honestly claim that all power resides in men's hands. Moreover, the continuing existence of class structures, and their existence in the past, has meant that women have not been entirely excluded from participation in historical forms of power. I argued earlier that to wait for the disruption of all past forms of discourse in order to speak is to wait until the end of history. We cannot stand outside of language if we are to communicate. We are forced to use words with their historic meanings, and though those meanings are fluid and changing, no one can make a complete and discontinuous break with what has gone before. Women are socially constructed, but so too are men. Taking responsibility for ourselves, for our history and for our future must then involve asking how it is that the most oppressive of men come into being, and how women may come to participate in the construction of new men who are, if not more like women, at least comfortable with and respecting of women's independence and difference. This might seem naive if one thinks that it is society rather than the individual that is responsible for the conditions which lead to the construction of an oppressive masculinity. But if a faceless and unchangeable social reality is to blame, there is little point in movements of liberation. Many changes in behaviour begin at the individual level, and so it is not utopian to attempt to understand how we, as women, can use the influence we have in order to promote an understanding of the generation of misogyny, sadism and violence towards women in men.

Object relations theory suggests that central to the difference in masculine and feminine gender identity is a different relationship to the first love object, the mother. Briefly put, the little girl learns that she is to identify with her mother and develops a sense of self that is connected and relational, while the little boy has to differentiate himself from the mother and develops a sense of self that is separate and disconnected. I surmise that the more completely a boy is forced to repress and deny the original relationship with the mother, the less he is motivated by the continuing sense of a desire for the mother's love, which, in the girl, remains a forceful motivator for her behaviour. The following suggestions have the status of empirical hypotheses which need to be carefully examined, and it may be that other forces are at work here, so they are offered as tentative suggestions that need greater exploration and elaboration. The little girl is never required to repress her primary affection for the mother, or her dependence on the mother's goodwill. As Freud observed, at some stage in her development towards moral maturity, she transfers her affections from her mother to her father. This means that the little girl can distance herself from her mother, without distancing herself from the kind of affective relationship she has had with her. She reproduces this affective relationship in her relations with her father and continues to be motivated, and to expect others to be motivated, through the processes of affection and withdrawal of affection which have always strongly motivated her. This means in particular that she is not likely to experience her sexuality and her emotional self as in conflict with her moral self. Sexual desire, as has often been observed, tends to be connected in women with the desire for close emotional relationships and strong moral ties. It appears that this is connected to the fact that the girl's relationship with her father, and later with other men, is, in a sense, a reproduction of an earlier affective relationship with the mother.

By contrast, the incest taboo places a constraint on the mother's relationship with her son. His affective relationship with her cannot be allowed to develop its sexual aspect. Often the sexual aspect of a little boy's embraces will be a reason for not offering him the physical affection that is easily offered to little girls. And in any case, the little boy has to split his affection for his mother from his sexual desire for her. This leads, as Freud notes, to a tendency among men to disassociate sexuality and affection. In the extreme cases which Freud notes, men are impotent with the women they love and admire, and can only enjoy sex with prostitutes.[37] Different societies negotiate this difficulty in different ways. In many societies little boys stay with their mothers and the other women until a designated age just before puberty, at which they are wrenched away, often in a ceremony of kidnapping which symbolically registers the boy's loss, to become men. If Freud is right, it is the castration threat which induces a boy to give up his sexual attachment to his mother, but at a price, for it may lead him to give up affection for women altogether, if his resentment at his loss is too great. However society treats this transition, the facts suggest that Freud was mistaken with regard to the genesis of moral motivation, and that contrary to his views, the internalization of moral motives is more complex for men than for women. Because the first love object is a woman, boys have to go through a tricky transition in which their sexual desire for their mother is repressed, without this involving either a loss of affection for the mother and other women, or an excessive loathing of their sexual urges. How this is best achieved seems an urgent matter for careful research.

Chodorow has suggested that the difficulties implicit in the development of both girls and boys would be mitigated if there were more egalitarian parenting arrangements.[38] But her claims, while they may be true, are based on a theoretical model rather than on detailed empirical data, and there is a need for more investigation into this area. Feminist humanism thus becomes a research project. The tradition of feminist humanists, I have argued, has been one in which women have seen humans as rational and embodied. It has seen them as moral individuals whose morality is grounded in sentiments, which are reproduced through the practices of parenting, particularly mothering, and education. It has seen them also as rational individuals who need reason to judge what is genuinely good. Women's participation in child-rearing has tended to lead to assumptions concerning human nature which implicitly reject the idea that we are infinitely malleable. Babies come into the world with certain tendencies towards development which are universal. De Pisan and Wollstonecraft both place great emphasis on education, relying on observation to derive some simple principles concerning the development of moral motivation in children. They do not assume that citizens spring up like mushrooms in the night. Nor do they assume that we can do without reason. In fact, understanding how our actions will have different consequences for the moral development of others, and how our institutions can foster this moral development, is part of the rational exercise of creating a better society. Feminists cannot give up on justice, for it is the claim that, given the equal worth of men and women, their unequal power is unjustified which lies at the heart of feminism. But feminists have never assumed that the totality of the ethical is covered by principles of justice alone. Because of their traditional connections with children, motherhood and education, feminist humanists have been particularly sensitive to the place of emotion, sympathy, imagination and love, both in the exercise of ethical judgement and in the reproduction of ethical motivation. A just society needs to reproduce itself. Doing so requires institutions, like the family, within which love and sexual desire contribute to the reproduction of morally motivated citizens. These institutions need to be just from women's point of view (as well as men's). They need to reproduce women and men who are economically independent and who regard each other as equals. We still understand too little about the dynamics of such institutions and the means that are available to us to reproduce a society in which men fail to dominate women. But attempting to construct such a society is pursuing transcendence, without any commitment to the existence of disembodied or ahistorical selves. It requires honest and detailed research, and communication between women. It requires a certain faith that as humans we have sufficient potential for reasonableness and morality to be able to put in place less oppressive structures than those which have existed in the past. This is the secular equivalent of Wollstonecraft's faith in a reasonable and virtuous God. It connects such humanism to the tradition of Enlightenment thought. But this faith does not have to claim that some of us have a privileged access to the truth. A belief in the potential of reason can remain just that: not a certainty that truth has been attained and may be imposed on others, but a faith that a constant attempt to eradicate errors, prejudice and gross injustice through rational means is the only way to avoid their luxuriant growth. One does not need to be committed to a grand narrative in order to think that reason is the only means we have for making partial sense of our existence. And, as I hope this book has demonstrated, conceptualizing humanity as rational is quite compatible with understanding ourselves as embodied, emotional creatures whose sense of self is made up of a mixture of reason and feeling which cannot be sharply separated.

Notes

Introduction

1 Millett, *Sexual Politics*, pp. 23–6.
2 A recent discussion of the political effects of these confusions is given, from a socialist feminist perspective, by Segal, *Is the Future Female?*.
3 Jaggar, *Feminist Politics and Human Nature*, provides a thorough introduction, from a socialist feminist perspective, to four main strands: liberal, Marxist, radical and socialist feminism.
4 This definition goes back as far as de Pisan, *The Book of the City of Ladies*, p. 187.
5 J. Butler, *Gender Trouble*, p. 148.
6 Plato, *Republic*, pp. 225–59. A description of the society also occurs at 17c–19a in Plato, *Timeus*, pp. 3–5.
7 Plato, *Republic*, pp. 232–6.
8 Aristotle, *Politics*, book II §i–iv, pp. 101–12.
9 Ibid., book I § xii, pp. 91–2.
10 Elshtain, *Public Man, Private Woman*, Okin, *Women in Western Political Thought*, and Coole, *Women in Political Theory*, all discuss in detail this theme in western political thinking.
11 This theme is particularly strong in the contributions to Trebilcot, *Mothering: Essays in Feminist Theory*.
12 Jaggar, *Feminist Politics and Human Nature*, pp. 39–48; Pateman, *The Sexual Contract*, pp. 39–76.
13 Gilligan, *In a Different Voice: Psychological Theory and Women's Development*.
14 Reuther, *New Woman, New Earth*, pp. 186–204.
15 De Pisan, *The Book of the Duke of True Lovers*.
16 Sapiro, *A Vindication of Political Virtue*, ch. 2, pp. 43–76, does much to dispel current misrepresentations of Wollstonecraft's thought on these matters. See also my 'Reason and Feeling: Resisting the Dichotomy'.

Chapter 1 Against Feminist Anti-humanism

1 Rose, 'Hand, Brain, and Heart'.
2 Le Doeuff, 'Women, Reason, Etc.', p. 8, and *Hipparchia's Choice*, pp. 189–92.
3 Flax, 'Political Philosophy and the Patriarchal Unconscious'; Gallop, *The Daughter's Seduction: Feminism and Psychoanalysis*; Bordo, 'The Cartesian Masculinization of Thought'; Irigaray, *Speculum of the Other Woman*; Ruddick, 'Maternal Thinking' and 'Remarks on the Sexual Politics of Reason'.
4 Gilligan, 'In a Different Voice: Women's Conceptions of Self and Morality', *In a Different Voice*, and 'The Conquistador and the Dark Continent'; Keller, *Reflections on Gender and Science*.
5 Seigfried, 'Gender Specific Values', and '*Second Sex*: Second Thoughts' takes this attitude to de Beauvoir; Jacobus, 'The Difference of View', is critical of Wollstonecraft, suggesting that she speaks against women; and Jaggar, *Feminist Politics and Human Nature*, pp. 39–48, assumes that criticisms which have been made against male liberal theorists carry over to feminist liberal theorists.
6 Ruddick, 'Remarks on the Sexual Politics of Reason', p. 240.
7 Okin, *Justice, Gender and the Family*, pp. 170–1, see also Okin, 'Thinking like a Woman'.
8 Foucault, 'What is Enlightenment?', p. 44.
9 The excessive faith in a pure reason which conceives of itself as independent of all contingent and imaginary elements has been developed by Michèle Le Doeuff, who nevertheless does not see this as justifying the rejection of reason. Le Doeuff, 'Women, Reason, Etc.'.
10 A useful introduction to the contemporary debate between those who believe we should abandon philosophical humanism and those who believe that our idea of the rational subject can be transformed is to be found in Baynes et al., *After Philosophy: End or Transformation*, pp. 1–18.
11 Fuss, *Essentially Speaking*, pp. 2–4.
12 Le Doeuff, 'Simone de Beauvoir and Existentialism', p. 287.
13 Le Doeuff, 'Women, Reason, Etc.', p. 6. Sartre, *Existentialism and Humanism*, pp. 54–5, discusses two senses of humanism. Existentialist humanism emphasizes human freedom against essentialist or determinist humanisms.
14 Jagger, *Feminist Politics and Human Nature*, pp. 52–9, gives an account of Marxism which gives it this humanist cast.
15 I take this term from Rorty, *Objectivity, Relativism and Truth*, p. 1.
16 A brief discussion of the humanist and anti-humanist tendencies within Marxism is given by Grosz, *Sexual Subversions*, pp. 6–16.
17 Saussure, *Course in General Linguistics*.
18 Ibid., pp. 101–22.
19 Lacan, 'The Meaning of the Phallus', pp. 74–85. Sayers, *Sexual Contradictions*, provides concise and readable critical introduction to Lacan's thought. Flax, *Thinking Fragments*, pp. 89–132, provides a useful comparison of Lacan and Winnicott.
20 A brief account of some difficulties with these aspects of structuralism is given in Cameron, *Feminism and Linguistic Theory*, pp. 93–100. I offer some

further thoughts on the assumptions behind post-structuralist thinking about language in my 'Brain Writing and Derrida'. An important defence of the idea that language is a biological categeory is Millikan, *Language, Thought and Other Biological Categories*.

21 Foucault, *The Order of Things*, pp. xv–xxiv, 'Nietzsche, Genealogy, History' and 'On the Genealogy of Ethics'. Foucault resists the label 'structuralist' (*The Order of Things*, p. xiv), but the similarities between his work and that of structuralists, which he admits, extend to the questioning of representation that derives from Saussure.
22 Foucault, *The Use of Pleasure*, p. 6.
23 Foucault, *The Order of Things*, p. 387.
24 Foucault, 'What is Enlightenment?', p. 50.
25 Foucault, 'On the Genealogy of Ethics', pp. 348–51.
26 Flax, *Thinking Fragments*, p. 7; Lyotard, 'The Post-modern Condition'.
27 Wheeler, 'Indeterminacy of French Interpretation', p. 484, notices this feature of Derrida's thought.
28 Derrida, *Of Grammatology*, pp. 27–73, and 'Différance', pp. 1–27.
29 Derrida, 'Le Facteur de la Verité, pp. 476–83, *Spurs: Nietzsche's Styles*, pp. 55–63; Demida and McDonald, 'Choreographies', p. 76; Cornell, *Beyond Accommodation*, pp. 79–88.
30 Examples of this can be found in Flax, *Thinking Fragments*, pp. 168–83, and Scott, 'Deconstructing Equality-versus-Difference', as well as Harding, *The Science Question in Feminism*, ch. 7.
31 Derrida, *Acts of Literature*, p. 63.
32 Heidegger, *Being and Time*, § 72 p. 428.
33 Derrida, *Acts of Literature*, p. 54.
34 Spender, *Man Made Language*, pp. 138–62; see Cameron, *Feminism and Linguistic Theory*, pp. 57–113, for some criticisms of the use Spender makes of structuralism. Sneja Gunew, 'Feminist Knowledge: Critique and Construct', assumes an explicitly Foucauldian epistemology despite recognizing that this leaves feminism faced with intractable 'riddles'. See also Grosz, 'Feminism and Anti-humanism'.
35 Irigaray, 'Woman's Exile', and 'This Sex Which is not One'.
36 For introductions to Irigaray's thought see: Grosz, *Sexual Subversions*, pp. 100–39; Cameron, *Feminism and Linguistic Theory*, pp. 114–33; Burke, 'Irigaray Through the Looking Glass'; Moi, *Sexual/Textual Politics*, pp. 127–49; Whitford, 'Luce Irigaray's Critique of Rationality'; and especially Whitford, *Luce Irigaray: Philosophy in the Feminine*.
37 The problematic relationship between feminism and post-structuralism has now been pointed out by a number of writers: Jardine, 'Gynesis' and *Gynesis*; Moi, *Sexual/Textual Politics*, pp. 137–49; Flax, *Thinking Fragments*, pp. 140–1; Poovey, 'Feminism and Deconstruction'; Benhabib, 'Feminism and the Question of Postmodernism'; and Harding, 'Feminism, Science and the Anti-Enlightenment Critiques'.
38 Jardine, *Gynesis*, p. 262; Grosz, *Sexual Subversions*, pp. 101–4; Burke, 'Irigaray Through the Looking Glass', p. 290; and Moi, *Sexual/Textual Politics*, p. 138.
39 Elizabeth Gross, 'What is Feminist Theory?' and 'Philosophy'. A particularly clear resumé of this position can be found in Michael Payne's introduction

to Moi, *Feminist Theory and Simone de Beauvoir*, p. 10. Toril Moi's chief criticism of de Beauvoir, in 'Intentions and Effects: Rhetoric and Identification in Simone de Beauvoir's "The Woman Destroyed" ', in this volume, pp. 61–93, is that de Beauvoir takes up a position of authorial authority.

40 Lovibond, in an excellent discussion, develops further reasons for feminists to be suspicious of post-modernism, bringing out the problematic nature of its Nietzschean legacies. Lovibond, 'Feminism and Post-modernism', and 'Feminism and Pragmatism'; see also the texts cited in n. 37.

41 Butler, *Gender Trouble*, p. 149.

42 Irigaray, *Speculum of the other Woman*, pp. 243–364.

43 Ibid., pp. 133–46.

44 Irigaray, 'Women-amongst-themselves: Creating a Woman-to-woman Sociality' and 'The Necessity for Sexuate Rights'.

45 Whitford, *Luce Irigaray: Philosophy in the Feminine*, pp. 67–8.

46 Irigaray, 'The Necessity for Sexuate Rights', p. 205, 'The Female Gender' and *Le Temps de la Différence*, pp. 103–23.

47 Irigaray, *Le Temps de la Différence*, pp. 42–3.

48 Irigaray, 'A Chance for Life', p. 205, 'How to Define Sexuate Rights?', p. 205, and 'Questions to Emmanual Levinas', p. 183; see also 'The Female Gender'. Whitford comments on this distancing from deconstruction in *Luce Irigaray: Philosophy in the Feminine*, pp. 96 and 124–9.

49 Lovibond, 'Feminism and Pragmatism', p. 71.

50 Irigaray, 'Is the Subject of Science Sexed?'.

51 Lloyd, *The Man of Reason*.

52 Young, 'Humanism, Gynocentrism and Feminist Politics', uses the terms 'humanist' and 'gynocentric'. H. Eisenstein discusses the same distinction using slightly different vocabulary in *Contemporary Feminist Thought*, pp. 45–7.

53 Jaggar, *Feminist Politics and Human Nature*, pp. 46–8 and 105–18.

54 Aristotle, *Politics*, book 1 §xiii, pp. 94–5.

55 Daly, *Gyn/Ecology*.

56 Plato, *Republic*, pp. 255–8. For a rejection of Plato's alleged feminism see Annas, 'Plato's *Republic* and Feminism', and *An Introduction to Plato's Republic*, pp. 181–7. Also, Okin, 'Philosopher Queens and Private Wives', and *Women in Western Political Thought*, pp. 15–70.

57 Jaggar, *Feminist Politics and Human Nature*, pp. 39–48.

58 I have given a detailed argument for this contention in my 'Femininity and Transcendence'.

59 Williams, 'The Idea of Equality', gives a classic defence of the ideal of equality despite our differences. Midgley, 'On Not Being Afraid of Natural Sex Differences', develops the argument that political equality does not demand indiscernibility for the particular case at hand.

Chapter 2 Women of *Virtù*

1 De Pisan, *The Book of the City of Ladies*, p. 4.

2 De Pisan, *Le Livre de la Mutation de Fortune*, p. 12.

3 De Pisan, *The Book of the City of Ladies*, p. 7.

4 Biographical sketches of Christine de Pisan are provided in the introduction to *The Book of the City of Ladies*, and by Willard, *Christine de Pisan: Her Life and Works*; Lucas, *Women in the Middle Ages*, pp. 161–9; and McLeod, *The Order of the Rose*. Gabriel, 'The Educational Ideas of Christine de Pisan', gives a useful outline of de Pisan's thought with particular emphasis on the modernity of her educational ideas.

5 De Meun and de Lorris, *The Romance of the Rose*, p. 103.

6 Ibid., p. 141.

7 Ibid., pp. 116–18.

8 Ibid., pp. 142–8.

9 Ibid., pp. 459–61.

10 Ibid., p. 156.

11 Ibid., p. 463.

12 Ibid., pp. 413–23.

13 Ibid., p. 289.

14 Ibid., p. 185.

15 De Pisan, 'Letter to Pierre Col (2nd October 1402)' and *The Book of the City of Ladies*, p. 187.

16 De Meun and de Lorris, *The Romance of the Rose*, pp. 171–91 and 349–54.

17 Ibid., pp. 177–8.

18 St Augustine, *The City of God*, book VIII, chs 4–12, pp. 303–15.

19 De Pisan, *The Book of the Duke of True Lovers*, p. 96.

20 St Augustine, *The City of God*, book IX, chs 17–22, pp. 448–54.

21 Ibid., book XIV, chs 21–4, pp. 583–7.

22 De Pisan, *The Book of the City of Ladies*, p. 16.

23 De Pisan, *The Treasure of the City of Ladies*, p. 172.

24 Ibid., pp. 59–79.

25 Ibid., p. 111.

26 De Pisan, 'An Epistle to the Queen of France'; see also *The Treasure of the City of Ladies*, pp. 50–2.

27 Lloyd, *The Man of Reason*, p. x.

28 De Pisan, *The Treasure of the City of Ladies*, p. 51, and 'An Epistle to the Queen of France', pp. 75–7.

29 Quilligan, *The Allegory of Female Authority*, provides a detailed account of the relationship of de Pisan's text to its sources and the method that she uses in constructing her allegory.

30 A useful summary of these arguments is provided by Maclean, *The Renaissance Notion of Women*, pp. 7–14.

31 De Pisan, *The Book of the City of Ladies*, p. 23. The original source of this view is Aristotle, *De Generatione animalium*.

32 Maclean, *The Renaissance Notion of Women*, pp. 11–14.

33 Augustine's views on women are discussed by Lloyd, *The Man of Reason*, pp. 28–33.

34 De Pisan, *The Book of the City of Ladies*, p. 28.

35 St Augustine, *The City of God*, book XXII, ch 17, p. 1057.

36 De Pisan, *The Book of the City of Ladies*, p. 187.

37 Ibid., p. 255.

38 Laigle, *Le Livre de Trois Virtus de Christine de Pisan*, pp. 120–3.

39 Delany, ' "Mothers to Think Back Through" ', pp. 177–97.

40 De Pisan, *The Book of the City of Ladies*, p. 14; Plato, *The Republic*, p. 66.
41 De Pisan, *Le Livre du Corps de Policie*, p. 61.
42 Plato, *Republic*, pp. 202–6 and 228–36.
43 De Pisan, *The Book of the City of Ladies*, p. 31.
44 Ibid., p. 119.
45 De Pisan, *Le Livre du Chemin de Long Estude*, pp. 8–11.
46 Laigle, *Le Livre de Trois Virtus de Christine de Pisan*, pp. 107–8.
47 This makes her reasoning in many ways similar to that devloped by McMillan, *Women, Reason and Nature*.
48 De Pisan, *The Treasure of the City of Ladies*, pp. 128–33.
49 Ibid., pp. 310–25.
50 Ibid., p. 159.
51 De Pisan, *The Book of the City of Ladies*, pp. 110–13.
52 Ibid., pp. 193–200.
53 De Pisan, *Le Livre du Chemin de Long Estude*, pp. 8–11.
54 De Pisan, *The Treasure of the City of Ladies*, pp. 133–34 and 61.
55 Delany, ' "Mothers to Think Back Through" '.
56 De Pisan, *The Treasure of the City of Ladies*, pp. 62–5.
57 See for instance the anonymous *An Essay in Defence of the Female Sex*; Astell, *A Serious Proposal to the Ladies* and *Some Reflections upon Marriage*; and Poovey, *The Proper Lady and the Female Writer*.
58 De Pisan, *The Treasure of the City of Ladies*, pp. 43–6.
59 De Pisan, *Le Livre du Corps de Policie*, pp. 2–5.
60 Machiavelli, *The Prince*, p. 96; de Pisan, *The Treasure of the City of Ladies*, pp. 71–4.
61 Gabriel, 'The Educational Ideas of Christine de Pisan'.
62 Held, 'Non-contractual Society: A Feminist View'.

Chapter 3 Hobbes, Amazons and Sabine Women

1 De Pisan, *Le Livre du Fais et Bonnes Meurs du Sage Roy Charles*, p. 5.
2 Hobbes, *Leviathan*, ch. XIII, p. 63.
3 Hobbes, *Philosophical Elements of a True Citizen*, ch. vi, §11–13, pp. 78–80.
4 Hobbes, *Leviathan*, ch. XVII, pp. 87–90.
5 Brennan and Pateman, ' "Mere Auxiliaries to the Commonwealth" ', pp. 189–90; and Pateman, *The Sexual Contract*, pp. 43–53.
6 Hobbes, *Leviathan*, ch. XX, p. 105, and *Philosophical Elements of a True Citizen*, ch. IX, §3, p. 116.
7 Hobbes, *De Corpore Politico*, ch. IV, p. 154.
8 Hobbes, *Leviathan*, ch. XX, p. 105, *De Corpore Politico*, ch. IV, p. 154, and *Philosophical Elements of a True Citizen*, ch. IX, §4, p. 117.
9 Jaggar, *Feminist Politics and Human Nature*, p. 45; Brennan and Pateman, ' "Mere Auxiliaries to the Commonwealth" '; Flax, 'Political Philosophy and the Patriarchal Unconscious', pp. 261–4.
10 Midgley, *Beast and Man*, chs 5 and 6, argues persuasively for the existence of altruistic motives in animals.
11 Hobbes, *Philosophical Elements of a True Citizen*, ch I, §2, fn., p. 6.

12 Coady, 'Hobbes and "The Beautiful Axiom"'.
13 On one reading of Rousseau, this is Rousseau's view, which is discussed further below.
14 Hobbes, *Leviathan*, ch. XIII, p. 65.
15 Ibid., ch. XX, p. 105.
16 This is argued for in some detail in Chapman, '*Leviathan* Writ Small'.
17 Hobbes, *Leviathan*, ch. XX, p. 105.
18 Ibid., ch. XX, p. 107, and Hobbes, *Philosophical Elements of a True Citizen*, ch. 4, §15, fn. p. 84. Hobbes's view is based on the introduction to Thucydides, *The Peloponesian War*, pp. 35–40; *Leviathan*, ch. X, p. 47, is particularly reminiscent of this source.
19 Lerner, *The Creation of Patriarchy*, chs 4 and 5, esp. pp. 89 and 121–2.
20 I discuss this difference in natural liberty in a slightly different context in 'Rawls, Women and the Priority of Liberty'.
21 Hobbes, *Philosophical Elements of a True Citizen*, ch. IX, §2, p. 115.
22 Lerner, *The Creation of Patriarchy*, pp. 78–89.
23 Rousseau, *Emile*, pp. 321–4.
24 Hobbes, *Philosophical Elements of a True Citizen*, ch. IX, §2, p. 115.
25 Pateman, *The Sexual Contract*, p. 49.
26 Pateman, '"God Hath Ordained to Man a Helper"', p. 70.
27 Pateman, *The Sexual Contract*, chs 4 and 5.
28 Freud, *Civilisation and its Discontents*.
29 Green, 'Rawls, Women and the Priority of Liberty'; and Okin, *Justice, Gender and the Family*.
30 Du Bois, *Centaurs and Amazons*, pp. 67–71; and Tyrell, *Amazons: A Study of Athenian Myth Making*, pp. 113–28.
31 De Pisan, *The Book of the City of Ladies*, pp. 40–52, and *Le Livre de la Mutation de Fortune*, book V, vol. 2, pp. 201–10, book VI, vol. 3, pp. 5–25 and 141–63, and book VII, vol. 4, pp. 50 2. See also Hindman, *Christine de Pisan's "Epistre Othea"*; and Kleinbaum, *The War Against the Amazons*, pp. 64–9.
32 Plutarch, *Life of Romulus*, 19, quoted by Bryson, 'Two Narratives of Rape in the Visual Arts', pp. 155–6.
33 The possibility of this is illustrated by a slightly different story of the abduction of women related by Herodotus, *The History of Herodotus*, pp. 113–14.
34 Bryson, 'Two Narratives of Rape in the Visual Arts' calls the story a fable of the ways in which law had emerged out of violence, p. 158.
35 De Pisan, *The Book of the City of Ladies*, pp. 147–50.
36 For a sketch of three possible interpretations see Greenleaf, 'Hobbes: The Problem of Interpretation'.
37 Hobbes, *Leviathan*, ch. XXXI, p. 197.
38 Hobbes, *De Corpore Politico*, ch. IX, pp. 213–20.
39 Ibid., p. 215.
40 Sir Thomas Smith, *De Republica Anglorum*, quoted by Hinton, 'Husbands, Fathers and Conquerers', pp. 292–3.
41 Hobbes, *Leviathan*, ch. XX, p. 105.
42 Hobbes, *Philosophical Elements of a True Citizen*, ch. IV, §11, p. 78.
43 Herodotus, *The History of Herodotus*, p. 114.
44 Rawls, *A Theory of Justice*, pp. 11–17.

45 See for instance the account of the theme of fortune in politics in Hindman, *Christine de Pisan's "Epistre Othea"*, pp. 123–8.
46 De Pisan, *Le Livre du Corps de Policie*, p. 16.
47 Gilligan, *In a Different Voice*, and 'In a Different Voice: Women's Conceptions of Self and Morality'; Ruddick, 'Maternal Thinking', and 'Preservative Love and Military Destruction'.
48 An early discussion of this difficulty is to be found in Blum et al., 'Altruism and Woman's Oppression'. Ruddick is also aware of the problem, but does not offer a clear solution in 'Maternal Thinking' and 'Preservative Love and Military Destruction'.
49 Noddings, *Caring*, p. 5.
50 Filmer, *Patriarcia*, pp. 1–68.
51 Locke, *Two Treatises of Government*, 'The Second Treatise', §4, pp. 287–8. The feminist implications of Locke's work are discussed in M. Butler, 'Early Liberal Roots of Feminism'.
52 Locke, *Two Treatises of Government*, 'The Second Treatise', §82, p. 339.
53 Ibid., 'The First Treatise', §61, pp. 202–3.
54 Ibid., 'The Second Treatise', §52–76, pp. 321–36.
55 Ibid., 'The Second Treatise', §65, pp. 328–9.
56 Rousseau, *Emile*, p. 363.
57 Locke, *Two Treatises of Government*, 'The Second Treatise', §124, pp. 368–9.
58 Rousseau, *The Social Contract*, book I, ch. 6, p. 62.
59 Ibid, book II, ch. 1, pp. 69–70, and Rousseau, *A Discourse on Political Economy*, pp. 256–8.

Chapter 4 Virtuous Women and the Citizen of Geneva

1 There is some controversy over whether Rousseau should be considered a liberal, but this need not concern us, since it is clear that Rousseau's thought had a considerable influence on the way in which liberal democratic society actually developed, as is usefully outlined by Figes, *Patriarchal Attitudes*, ch. 4.
2 Lange, 'Rousseau and Modern Feminism', p. 96. P. Thomas, 'Jean-Jacques Rousseau, Sexist?', p. 6, also notices that it is a mistake to treat Rousseau as simply another Lockean liberal.
3 An account of the influence of Rousseau's views on advocates of suffrage is provided in Holton, *Feminism and Democracy*. A more general account of his influence is that by Pope, 'The Influence of Rousseau's Ideology of Domesticity'.
4 Rousseau, *Emile*, p. 5.
5 Cassirer, *The Question of Jean-Jacques Rousseau*, pp. 37–8.
6 Wollstonecraft, *Vindication of the Rights of Woman*, pp. 93–9 and 178–90.
7 Pateman, '"The Disorder of Women"'; and Flax, 'Political Philosophy and the Patriarchal Unconscious'. See also Gatens, 'Rousseau and Wollstonecraft: Nature vs. Reason'; Coole, *Women in Political Theory*, pp. 103–19.
8 Pateman, '"The Disorder of Women"', pp. 20–34.
9 Ibid., p. 22.

10 A more accurate picture of the relationship between reason, nature and women in Rousseau's thought is provided by Lloyd, 'Rousseau on Reason, Nature and Women', and by Schwartz, *The Sexual Politics of Jean-Jacques Rousseau*. In what follows I am indebted to their work.

11 Rousseau, *The Social Contract*, book I, ch. 2, p. 50.

12 Rousseau, *A Discourse on Political Economy*, p. 250, and *A Discourse on Inequality*, p. 65.

13 Okin, *Women in Western Political Thought*, pp. 99–102, places Rousseau in the Aristotelian tradition, and Coole, *Women in Political Theory*, p. 103, notes the analogy.

14 Rousseau, *The Social Contract*, p. 112.

15 Pateman, '"The Disorder of Women"', pp. 21–4.

16 Rousseau, *A Discourse on Inequality*, pp. 98–102, and *The Social Contract*, pp. 49–58.

17 Rousseau, *A Discourse on Inequality*, p. 101.

18 This is ambiguous. There could be basic altruistic desires, according to Hobbes, but they would not count as ethical.

19 Most translators and commentators on Rousseau remark on the difficulty of translating *'amour de soi'* and *'amour-propre'* as they occur in Rousseau's texts. *Amour de soi* is for Rousseau a legitimate and natural self-love which, extended to others, transforms into virtue: Rousseau, *Emile*, p. 215. *Amour-propre* is a corrupted self-love which leads men and women to seek power and glory. I have chosen to translate these terms by 'self-esteem' and 'self-importance' respectively because these are the more commonly used contemporary terms for making the kind of psychological observation that Rousseau develops in his work.

20 Rousseau, *A Discourse on Inequality*, p. 112.

21 McMillan, *Woman, Reason and Nature*, is critical of feminism largely because she assumes that feminists reject the importance of the maternal role. She is impressed by Rousseau's observations and accepts to a large degree the conclusions that he draws from them. Midgley, *Beast and Man*, ch. 6, discusses, in the context of sociobiology, the view that all human action is egoistic, and gives a sustained refutation of this view very much in the spirit of Rousseau's less-developed comments.

22 Sénéchal, 'J.-J. Rousseau, Secrétaire de Madame Dupin'.

23 Rousseau, 'Sur les Femmes', and 'Essai sur les Evénements dont les Femmes ont été la Cause Secrette'.

24 Rousseau, *Emile*, book V, esp. pp. 321–72.

25 Ibid., pp. 5–6.

26 Ibid., pp. 328, 333, 334 and 349.

27 Ibid., p. 353.

28 Ibid., p. 370.

29 Rousseau, *A Discourse on Inequality*, p. 65.

30 Schwartz, *The Sexual Politics of Jean-Jacques Rousseau*, pp. 56–8; Okin, *Women in Western Political Thought*, pp. 104, 121 and 130–1.

31 Rousseau, *Emile*, p. 5.

32 Rousseau, *Confessions*, book 7, pp. 320–2 and book 8, p. 333. Schwartz, *The Sexual Politics of Jean-Jacques Rousseau*, pp. 152–4, suggests that Rousseau differentiated what was appropriate for the masses from what is allowable

to the extraordinary individual, but the interpretation offered here is suggested by Rousseau's self-reproaches in the *Confessions*, book 12, p. 549, where he refers to *Emile*, book 1.

33 See Figes, *Patriarchal Attitudes*, ch. 4; and Pope, 'The Influence of Rousseau's Ideology of Domesticity'. And for interesting data on the relationship between infant mortality and wet-nursing, Badinter, 'Maternal Indifference'.

34 Rousseau, *A Discourse on Inequality*, pp. 112–13.

35 Rousseau, *Emile*, pp. 321–6. Weiss, 'Rousseau, Antifeminism and Woman's Nature', and McMillan, *Woman, Reason and Nature*, both recognize the importance of this argument in Rousseau's thinking.

36 Rousseau, *Emile*, book V, pp. 321–6.

37 Okin, *Women in Western Political Thought*, p. 22.

38 Viroli, *Jean-Jacques Rousseau and the 'Well-ordered Society'*, p. 21, points out that in Rousseau's text, 'Virtue is always defined, as it is in St Augustine, as "the love of order,".

39 Rousseau, *A Discourse on Inequality*, p. 67.

40 Ibid, pp. 7–9.

41 Rousseau, *Emile*, p. 249.

42 Ibid., p. 249.

43 Ibid, p. 408.

44 Ibid., p. 353.

45 Ibid., p. 354 and 443.

46 Ibid., p. 276.

47 Rousseau, *A Discourse on Inequality*, pp. 99–101.

48 Ibid., pp. 102–3.

49 Rousseau, *Emile*, p. 348.

50 Rousseau, *A Discourse on Inequality*, p. 114, and also *Emile*, pp. 175–6.

51 Rousseau, *Emile*, p. 370.

52 Ibid., p. 443; see also Schwartz, *The Sexual Politics of Jean-Jacques Rousseau*, pp. 89–98.

53 This seems to be the intention of the rather enigmatic passage in which it is claimed that 'it is only fair that woman should bear her share of the ills she has brought upon man': Rousseau, *Emile*, p. 332.

54 Rousseau, *Politics and the Arts*, p. 84. Lange, 'Rousseau and Modern Feminism', recognises the rather modern sociobiological aspects of this argument.

55 Rousseau, *Politics and the Arts*, p. 84.

56 For some earlier thoughts of mine on sexuality and the reproduction of society see my 'Prostitution, Exploitation and Taboo'.

57 Rousseau, *A Discourse on Inequality*, pp. 131–7.

58 Rousseau, *The Social Contract*, pp. 59–68.

59 Rousseau, *Politics and the Arts*, p. 117.

60 Ibid., pp. 117–18; see also ibid., p. 110.

61 Rousseau, *Emile*, pp. 407–14.

62 Rousseau, *A Discourse on Inequality*, p. 103.

63 Rousseau, *The Social Contract*, pp. 61–2 and fn. p. 61.

64 Ibid., p. 59.

65 Rousseau, *Politics and the Arts*, pp. 100–1.

66 Rousseau, *Emile*, p. 326.

67 Pateman, 'The Fraternal Social Contract', p. 50, points to the connections between citizenship and the fraternity of men as defenders of 'their' state.
68 See Holton, *Feminism and Democracy*, for an account of this theme in suffrage writings.
69 See Lloyd, *The Man of Reason*, pp. 64–85, for an account of the development
   of this theme in the writings of Kant and Hegel. See also Mill, *The Subjection
   of Women*, ch. 3. A feminist who develops the same association is Benhabib,
   'The Generalised and the Concrete Other'.
70 De Sade, 'Selections', p. 135.
71 De Sade, *The Complete Justine*.
72 De Beauvoir, 'Must we Burn de Sade?', and Klossowski, 'Nature as Destructive Principle', provide interesting discussions of de Sade's views on nature.
   A readable discussion of his work is Carter, *The Sadeian Woman*.
73 Foucault, *The History of Sexuality*, vol. 1, pp. 17–35.

Chapter 5 The Female Citizen

1 Wollstonecraft, *Mary and The Wrongs of Woman*, pp. 1–68.
2 The account of Wollstonecraft's life most contemporary with it is William
   Godwin's memoir in Wollstonecraft and Godwin, *A Short Residence in
   Sweden, Norway and Denmark*, pp. 205–73. A comprehensive bibliography
   of biographical works is available in Sapiro, *A Vindication of Political
   Virtue*, pp. 344–6.
3 A contemporary summary of these criticisms is provided by Jaggar, *Feminist
   Politics and Human Nature*, pp. 39–48.
4 See Elizabeth Badinter's discussion in Thomas et al., *Qu'est-ce qu'une
   Femme?*, p. 44, and that of Celia Amorós, 'Cartesianism and Feminism'.
5 This way of understanding the contrast is suggested by Carol Gilligan and
   Sarah Ruddick's views. See in particular Gilligan, 'The Conquistador and the
   Dark Continent'; and Ruddick, 'Maternal Thinking', and 'Remarks on the
   Sexual Politics of Reason'.
6 Wollstonecraft, *The French Revolution*, pp. 21–2.
7 Wollstonecraft, *Vindication of the Rights of Men*, pp. 11 and 31.
8 Wollstonecraft, *The French Revolution*, p. 22.
9 Ibid., p. 21.
10 Flax, 'Political Philosophy and the Patriarchal Unconscious', p. 269.
11 This is essentially the interpretation offered by Korsmeyer, 'Reason and
   Morals in the Early Feminist Movement: Mary Wollstonecraft', and by
   Coole, *Women in Political Theory*, pp. 119–32.
12 Jacobus, 'The Difference of View', pp. 32–3.
13 This point is also made by Grimshaw, 'Mary Wollstonecraft and the Tensions
   in Feminist Philosophy'.
14 Sapiro, *A Vindication of Political Virtue*, ch. 2.
15 For the first see particularly Mary Wollstonecraft's letters in Wollstonecraft
   and Godwin, *A Short Residence in Sweden, Norway and Denmark*, pp. 122
   and 131. Wollstonecraft's thought on these matters was undoubtedly deeply

influenced by Rousseau; in one of her letters to Imlay she jokingly says of Rousseau that she has always been half in love with him: 'Letters to Imlay', p. 387.

16 This is the heart of socialist criticisms of liberal feminist views. See Coole, *Women in Political Theory*, p. 130.
17 Wollstonecraft, *Vindication of the Rights of Woman*, p. 94.
18 Ibid., pp. 94–5. A brief outline of the Irenaean theodicy is provided by Hick, *Philosophy of Religion*, p. 45; see also Sapiro, *A Vindication of Political Virtue*, p. 48.
19 Wollstonecraft, *Vindication of the Rights of Woman*, pp. 105–7 and 131–2.
20 Wollstonecraft, *Vindication of the Rights of Men*, pp. 10 and 20–3.
21 Wollstonecraft, *Vindication of the Rights of Woman*, p. 88.
22 Ibid., pp. 102–3.
23 Ibid., p. 100.
24 Rousseau, *Emile*, p. 328.
25 Ibid., p. 345.
26 Wollstonecraft, *Vindication of the Rights of Woman*, pp. 104, 117–18 and 184.
27 Ibid., p. 104.
28 Ibid., p. 135.
29 Ibid., p. 189.
30 Rousseau, *Confessions*, p. 413.
31 Wollstonecraft, *Vindication of the Rights of Woman*, pp. 134–5.
32 Ibid., p. 135.
33 Wollstonecraft, *Vindication of the Rights of Men*, p. 14.
34 Wollstonecraft, *The French Revolution*, pp. 20–3, and *Vindication of the Rights of Men*, pp. 10–11. In her own life Wollstonecraft's experience with Imlay showed her that there was reason to doubt her optimism, yet to the end she continued to believe of him that he was not what he appeared to be: 'Letters to Imlay', p. 437–8.
35 Wollstonecraft, 'Hints', p. 273.
36 Rousseau, *Emile*, pp. 146–62.
37 Schwartz, *The Sexual Politics of Jean-Jacques Rousseau*, pp. 70–3.
38 Wollstonecraft, *The French Revolution*, p. 17.
39 Wollstonecraft, *Vindication of the Rights of Woman*, p. 258.
40 Ibid., p. 259.
41 Ibid., p. 188; see also pp. 110–11.
42 Ibid., pp. 188–9.
43 Ibid., pp. 195–6.
44 This is part of the thrust of Cora Kaplan's criticism in *Sea Changes*, pp. 31–56.
45 These figures come from Badinter, 'Maternal Indifference', pp. 170–3.
46 Quoted in Wollstonecraft and Godwin, *A Short Residence in Sweden, Norway and Denmark*, p. 222. See also her comments on boarding schools in Wollstonecraft, *Thoughts on the Education of Daughters*, p. 22.
47 Wollstonecraft, *Vindication of the Rights of Woman*, pp. 252–8, and the implied criticism in *Mary* chs. 1 and 2.
48 Ibid., pp. 167, 113–16.
49 Ibid., p. 259.
50 Coole, *Women in Political Theory*, p. 130.

51 Green, 'Rawls, Women and the Priority of Liberty'; and Okin, *Justice, Gender and the Family*, pp. 170–86.
52 Z. Eisenstein, *The Radical Future of Liberal Feminism*, p. 248. This and other objections to liberal feminist politics are discussed by Jaggar, *Feminist Politics and Human Nature*, pp. 185–206.
53 Wollstonecraft, *The French Revolution*, p. 17
54 Wollstonecraft, *Vindication of the Rights of Woman*, p. 260.
55 Green, 'Rawls, Women and the Priority of Liberty', p. 35.
56 I have not here discussed another criticism of feminist liberalism which has often been raised: the claim that liberalism is committed to abstract individualism. See for instance Jaggar, *Feminist Politics and Human Nature*, pp. 39–44 and 86. It is so clear that Wollstonecraft is centrally concerned with the fact that individual character is deeply affected by society that this objection has no purchase against her views. A more general defence of liberalism against this charge is developed by Kymlicka, *Liberalism, Community and Culture*, pp. 9–20.
57 C. Kaplan, *Sea Changes*, pp. 45–7.
58 Jacobus, 'The Difference of View', pp. 32–3.
59 Jaggar, *Feminist Politics and Human Nature*, p. 40, accuses liberal feminists in general of some such commitment. She claims that for liberals 'what is specially valuable about human beings is their "mental" capacity for rationality', apparently assuming that it is impossible to value both reason and feeling.
60 Wollstonecraft, *Vindication of the Rights of Woman*, p. 199.
61 Wollstonecraft, *Thoughts on the Education of Daughters*, p. 9.
62 Wollstonecraft, *Original Stories from Real Life*. The method employed in these stories is clearly also influenced by Rev. C. G. Salzmann, whose *Elements of Morality* Wollstonecraft translated in 1790.
63 Wollstonecraft, *Vindication of the Rights of Woman*, pp. 212–15
64 Midgley, *Beast and Man*, pp. 250–83, gives an account of the relationship between feeling and reflection which might well have appealed to Wollstonecraft. See also Midgley, *Heart and Mind*, pp. 1–7.
65 See her 'Letters to Imlay', and the letters to Godwin in *Collected Letters of Mary Wollstonecraft*.
66 Wollstonecraft, *Mary and The Wrongs of Woman*, pp. 69–204.
67 Poovey, *The Proper Lady and the Woman Writer*, pp. 94–113.
68 Ibid., pp. 3–48.
69 Sapiro, *A Vindication of Political Virtue*, p. 43.
70 Wollstonecraft, 'Letters to Imlay', p. 387.
71 Wollstonecraft, *Mary and The Wrongs of Woman*, p. 176.
72 Wollstonecraft, 'Hints', p. 275.
73 Wollstonecraft, 'On Poetry', pp. 7–11.
74 Wollstonecraft and Godwin, *A Short Residence in Sweden, Norway and Denmark*, p. 123.

Chapter 6 Socialism, Sex and Savage Society

1 Thompson, *Appeal of One-half of the Human Race*, pp. xxvi–xxvii. Coole, *Women in Political Theory*, pp. 154–65, provides an introduction to the background of this book, and Pateman, *The Sexual Contract*, pp. 154–63 gives a short account of its arguments.
2 The feminist aspects of early utopian socialism are outlined by Easlea, *Science and Sexual Oppression*; there he develops the argument that the overthrow of exploitative capitalism requires the abolition of dominant masculine attitudes towards sexuality.
3 Engels, *The Origin of the Family, Private Property and the State*, p. 93.
4 Ibid., p. 8, letter to Kausky, quoted by Michèle Barrett in her introduction to Engels's book.
5 Ibid., pp. 84–7.
6 Ibid., pp. 105–15.
7 Schwarzer, *After "The Second Sex"*, p. 32.
8 Firestone, *The Dialectic of Sex*. Unfortunately, the relationship of Firestone's thought to that of Reich is somewhat obscure. She quotes him as an authority on pp. 213–14, but, as is discussed below, her understanding of the nature of sexual liberation is rather different to his, owing perhaps more to Marcuse.
9 Bebel, *Women under Socialism*.
10 Wollstonecraft, 'Letter on the Present Character of the French Nation', pp. 443–6. For some comments on the importance of the French Revolution for Hegel see Taylor, *Hégel*, ch. 2. A concise and easily read introduction to Hegel's thought is available in Singer's short book *Hegel*.
11 Marx and Engels, *The German Ideology*, p. 47, Marcuse, *Reason and Revolution*, pp. 273–87 and Plamenatz, *Ideology*, pp. 32–45, give introductory accounts of the notion which assume as in this description that ideology is illusory. This is not the only way in which the notion of ideology has been used in Marxism. A recent clear introduction to the debates centring on the notion of ideology is provided by Barrett, *The Politics of Truth*.
12 Reich, *The Sexual Revolution*, 'Preface to the Second Edition (1936)', p. xxiv.
13 Reich, *The Invasion of Compulsory Sex-morality*, pp. 70–1.
14 Mitchell, *Psychoanalysis and Feminism*, p. 413.
15 Freud, 'Femininity', pp. 128–35, 'Some Psychical Consequences of the Anatomical Distinction between the Sexes', pp. 257–8, and *The Ego and the Id*, pp. 28–39.
16 Freud, *Totem and Taboo*, pp. 141ff; see also *Civilisation and its Discontents*, pp. 100–1 and 131–3.
17 Reich, *The Sexual Revolution*, 'Preface to the Third Edition (1945)', p. xvi.
18 Reich, *The Function of the Orgasm*, pp. 108–9.
19 Malinowski, *The Sexual Life of Savages*, pp. 2–4.
20 Ibid., pp. 97–103 and 121–5, and Malinowski, *Sex and Repression in Savage Society*, p. 98.
21 Malinowski, *Sex and Repression in Savage Society*, p. 222.
22 Reich, *The Invasion of Compulsory Sex-morality*, pp. 145–8.
23 Malinowski, *Sex and Repression in Savage Society*, pp. 74–82.

24 Ibid., p. 46.
25 Malinowski, *The Sexual Life of Savages*, pp. 93–103, 258 and 179–99.
26 Reich, *The Invasion of Compulsory Sex-morality*, p. 33.
27 Engels, *The Origin of the Family, Private Property and the State*, p. 60.
28 Malinowski, *The Sexual Life of Savages*, p. xxv.
29 Jones, 'Mother-right and the Sexual Ignorance of Savages'. The view has recently been defended by Spiro, *Oedipus in the Trobriands*.
30 Malinowski, *Sex and Repression in Savage Society*, p. 144.
31 Ibid., p. 165.
32 Freud, *Civilisation and its Discontents*, p. 133.
33 Malinowski, *Sex and Repression in Savage Society*, p. 278.
34 Marcuse, *Eros and Civilisation*, pp. 190–214. To be fair to Reich, he argues on the basis of his clinical evidence that there is no justification for postulating a death drive: *The Function of the Orgasm*, pp. 133–44 and 247–53.
35 Malinowski, *Sex and Repression in Savage Society*, pp. 85–90.
36 Easlea, *Science and Sexual Oppression*, p. 275, cites Masters's and Johnson's evidence that male homosexuals are at least as inclined to fantasize being rapists as are male heterosexuals, and observes that, for many, homosexuality involves a cult of masculinity and casual, impersonal sex.
37 Dworkin, *Pornography: Men Possessing Women*, pp. 70–1, notes the respect that some advocates of sexual liberation have for de Sade, and while her own portrayal of him is quite distorted, she is surely correct in being suspicious of philosophies which are committed to glorifying either de Sade's life or his fantasies.
38 Firestone, *The Dialectic of Sex*, pp. 58 and 209. A similar analysis of egotistical love, this time reminiscent of Eric Fromm's, was offered by Greer, *The Female Eunuch*, pp. 153–61. For Fromm's analysis of the ideology of love under capitalism see *The Art of Loving*, pp. 72–89.
39 Dworkin, *Pornography: Men Possessing Women*, p. 99.
40 Ibid., p. 100.
41 Daly, *Gyn/Ecology*, esp. pp. 37–42.
42 Dworkin so distances herself and shows some sensitivity to the dangers inherent in endorsing biological essentialism in 'Biological Superiority. The World's Most Dangerous and Deadly Idea'. At the same time, her claim that de Sade embodies the common values and desires of men, and her constant emphasis on the most brutal features of male sexuality, tend to leave the impression that men are irredeemable. In her book *Intercourse*, p. 123, she intimates that penetration is intrinsically invasive, and if this is so it is difficult to see under what circumstances heterosexuality could be anything other than violation of women by men.
43 Jeffreys, *Anticlimax*, p. 3.
44 Rich, 'Compulsory Heterosexuality', p. 633. There is in fact a difference between Rich's view and that of Jeffreys. Rich talks of 'compulsory heterosexuality' thus suggesting the possibility of a non-oppressive, freely chosen heterosexuality. Jeffreys makes it clear that it is heterosexuality itself which she believes to be oppressive: Jeffreys, *Anticlimax*, pp. 294–7.
45 MacKinnon, 'Feminism, Marxism, Method and the State: An Agenda for Theory', p. 533.

46 Jeffreys, *Anticlimax*, p. 2.
47 MacKinnon, 'Feminism, Marxism, Method and the State: An Agenda for Theory'.
48 Ibid., p. 534. See also Jeffreys, *Anticlimax*, p. 104, and Dworkin, *Intercourse*, pp. 133–4.
49 Jeffreys, *Anticlimax*, pp. 5–32, and see also Jeffreys, ' "Free from All Uninvited Touch of Man" ', Jackson 'Sexology and the Social Construction of Male Sexuality', and 'Sexology: the Universalisation of Male Sexuality'.
50 Jeffreys, *Anticlimax*, p. 31.
51 Ibid., p. 253.
52 Ibid., p. 127.
53 Ibid, p. 315, and Jeffreys, ' "Free from All Uninvited Touch of Man" ', pp. 39–40.
54 Dworkin, *Intercourse*, p. 123.
55 Like many conservatives, these writers appear to be assuming that there is a sharp divide between male and female, which is not adequate to the facts. See for instance G. Kaplan and Rogers, 'The Definition of Male and Female'.
56 Malinowski, *The Sexual Life of Savages*, p. 111.
57 Ibid., pp. 80–3; and Reich, *The Invasion of Compulsory Sex-morality*, pp. 58–9.
58 See Green, 'Rawls, Women and the Priority of Liberty', pp. 26–36, for a more extended argument to the conclusion that lesbian separatism is not obviously in women's interests.
59 Mill, *On Liberty*, pp. 65–77.
60 Langton, 'Whose Right? Ronald Dworkin, Women and Pornographers'; and Dyzenhaus, 'John Stuart Mill and the Harm of Pornography'.
61 See the Muria ghotul referred to by Easlea, *Science and Sexual Oppression*, pp. 271–3. The society which Mead describes in *Coming of Age in Samoa*, is not as sexually open as the Trobriands, but similarly appears to tolerate adolescent sexuality.
62 Jeffreys, *Anticlimax*, p. 290.
63 Ibid., p. 145.
64 See Segal, *Is the Future Female?*, esp. pp. 154–5, for a defence of this position.
65 It seems that this was part of the point of the nineteenth-century emphasis on the value of spinsterhood. It was not that they were promoting the bizarre view that all women should be spinsters, but only the reasonable contention that if marriage is to be genuinely voluntary there need to be other socially recognized options for women. See Hamilton, *Marriage as a Trade*, pp. 141–5.
66 Griffin, *Pornography and Silence*, pp. 156–81.
67 Dworkin, *Intercourse*.
68 Ibid., p. 123.
69 Irigaray, *Ethique de la Différence Sexuelle*, and 'Sexual Difference'.
70 Foucault, 'Truth and Power', pp. 51 and 60.
71 MacKinnon, 'Feminism, Marxism, Method and the State: Toward Feminist Jurisprudence' p. 637, fn. 5.
72 MacKinnon, 'On Collaboration', p. 205.
73 Harding, *The Science Question in Feminism*, pp. 136–62, gives some related criticisms of the extension of Marxist epistemology to be found in Hartsock, 'The Feminist Standpoint', and *Money, Sex, Power*.

74 Examples of this are numerous: to cite but a few, Jaggar, *Feminist Politics and Human Nature*, pp. 39–48; Tapper, 'Can a Feminist be a Liberal?'; and Jeffreys, *Anticlimax*, p. 239.
75 Singer, *Hegel*, pp. 29–39, gives a useful introduction to this problem.
76 Foucault, *The Use of Pleasure*, p. 6.
77 Foucault, *Madness and Civilization*, pp. ix–xii.
78 Foucault, *The History of Sexuality*, vol. 1, pp. 17–49, and 'Truth and Power', p. 62.
79 Taylor, 'Foucault on Freedom and Truth'.
80 Foucault, 'On the Genealogy of Ethics', pp. 348–51.
81 Wollstonecraft, *Collected Letters of Mary Wollstonecraft*, p. 397.

Chapter 7 Flight from the Other

1 De Beauvoir, *Le Deuxième Sexe*, vol. 1, p. 19 (*The Second Sex*, p. 19). In references to this work hereafter, page numbers in parentheses are those of Parshley's translation.
2 Irigaray, *Speculum of the Other Woman*, p. 133.
3 Irigaray, 'Equal or Different'; Grosz, 'Philosophy', pp. 158–9; and Moi, *Feminist Theory and Simone de Beauvoir*, pp. 66–7.
4 The earliest discussion of the sexism of existentialism is Collins and Pierce, 'Holes and Slime: Sexism in Sartre's Psychoanalysis'. This imagery is also discussed by Le Doeuff, 'Simone de Beauvoir and Existentialism', and *Hipparchia's Choice*, pp. 45–165, esp. p. 84, where she suggests that de Beauvoir effectively escapes this legacy. Reservations over the cogency of using existentialist conceptions of transcendence as a basis for feminism are expressed by Lloyd, *The Man of Reason*, pp. 74–102, and 'Masters, Slaves and Others'; and by Seigfried, 'Gender Specific Values', and 'Second Sex: Second Thoughts'.
5 Sartre, *Being and Nothingness*, pp. 773–9.
6 Simone de Beauvoir, *Le Deuxième Sexe*, vol. 1, p. 13. In one of the lapses of good judgement characteristic of Parshley's abridged translation this sentence does not occur in the English version.
7 Ibid., p. 19 (p. 19).
8 Ibid., p. 19 (p. 20).
9 Ibid., p. 21 (p. 21).
10 Ibid., pp. 111–12 (pp. 95–6); for de Beauvoir's longer account of pregnancy as immersion in mere species life, see ibid., vol. 2, pp. 306–11 (pp. 512–15).
11 Le Doeuff, 'Simone de Beauvoir and Existentialism'; and for a similar criticism in relation to a different de Beauvoir text see Moi, *Feminist Theory and Simone de Beauvoir*, pp. 61–93.
12 De Beauvoir, *Le Deuxième Sexe*, vol. 1, pp. 20–1 (pp. 20–1), and for further discussion of the master/slave dialectic in regard to men and women see ibid., vol. 2, pp. 287–9 (pp. 500–1).
13 Ibid., vol. 1, p. 31 (p. 29).
14 See in particular Lloyd, *The Man of Reason*, pp. 74–102, and 'Masters, Slaves and Others'; and Seigfried, 'Gender Specific Values', and 'Second Sex: Second Thoughts'.

15 Irigaray, *Speculum of the Other Woman*, p. 133; see also de Beauvoir, *Le Deuxième Sexe*, vol. 1, pp. 91–3 (pp. 82–3).
16 Moi, *Sexual/Textual Politics*, pp. 127–49.
17 De Beauvoir, *Le Deuxième Sexe*, vol. 1, p. 93 (p. 83).
18 Ibid., p. 95 (p. 84).
19 Ibid., pp. 98–9 (pp. 86–8).
20 Ibid., p. 101 (p. 89).
21 De Beauvoir, *The Ethics of Ambiguity*, esp. pp. 7–24.
22 J. Butler, 'Sex and Gender in Simone de Beauvoir's *The Second Sex*', pp. 35–42, points out that de Beauvoir's insistence that there is no culturally uninterpreted body points in directions taken up by Michel Foucault and Monique Wittig, a direction which is radically anti-essentialist but, according to my discussion in the introduction, not necessarily anti-humanist.
23 Lévi-Strauss, *The Elementary Structures of Kinship*, ch. 29.
24 Irigaray, 'Women on the Market', pp. 171–2.
25 I argue this case in greater detail in 'Femininity and Transcendence'.
26 Lerner, 'Women and History', makes much of this distinction and while I think that she rather overestimates the importance of history when she says (p. 156) that 'it is the relationship of women to history which explains the nature of female subordination', it does appear to me that reconstituting our relationship to history is a necessary part of the overcoming of our subordination.
27 For example Sanday, *Female Power and Male Dominance*, pp. 113–34.
28 Bell, *Daughters of the Dreaming*, pp. 41–59.
29 Lévi-Strauss, *The Elementary Structures of Kinship*, p. 479.
30 Bell, *Daughters of the Dreaming*, appendix 2, pp. 256–72.
31 Ibid., p. 237.
32 Ibid., p. 212.
33 Ibid., p. 166.
34 For evidence that de Beauvoir implicitly makes this assumption see my 'Femininity and Transcendence', p. 92.
35 For an account of this aspect of Sartre's writing see Le Doeuff, *Hipparchia's Choice*, pp. 189–91.
36 Mathieu, 'When Yielding is Not Consenting', parts 1 and 2.
37 Ibid., part 2, p. 54.
38 Godelier, 'La Part Idéélle du Réel: Essai sur l'Idéologique', quoted by Mathieu, 'When Yielding is Not Consenting', part 2, p. 68.
39 Mathieu, 'When Yielding is Not Consenting', part 2, pp. 77–8.
40 E. Mackenzie, *Memoirs of Mrs Caroline Chisholm*, p. 95.
41 Lerner, *The Creation of Patriarchy*, pp. 69–74, illustrates this process.
42 See my 'Prostitution, Exploitation and Taboo'.
43 A number of feminist theorists have taken up the theme of the patriarchal nature of the state, in particular Pateman, *The Sexual Contract*, pp. 77–105, and 'The Fraternal Social Contract'. Her analysis captures much that is true with regard to the development of the historical state, but it leaves little basis for a positive transformation. It seems more accurate to assert with Connell, *Gender and Power*, p. 129, that 'the state is not inherently patriarchal, but is historically constructed as patriarchal in a political process whose outcome is open.'

44 De Beauvoir, *Le Deuxième Sexe*, vol. 2, p. 506, quoted by Béatrice Slama, 'Simone de Beauvoir: Feminine Sexuality and Liberation', p. 220. Parshley translates the passage thus: 'For woman love is a supreme effort to survive by accepting the dependence to which she is condemned' (p. 678).
45 De Beauvoir, *Le Deuxième Sexe*, vol. 2, p. 478 (p. 653).
46 Ibid., p. 480 (p. 655).
47 Ibid., p. 478 (p. 653).
48 Okin, *Justice, Gender and the Family*, pp. 175–80.
49 Wittig, 'The Social Contract'; Jeffreys, *Anticlimax*.
50 Irigaray, *Le Temps de la Différence*, and 'How to Define Sexuate Rights?'.
51 Le Doeuff, *Hipparchia's Choice*, pp. 230–54.

Chapter 8 Reason, Femininity, Love and Morality

1 This is a danger which is pertinently discussed by Jaggar, 'Feminist Ethics', and of which Ruddick is clearly aware: see her 'Remarks on the Sexual Politics of Reason', and 'Maternal Thinking'.
2 Harding, *The Science Question in Feminism*, p. 141.
3 Gilligan, 'In a Different Voice: Women's Conceptions of Self and Morality', and *In a Different Voice*.
4 Chodorow, 'Gender Relations and Difference', and *The Reproduction of Mothering*.
5 Miller, *Toward a New Psychology of Women*.
6 It is assumed, for instance, by Jane Flax, 'Political Philosophy and the Patriarchal Unconscious', that showing that aspects of a man's theory correspond to a masculine gender orientation constitutes a criticism of the theory, and Nancy Chodorow describes the object-relations perspective as a 'critique of masculinity': 'Psychoanalytic Feminism', p. 185.
7 Halberg, 'Feminist Epistemology: An Impossible Project?', discusses the tension between relativism and objectivism in much of the writing in this area. See also Pierce, 'Postmodernism and Other Scepticisms'.
8 See Nye, *Feminist Theory and the Philosophies of Man*, pp. 115–71; and my 'Freud, Wollstonecraft, and Ecofeminism'.
9 This analogy, and much of the discussion which follows, has been developed in my 'Reason and Feeling: Resisting the Dichotomy'.
10 Haan, 'Hypothetical and Actual Moral Reasoning in a Situation of Civil Disobedience'; and Holstein, 'Irreversible, Stepwise Sequence in the Development of Moral Judgement'. A good critical account of this material is that by Okin, 'Thinking like a Woman'.
11 It also classed non-western boys lower than western boys, which might lead one to wonder if something other than a sex difference was being picked up.
12 Gilligan, 'The Conquistador and the Dark Continent', p. 76.
13 Kohlberg and Kramer, 'Continuities and Discontinuities in Childhood and Adult Moral Development'.
14 Lyons, 'Two Perspectives: On Self, Relationships, and Morality'.
15 Gilligan, 'The Conquistador and the Dark Continent', pp. 78–9.
16 See in particular Noddings, *Caring*, p. 5. It should be noted that Ruddick is

careful to avoid this tendency; see in particular 'Remarks on the Sexual Politics of Reason'.

17 Gilligan et al., *Mapping the Moral Domain*, pp. xvii and 8–9.
18 Ibid., p. xxvi.
19 Hume, *A Treatise of Human Nature*, book 3, part 1, pp. 165–78.
20 Baier, 'Hume: The Women's Moral Theorist?'.
21 Tiles, 'The Combat of Passion and Reason'.
22 Foot argued this case in her influential 'Morality as a System of Hypothetical Imperatives'.
23 Grimshaw, *Philosophy and Feminist Thinking*, pp. 42–9.
24 Ruddick, 'Maternal Thinking', pp. 350–3.
25 Murdoch, *The Sovereignty of Good*, pp. 28–9.
26 Exceptions are Oakley, *Morality and the Emotions*, and de Sousa, *The Rationality of Emotion*. De Sousa argues the case for seeing emotion as both cognitive and affective; imagination similarly involves both content and affect.
27 Murdoch, *The Sovereignty of Good*, p. 35.
28 Hare, *Moral Thinking*, p. 99.
29 Foot, 'Morality as a System of Hypothetical Imperatives'.
30 Freud, 'Some Psychical Consequences of the Anatomical Distinction between the Sexes', pp. 257–8, quoted by Gilligan, 'In a Different Voice: Women's Conceptions of Self and Morality', p. 277.
31 Freud, *The Ego and the Id*, p. 37, 'Femininity', p. 129, and 'Some Psychical Consequences of the Anatomical Distinction between the Sexes', pp. 257–8.
32 Pateman, *The Sexual Contract*, pp. 103–15.
33 Freud, *The Ego and the Id*, pp. 30–3.
34 Rousseau, *Confessions*, p. 26.
35 Carter attributes to de Sade 'a hatred of the mothering function' in *The Sadeian Woman*, p. 37, following Klossowski, *Sade My Neighbour*, pp. 127–35.
36 De Sade, *Selected Letters*, pp. 33 and 53.
37 Freud, 'On the Universal Tendency to Debasement in the Sphere of Love', pp. 179–83.
38 Chodorow, *The Reproduction of Mothering*, pp. 217–19.

Bibliography

Amorós, Celia. 'Cartesianism and Feminism. What Reason Has Forgotten; Reasons for Forgetting', *Hypatia* 9 (1994), pp. 147–63.

Annas, Julia. 'Plato's *Republic* and Feminism', *Philosophy* 51 (1976), pp. 307–21.

—. *An Introduction to Plato's Republic*, Clarendon Press, Oxford, 1981.

Anonymous. *An Essay in Defence of the Female Sex*, Source Book Press, New York, 1970 (1696).

Aristotle. *De Generatione animalium*, trans. A.L. Peck, Heinemann, London, 1943.

—. *Politics*, trans. T.A. Sinclair, Penguin, Harmondsworth, 1962.

Astell, Mary. *A Serious Proposal to the Ladies*, Source Book Press, New York, 1970 (1701).

—. *Some Reflections upon Marriage*, Source Book Press, New York, 1970 (1730).

St Augustine. *The City of God*, trans. Henry Bettenson, Penguin, Harmondsworth, 1972.

Badinter, Elizabeth. 'Maternal Indifference' in *French Feminist Thought*, ed. Toril Moi, Blackwell, Oxford, 1987, pp. 150–78.

Baier, Annette. 'Hume: The Women's Moral Theorist?' in *Women and Moral Theory*, eds Eva Kittay and Diana Meyers, Rowman and Littlefield, Totowa, NJ, 1987, pp. 37–55.

Baird, Joseph and John Kane, eds. *La Querelle de la Rose*, North Carolina Studies in the Romance Languages and Literatures, Chapel Hill, 1978.

Barrett, Michèle. *The Politics of Truth: From Marx to Foucault*, Stanford University Press, Stanford, California, 1991.

Baynes, Kenneth, James Bohman and Thomas McCarthy, eds. *After Philosophy: End or Transformation*, MIT Press, Cambridge, MA, 1987.

de Beauvoir, Simone. *The Ethics of Ambiguity*, trans. Bernard Frechtman, Philosophical Library, New York, 1948.

—. *Le Deuxième Sexe*, Gallimard, Paris, 1949.

—. 'Must we Burn de Sade?', trans. Annette Michelson in *The Marquis de Sade*, ed. Paul Dinnage, John Calder, London, 1962, pp. 11–82.

—. *The Second Sex*, trans. H.M. Parshley, Penguin, Harmondsworth, 1972 (1949).

Bebel, August. *Women under Socialism*, Source Book Press, New York, 1970.

Bell, Dianne. *Daughters of the Dreaming*, McPhee Gribble/George Allen and Unwin, Melbourne and Sydney, 1983.

Benhabib, Selya. 'The Generalised and the Concrete Other: The Kohlberg–Gilligan Controversy and Moral Theory' in *Women and Moral Theory*, eds Eva Kittay and Diana Meyers, Rowman and Littlefield, Totowa, NJ, 1987, pp. 154–77.

—. 'Feminism and the Question of Postmodernism' in *Situating the Self: Gender, Community and Postmodernism in Contemporary Ethics*, Routledge, London, 1992, pp. 203–41.

Blum, Larry, Marcia Homiak, Judy Housman and Naomi Scheman, 'Altruism and Woman's Oppression', *Philosophical Forum*, 5, (1974), pp. 222–35.

Du Bois, Page. *Centaurs and Amazons*, University of Michigan Press, Ann Arbor, 1982.

Bordo, Susan. 'The Cartesian Masculinization of Thought', *Signs* 11 (1986), pp. 439–56.

Boxer, Marilyn and Jean Quataert, eds. *Connecting Spheres: Women in the Western World 1500 – the Present*, Oxford University Press, New York, 1987.

Brennan, Teresa and Carole Pateman. '"Mere Auxiliaries to the Commonwealth": Women and the Origins of Liberalism', *Political Studies* 27 (1979), pp. 183–200.

Bryson, Norman. 'Two Narratives of Rape in the Visual Arts: Lucretia and the Sabine Women', in *Rape*, eds Sylvana Tomasselli and Roy Porter, Blackwell, Oxford, 1986, pp. 152–73.

Burke, Carolyn. 'Irigaray Through the Looking Glass', *Feminist Studies* 7 (1981), pp. 288–306.

Butler, Judith. 'Sex and Gender in Simone de Beauvoir's *Second Sex*' in

'Simone de Beauvoir: Witness to a Century', ed. Hélène Wenzel, special issue of *Yale French Studies* 72 (1986), pp. 35–49.

—. *Gender Trouble*, Routledge, New York and London, 1990.

Butler, Melissa A. 'Early Liberal Roots of Feminism: John Locke and the Attack on Patriarchy', *American Political Science Review* 72 (1978), pp. 135–50.

Cameron, Deborah. *Feminism and Linguistic Theory*, Macmillan, Basingstoke and London, 1985.

Card, Claudia, ed. *Feminist Ethics*, University Press of Kansas, Lawrence, KS, 1991.

Carter, Angela. *The Sadeian Woman*, Virago Press, London, 1979.

Cassirer, Ernst. *The Question of Jean-Jacques Rousseau*, trans. Peter Gay, Indiana University Press, Bloomington, 1963.

Chapman, Richard. '*Leviathan* Writ Small: Thomas Hobbes on the Family', *American Political Science Review* 69 (1975), pp. 76–90.

Chodorow, Nancy. *The Reproduction of Mothering: Psychoanalysis and the Sociology of Gender*, University of California Press, Berkeley and Los Angeles, 1978.

—. 'Gender Relations and Difference' in *The Future of Difference*, eds Hester Eisenstein and Alice Jardine, G.K. Hall, Boston, 1980, pp. 3–19.

—. 'Psychoanalytic Feminism and the Psychoanalytic Psychology of Women' in *Feminism and Psychoanalytic Theory*, Yale University Press, New Haven and London, 1989, pp. 178–98.

Coady, C.A.J. 'Hobbes and "The Beautiful Axiom"', *Philosophy* 65 (1990), pp. 5–17.

Collins, Margery and Christine Pierce. 'Holes and Slime: Sexism in Sartre's Psychoanalysis', *Philosophical Forum* 5 (1973–4), pp. 112–27, reprinted in *Women and Philosophy: Towards a Theory of Liberation*, eds Carol C. Gould and Marx W. Wartofsky, G.P. Putnam and Sons, New York, 1976, pp. 112–21.

Connell, R.W. *Gender and Power*, Allen and Unwin, Sydney, 1987.

Coole, Diana H. *Women in Political Theory*, Wheatsheaf Books, Brighton, 1988.

Cornell, Drucilla. *Beyond Accommodation: Ethical Feminism, Deconstruction and the Law*, Routledge, New York and London, 1991.

Coveney, Lal, Margaret Jackson, Sheila Jeffreys, Leslie Kay and Pat Mahony. *The Sexuality Papers*, Hutchinson, London, 1984.

Daly, Mary. *Gyn/Ecology*, Beacon Press, Boston, 1978.

Delany, Sheila. ' "Mothers to Think Back Through": Who are They? The Ambiguous Example of Christine de Pisan' in *Medieval Texts and*

Contemporary Readers, eds Laurie A. Fink and Martin B. Shichtman, Cornell University Press, Ithaca, NY, 1987, pp. 177–97.

Derrida, Jacques. *Of Grammatology*, trans. Gayatri Spivak, Johns Hopkins University Press, Baltimore, 1974 (1967).

—. *Spurs: Nietzsche's Styles*, trans. Barbara Harlow, Chicago, University of Chicago Press, 1979 (1978).

—. 'Différance' in *Margins of Philosophy*, trans. Alan Bass, University of Chicago Press, Chicago, 1982 (1972), pp. 1–27.

—. 'Le Facteur de la Vérité' in *The Post Card from Socrates to Freud and Beyond*, trans. Alan Bass, University of Chicago Press, Chicago, 1987 (1980), pp. 413–96.

—. *Acts of Literature*, ed. Derek Attridge, Routledge, New York and London, 1992.

Derrida, Jacques and Christine McDonald. 'Choreograpies', *Diacritics* 12 (1982), pp. 66–76.

Le Doeuff, Michèle. 'Simone de Beauvoir and Existentialism', *Feminist Studies* 6 (1980), pp. 277–89.

—. *Hipparchia's Choice*, trans. Trista Selous, Blackwell, Oxford, 1989.

—. 'Women, Reason, Etc.', *Differences: A Journal of Feminist Cultural Studies* 2 (1990), pp. 1–13.

Dworkin, Andrea. *Pornography: Men Possessing Women*, Women's Press, London, 1981.

—. *Intercourse*, Free Press, New York, 1987.

—. 'Biological Superiority: The World's Most Dangerous and Deadly Idea', (1977) in *Letters from a War Zone*, Secker and Warburg, London, 1988, pp. 110–15.

Dyzenhaus, David. 'John Stuart Mill and the Harm of Pornography', *Ethics* 102 (1992), pp. 534–51.

Easlea, Brian. *Science and Sexual Oppression*, Weidenfeld and Nicolson, London, 1981.

Eisenstein, Hester. *Contemporary Feminist Thought*, Unwin Paperbacks, London and Sydney, 1984.

Eistenstein, Zillah. *The Radical Future of Liberal Feminism*, Longman, New York, 1981.

Elshtain, Jean Bethke. *Public Man, Private Woman*, Princeton University Press, Princeton, NJ, 1981.

Engels, Frederick. *The Origin of the Family, Private Property and the State*, Penguin, Harmondsworth, Middlesex, England, 1985 (1884).

Figes, Eva. *Patriarchal Attitudes*, Stein and Day, New York, 1970.

Filmer, Sir Robert. *Patriarcia and Other Writings*, ed. Johann Sommerville, Cambridge University Press, Cambridge, 1991 (1680).

Firestone, Shulamith. *The Dialectic of Sex*, Bantam Books, New York, 1971.

Flax, Jane. 'Political Philosophy and the Patriarchal Unconscious: A Psychoanalytic Perspective on Epistemology and Metaphysics' in *Discovering Reality*, eds Sandra Harding and Merrill B. Hintikka, Reidel, Dordrecht, 1983, pp. 245–81.

—. *Thinking Fragments*, University of California Press, Berkeley, Los Angeles, Oxford, 1990.

Foot, Philippa. 'Morality as a System of Hypothetical Imperatives' in *Virtue and Vices*, Oxford University Press, Oxford, 1978, pp. 157–73.

Foucault, Michel. *Madness and Civilization*, trans. Richard Howard, Tavistock, London, 1967 (1961).

—. *The Order of Things*, Tavistock, London, 1970 (1966).

—. *Power/Knowledge: Selected Interviews and Other Writings, 1972–1977*, ed. Colin Gordon, Harvester Press, Brighton, 1980.

—. *The History of Sexuality*, vol. 1, trans. Robert Hurley, Penguin, Harmondsworth, 1984 (1976).

—. 'Nietzsche, Genealogy, History' in *The Foucault Reader*, ed. Paul Rabinow, Penguin, Harmondsworth, 1984, pp. 76–100.

—. 'On the Genealogy of Ethics' in *The Foucault Reader*, ed. Paul Rabinow, Penguin, Harmondsworth, 1984, pp. 340–72.

—. 'Truth and Power' in *The Foucault Reader*, ed. Paul Rabinow, Penguin, Harmondsworth, 1984, pp. 51–75.

—. 'What is Enlightenment?' in *The Foucault Reader*, ed. Paul Rabinow, Penguin, Harmondsworth, 1984, pp. 32–50.

—. *The Use of Pleasure*, vol. 2 of *The History of Sexuality*, trans. Robert Hurley, Penguin, Harmondsworth, 1987 (1984).

Freud, Sigmund. *Totem and Taboo*, in *The Standard Edition of the Complete Psychological Works of Sigmund Freud*, vol. 13, trans. James Strachey, Hogarth Press, London, 1955 (1913), pp. 1–161.

—. 'On the Universal Tendency to Debasement in the Sphere of Love', in *The Standard Edition of the Complete Psychological Works of Sigmund Freud*, vol. 11, ed. James Strachey, Hogarth Press, London, 1957 (1912), pp. 179–90.

—. *Civilisation and its Discontents*, in *The Standard Edition of the Complete Psychological Works of Sigmund Freud*, vol. 21, ed. James Strachey, Hogarth Press, London, 1961 (1930), pp. 64–145.

—. *The Ego and the Id*, in *The Standard Edition of the Complete Psychological Works of Sigmund Freud*, vol. 19, trans. James Strachey, Hogarth Press, London, 1961 (1923), pp. 12–66.

—. 'Some Psychical Consequences of the Anatomical Distinction between the Sexes', in *The Standard Edition of the Complete Psychological Works of Sigmund Freud*, vol. 19, trans. James Strachey, Hogarth Press, London, 1961 (1925), pp. 248–58.

—. 'Femininity', in *The Standard Edition of the Complete Psychological Works of Sigmund Freud*, vol. 22, trans. James Strachey, Hogarth Press, London, 1964 (1932), pp. 112–35.

Fromm, Eric. *The Art of Loving*, Unwin, London, 1975.

Fuss, Diana. *Essentially Speaking*, Routledge, New York, 1989.

Gabriel, Astrik. 'The Educational Ideas of Christine de Pisan', *Journal of the History of Ideas* 16 (1955), pp. 3–21.

Gallop, Jane. *The Daughter's Seduction: Feminism and Psychoanalysis*, Cornell University Press, Ithaca, NY, 1982.

Gatens, Moira. 'Rousseau and Wollstonecraft: Nature vs. Reason', *Australasian Journal of Philosophy* 64, suppl. (1986), pp. 1–15.

Gilligan, Carol. 'In a Different Voice: Women's Conceptions of Self and Morality' in *The Future of Difference*, eds Hester Eisenstein and Alice Jardine, G.K. Hall, Boston, 1980, pp. 274–317.

—. *In a Different Voice: Psychological Theory and Women's Development*, Harvard University Press, Cambridge, MA, 1983.

—. 'The Conquistador and the Dark Continent: Reflections on the Psychology of Love', *Daedalus* 113 (1984), pp. 75–93.

Gilligan, Carol, Janie Victoria Ward and Jill McLean Taylor. *Mapping the Moral Domain*, Harvard University Press, Cambridge, MA, 1988.

Godelier, Maurice, 'La Part Ideélle du Réel: Essai sur l'Idéologique', *L'Homme* 18 (1978), pp. 155–188.

Gould, Carol C. and Marx W. Wartofsky, eds. *Women and Philosophy: Towards a Theory of Liberation*, G.P. Putnam and Sons, New York, 1976.

Green, Karen. 'Rawls, Women and the Priority of Liberty', *Australasian Journal of Philosophy* 64 suppl. (1986), pp. 26–36.

—. 'Femininity and Transcendence', *Australian Feminist Studies* 10 (1989), pp. 85–107.

—. 'Prostitution, Exploitation and Taboo', *Philosophy* 64 (1989), pp. 525–34.

—. 'Brain Writing and Derrida', *Australasian Journal of Philosophy* 71 (1993), pp. 238–55.

—. 'Reason and Feeling: Resisting the Dichotomy', *Australasian Journal of Philosophy* 71 (1993), pp. 385–99.

—. 'Freud, Wollstonecraft, and Ecofeminism: A Defence of Liberal Feminism', *Environmental Ethics* 16 (1994), pp. 117–34.

Greenleaf, W.H. 'Hobbes: The Problem of Interpretation' in *Hobbes and*

Rousseau, eds Maurice Cranston and Richard S. Peters, Anchor Books, New York, 1972, pp. 5–36.

Greer, Germaine. *The Female Eunuch*, Paladin, St. Albans, 1971.

Griffin, Susan. *Pornography and Silence*, Women's Press, London, 1981.

Griffiths, Morwenna and Margaret Whitford, eds. *Feminist Perspectives in Philosophy*, Macmillan, London, 1988.

Grimshaw, Jean. *Philosophy and Feminist Thinking*, University of Minnesota Press, Minneapolis, 1986.

—. 'Mary Wollstonecraft and the Tensions in Feminist Philosophy', *Radical Philosophy* 52 (1989), pp. 11–17.

Gross (Grosz), Elizabeth. 'What is Feminist Theory?' in *Feminist Challenges*, eds Carole Pateman and Elizabeth Gross, Allen and Unwin, Sydney, 1986, pp. 190–204.

—. *Sexual Subversions*, Allen and Unwin, Sydney, 1989.

—. 'Feminism and Anti-humanism' in *Discourse and Difference*, eds Andrew Milner and Chris Worth, Centre for General and Comparative Literature, Monash University, Melbourne, 1990, pp. 63–75.

—. 'Philosophy' in *Feminist Knowledge; Critique and Construct*, ed. Sneja Gunew, Routledge, London and New York, 1990, pp. 147–74.

Gunew, Sneja, ed. *Feminist Knowledge: Critique and Construct*, Routledge, London and New York, 1990.

—. 'Feminist Knowledge: Critique and Construct' in *Feminist Knowledge: Critique and Construct*, ed. Sneja Gunew, Routledge, London and New York, 1990.

Haan, N. 'Hypothetical and Actual Moral Reasoning in a Situation of Civil Disobedience', *Journal of Personality and Social Psychology* 32 (1975), pp. 255–70.

Halberg, Margareta. 'Feminist Epistemology: An Impossible Project?', *Radical Philosophy*, 53, (1989), pp. 3–7.

Hamilton, Cicely. *Marriage as a Trade*, Women's Press, London, 1981 (1909).

Hampshire, Stuart. *Thought and Action*, Chatto and Windus, London, 1960.

Harding, Sandra. *The Science Question in Feminism*, Cornell University Press, Ithaca, NY, and London, 1986.

—. 'Feminism, Science and the Anti-Enlightenment Critiques' in *Feminisim/Postmodernism*, ed. Linda Nicholson, Routledge, New York and London, 1990, pp. 83–106.

Harding, Sandra and Merrill B. Hintikka, eds. *Discovering Reality*, Reidel, Dortrecht, 1983.

Hare, R.M. *Moral Thinking*, Oxford University Press, Oxford, 1981.

Hartsock, Nancy. 'The Feminist Standpoint: Developing the Ground for a Specifically Feminist Historical Materialism' in *Discovering Reality*, eds Sandra Harding and Merrill B. Hintikka, Reidel, Dortrecht, 1983, pp. 283–310.

—. *Money, Sex, Power*, Northeastern University Press, Boston, 1984.

Heidegger, Martin. *Being and Time*, trans. John Macquarie and Edward Robinson, Blackwell, Oxford, 1962 (1927).

—. 'Letter on Humanism' (1947) in *Martin Heidegger: Basic Writings*, ed. David Farrell Krell, Harper and Row, New York, 1977.

Held, Virginia. 'Non-contractual Society: A Feminist View', *Canadian Journal of Philosophy* 13 suppl. (1987), pp. 111–37.

Herodotus. *The History of Herodotus*, trans. George Rawlinson, J.M. Dent and Sons, London and New York, 1948.

Hick, John. *Philosophy of Religion*, 3rd edn, Prentice-Hall, Englewood Cliffs, NJ, 1983.

Hindman, Sandra. *Christine de Pisan's "Epistre Othea"*, Universa, Wetteren, 1986.

Hinton, R.W.K. 'Husbands, Fathers and Conquerors', *Political Studies* 15 and 16 (1967 and 1968), pp. 291–300, 55–67.

Hobbes, Thomas. *Philosophical Elements of a True Citizen* (1642) in *The English Works of Thomas Hobbes*, vol. 2, ed. Sir William Molesworth, John Bohn, London, 1841, reprinted Scientia Verlag, Aalen, 1966.

—. *De Corpore Politico*, (1650) in *The English Works of Thomas Hobbes*, vol. 4, ed. Sir William Molesworth, John Bohn, London, 1841, reprinted Scientia Verlag, Aalen, 1966.

—. *Leviathan*, J.M. Dent and Sons, London, 1979 (1651).

Holstein, Constance. 'Irreversible, Stepwise Sequence in the Development of Moral Judgement: A Longitudinal Study of Males and Females', *Child Development* 47 (1976), pp. 51–61.

Holton, Sandra. *Feminism and Democracy*, Cambridge University Press, Cambridge, 1986.

Hume, David. *A Treatise of Human Nature*, ed. A.D. Lindsay, J.M. Dent and Sons, New York, 1966.

Irigaray, Luce. 'Woman's Exile', *Ideology and Consciousness* 1 (1977), pp. 62–76.

—. *Ethique de la Différence Sexuelle*, Minuit, Paris, 1984.

—. *Speculum of the Other Woman*, trans. Gillian Gill, Cornell University Press, Ithaca, NY, 1985 (1974).

—. 'This Sex Which Is Not One' in *This Sex Which Is Not One*, trans.

Catherine Porter with Carolyn Burke, Cornell University Press, Ithaca, NY, 1985 (1977), pp. 23–33.

—. 'Women on the Market' in *This Sex Which Is Not One*, trans. Catherine Porter with Carolyn Burke, Cornell University Press, Ithaca, NY, 1985 (1977), pp. 170–91.

—. 'Is the Subject of Science Sexed?' in *Feminism and Science*, ed. Nancy Tuana, Indiana University Press, Bloomington, 1989, pp. 58–68.

—. *Le Temps de la Différence*, Livre de Poche, Paris, 1989.

—. 'Equal or Different' in *The Irigaray Reader*, ed. Margaret Whitford, Blackwell, Oxford, 1991, pp. 30–3.

—. 'Sexual Difference' in *The Irigaray Reader*, ed. Margaret Whitford, Blackwell, Oxford, 1991, pp. 165–77.

—. 'Questions to Emmanual Levinas' in *The Irigaray Reader*, ed. Margaret Whitford, Blackwell, Oxford, 1991, pp. 178–89.

—. 'Women-amongst-themselves: Creating a Woman-to-woman Sociality' in *The Irigaray Reader*, ed. Margaret Whitford, Blackwell, Oxford, 1991, pp. 190–7.

—. 'The Necessity for Sexuate Rights' in *The Irigaray Reader*, ed. Margaret Whitford, Blackwell, Oxford, 1991, pp. 198–203.

—. 'How to Define Sexuate Rights?' in *The Irigaray Reader*, ed. Margaret Whitford, Blackwell, Oxford, 1991, pp. 204–12.

—. 'The Female Gender' in *Sexes and Genealogies*, trans. Gillian G. Gill, Columbia University Press, New York, 1993 (1987), pp. 107–23.

—. 'A Chance for Life' in *Sexes and Genealogies*, trans. Gillian G. Gill, Columbia University Press, New York, 1993 (1987), pp. 185–206.

Jackson, Margaret. 'Sexology and the Social Construction of Male Sexuality (Havelock Ellis)' in *The Sexuality Papers*, eds Lal Coveney, Margaret Jackson, Sheila Jeffreys, Leslie Kay and Pat Mahony, Hutchinson, London, 1984, pp. 45–68.

—. 'Sexology: The Universalisation of Male Sexuality (from Ellis to Kinsey and Masters and Johnson)' in *The Sexuality Papers*, eds Lal Coveney, Margaret Jackson, Sheila Jeffreys, Leslie Kay and Pat Mahony, Hutchinson, London, 1984, pp. 69–84.

Jacobus, Mary. *Reading Woman: Essays in Feminist Criticism*, Columbia University Press, New York, 1986.

—. 'The Difference of View' in *Reading Women: Essays in Feminist Criticism*, Columbia University Press, New York, 1986.

Jaggar, Alison M. *Feminist Politics and Human Nature*, Harvester Press, Brighton, 1983.

—. 'Feminist Ethics' in *Feminist Ethics*, ed. Claudia Card, University Press of Kansas, Lawrence, KS, 1991, pp. 78–104.

Jardine, Alice. 'Gynesis', *Diacritics* 12 (1982), pp. 54–65.

—. *Gynesis*, Cornell University Press, Ithaca, NY, and London, 1985.

Jeffreys, Sheila. '"Free from All Uninvited Touch of Man": Women's Campaigns around Sexuality, 1880–1914' in *The Sexuality Papers*, eds Lal Coveney, Margaret Jackson, Sheila Jeffreys, Leslie Kay and Pat Mahony, Hutchinson, London, 1984, pp. 22–44.

—. *Anticlimax*, Women's Press, London, 1990.

Jones, Ernest. 'Mother-right and the Sexual Ignorance of Savages', *International Journal of Psychoanalysis* 4 (1925), pp. 109–30.

Kaplan, Cora. *Sea Changes*, Verso, London, 1986.

Kaplan, Gisela T. and Leslie J. Rogers: 'The Definition of Male and Female: Biological Reductionism and the Sanctions of Normality' in *Feminist Knowledge: Critique and Construct*, ed. Sneja Gunew, Routledge, London and New York, 1990, pp. 205–28.

Keller, Evelyn Fox. *A Feeling for the Organism*, Freeman, San Francisco, 1983.

—. 'Gender and Science' in *Discovering Reality*, eds Sandra Harding and Merrill B. Hintikka, Reidel, Dortrecht, 1983, pp. 187–205.

—. *Reflections on Gender and Science*, Yale University Press, New Haven, CT, 1984.

Kittay, Eva and Diana Meyers, eds. *Women and Moral Theory*, Rowman and Littlefield, Totowa, NJ, 1987.

Kleinbaum, Abby. *The War Against the Amazons*, McGraw-Hill, New York, 1983.

Klossowski, Pierre. 'Nature as Destructive Principle', trans. Joseph H. McMahon, in Marquis de Sade, *The 120 Days of Sodom and Other Writings*, Grove Press Inc., New York, 1966.

—. *Sade My Neighbour*, trans. Alphonse Lingis, Quartet Books, London, 1992 (1947).

Knottenbelt, Maaike. 'A Woman's Place: Wollstonecraft on Woman in Society', *Political Theory Newsletter* 3 (1991), pp. 47–59.

Kohlberg, Lawrence and R. Kramer. 'Continuities and Discontinuities in Childhood and Adult Moral Development', *Human Development* 12 (1969), pp. 93–120.

Korsmeyer, Carolyn. 'Reason and Morals in the Early Feminist Movement: Mary Wollstonecraft', *Philosophical Forum* 5 (1974), pp. 97–111.

Kymlicka, Will. *Liberalism, Community and Culture*, Clarendon Press, Oxford, 1989.

Lacan, Jacques. 'The Meaning of the Phallus' in *Feminine Sexuality*, eds Juliet Mitchell and Jacqueline Rose, Macmillan, Basingstoke and London, 1982, pp. 74–85.

Laigle, Mathilde. *Le Livre de Trois Virtus de Christine de Pisan et son Milieu Historique et Litéraire*, Librairie Spécial pour l'Histoire de France, Paris, 1912.

Lange, Lynda. 'Rousseau and Modern Feminism' in *Feminist Interpretations of Political Theory*, eds Mary Shanley and Carole Pateman, Pennsylvania State University Press, University Park, PA, 1991, pp. 95–111.

Langton, Rae. 'Whose Right? Ronald Dworkin, Women and Pornographers', *Philosophy and Public Affairs* 19 (1990), pp. 311–59.

Lerner, Gerda. *The Creation of Patriarchy*, Oxford University Press, Oxford, 1986.

—. 'Women and History' in *Critical Essays on Simone de Beauvoir*, ed. Elaine Marks, G.K. Hall, Boston, 1987, pp. 154–68.

Lévi-Strauss, Claude. *The Elementary Structures of Kinship*, trans. James Hurle Bell, John Richard von Sturmer and Rodney Needham, Eyre and Spottiswoode, London, 1969 (1949).

Lloyd, Genevieve. 'The Man of Reason', *Metaphilosophy* 10 (1979), pp. 18–37.

—. 'Masters, Slaves and Others', *Radical Philosophy* 34 (1983), pp. 2–9.

—. 'Rousseau on Reason, Nature and Woman', *Metaphilosophy* 14 (1983), pp. 308–26.

—. *The Man of Reason*, Methuen, London, 1984.

Locke, John. *Two Treatises of Government*, ed. Peter Laslett, Cambridge University Press, Cambridge, 1970 (1690).

Lovibond, Sabina. 'Feminism and Post-modernism', *New Left Review* 178 (1989), pp. 5–28.

—. 'Feminism and Pragmatism: A Reply to Richard Rorty', *New Left Review* 193 (1992), pp. 56–74.

Lucas, Angela M. *Women in the Middle Ages*, Harvester Press, Brighton, 1983.

Luria, Maxwell. *A Reader's Guide to the Roman de la Rose*, Archon Books, Hamden, CT, 1982.

Lyons, Nona. 'Two Perspectives: On Self, Relationships, and Morality', *Harvard Education Review* 53 (1983), pp. 125–45.

Lyotard, Jean-François. 'The Post-modern Condition' in *After Philosophy: End or Transformation*, eds Kenneth Baynes, James Bohman and Thomas McCarthy, MIT Press, Cambridge, MA, 1987, pp. 73–94.

Machiavelli, Niccolò. *The Prince*, trans. George Bull, Penguin, Harmondsworth, 1961 (1514).

Mackenzie, Catriona. 'Philosophy and/or the Female Body' in *Feminist Challenges*, eds Carole Pateman and Elizabeth Gross, Allen and Unwin, Sydney, 1986, pp. 144–56.

Mackenzie, Eneas. *Memoirs of Mrs Caroline Chisholm*, 2nd edn, Webb, Millington and Co., London, 1852.

MacKinnon, Catharine. 'Feminism, Marxism, Method and the State: An Agenda for Theory', *Signs* 7 (1982), pp. 515–44.

—. 'Feminism, Marxism, Method and the State: Toward Feminist Jurisprudence', *Signs* 8 (1983), pp. 635–58.

—. 'On Collaboration' in *Feminism Unmodified*, Harvard University Press, Cambridge, MA, and London, 1987, pp. 198–213.

Maclean, Ian. *The Renaissance Notion of Women*, Cambridge University Press, Cambridge, 1980.

McLeod, Enid. *The Order of the Rose*, Chatto and Windus, London, 1976.

McMillan, Carol. *Women, Reason and Nature*, Blackwell, Oxford, 1982.

Malinowski, Bronislaw. *Sex and Repression in Savage Society*, Routledge and Kegan Paul, London, 1927.

—. *The Sexual Life of Savages in North-western Melanesia*, Routledge and Kegan Paul, London, 1929.

Marcuse, Herbert. *Reason and Revolution*, 2nd edn, Routledge and Kegan Paul, London, 1955.

—. *Eros and Civilisation*, Sphere, London, 1969.

Marks, Elaine, ed. *Critical Essays on Simone de Beauvoir*, G.K. Hall, Boston, 1987.

Marx, Karl and Frederick Engels. *The German Ideology*, ed. C.J. Arthur, International Publishers, New York, 1970.

Mathieu, Nicole-Claude. 'When Yielding is not Consenting', parts 1 and 2, *Feminist Issues* 9 and 10, (1989 and 1990), pp. 3–49, 38–51, originally published in *L'Arraisonnement des Femmes*, ed. Claude-Nicole Mathieu, Editions de l'Ecole des Hautes Etudes en Sciences Sociales, Paris, 1985.

Mead, Margaret. *Coming of Age in Samoa*, Penguin, Harmondsworth, 1943. (1928).

de Meun, Jean and Guillaume de Lorris. *The Romance of the Rose*, trans. Harry W. Robbins, E.P. Dutton, New York, 1962 (c.1237).

Midgley, Mary. *Beast and Man*, Cornell University Press, Ithaca, NY, 1978.

—. *Heart and Mind*, Methuen, London, 1981.

—. 'On Not Being Afraid of Natural Sex Differences' in *Feminist Perspectives in Philosophy*, eds Morwenna Griffiths and Margaret Whitford, Macmillan, London, 1988, pp. 29–41.

Mill, John Stuart. *On Liberty* in *Utilitarianism, Liberty, Representative Government*, J.M. Dent and Sons, London, 1964 (1859).
—. *The Subjection of Women*, MIT Press, Cambridge, MA, and London, 1989 (1869).
Miller, Jean Baker. *Toward a New Psychology of Women*, Penguin, Harmondsworth, 1976.
Millett, Kate. *Sexual Politics*, Sphere, London, 1971.
Millikan, Ruth Garrett. *Language, Thought and Other Biological Categories: New Foundations for Realism*, MIT Press, Cambridge, MA, 1984.
Mitchell, Juliet. *Psychoanalysis and Feminism*, Penguin, Harmondsworth, 1974.
Mitchell, Juliet and Jacqueline Rose, eds. *Feminine Sexuality*, Macmillan, Basingstoke and London, 1982.
Moi, Toril. *Sexual/Textual Politics*, Methuen, London, 1985.
—. ed. *French Feminist Thought*, Blackwell, Oxford, 1987.
—. *Feminist Theory and Simone de Beauvoir*, Blackwell, Oxford, 1990.
Murdoch, Iris. *The Sovereignty of Good*, Routledge and Kegan Paul, London, 1970.
Nicholson, Linda, ed. *Feminisim/Postmodernism*, Routledge, New York and London, 1990.
Noddings, Nel. *Caring: A Feminine Approach to Ethics and Moral Education*, University of California Press, Berkeley, 1984.
Nye, Andrea. *Feminist Theory and the Philosophies of Man*, Croom Helm, London, 1988.
Oakley, Justin. *Morality and the Emotions*, Routledge, London and New York, 1992.
Okin, Susan Moller. 'Philosopher Queens and Private Wives: Plato on Women and the Family', *Philosophy and Public Affairs* 6 (1977), pp. 345–69.
—. *Women in Western Political Thought*, Princeton University Press, Princeton, NJ, 1979.
—. *Justice, Gender and the Family*, Basic Books, New York, 1989.
—. 'Thinking like a Woman' in *Theoretical Perspectives on Sexual Difference*, ed. Deborah Rhode, Yale University Press, New Haven, CT, 1990, pp. 145–59.
Pateman, Carole. ' "The Disorder of Women": Women, Love, and the Sense of Justice', *Ethics* 91 (1980), pp. 20–34.
—. *The Sexual Contract*, Polity Press, Cambridge, 1988.
—. *The Disorder of Women*, Polity Press, Cambridge, 1989.

—. 'The Fraternal Social Contract' in *The Disorder of Women*, Polity Press, Cambridge, 1989, pp. 33–57.

—. '"God hath Ordained to Man a Helper": Hobbes, Patriarchy and Conjugal Right' in *Feminist Interpretations of Political Theory*, eds Mary Shanley and Carole Pateman, Pennsylvania State University Press, University Park, PA, 1991, pp. 53–73.

Pateman, Carole and Elizabeth Gross, eds. *Feminist Challenges*, Allen and Unwin, Sydney, 1986.

Pierce, Christine. 'Postmodernism and Other Scepticisms' in *Feminist Ethics*, ed. Claudia Card, University Press of Kansas, Lawrence, KS, 1991, pp. 60–77.

de Pisan, Christine. *Le Livre du fais et Bonnes Meurs du Sage Roy Charles* in *Nouvelle Collection des Mémoires pour Servir à l'Histoire de France*, Series 1, vols 1–2, eds MM. Michaud and Poujoulat, Imprimerie d'Edouard Proux, Paris, 1836 (1404), pp. 591–637, 1–145.

—. *Le Livre de la Mutation de Fortune*, ed. Suzanne Solente, Editions A. and J. Picard, Paris, 1959 (1403).

—. *The Book of the Duke of True Lovers*, trans. Alice Kemp-Welch, Cooper Square Publishers, New York, 1966.

—. *Le Livre du Corps de Policie*, ed. Robert Lucas, Librarie Droz, Geneva, 1967 (1407).

—. *Le Livre du Chemin de Long Estude*, Slatkine Reprints, Geneva, 1974 (1402).

—. 'Letter to Pierre Col (2nd October 1402)' in *La Querelle de la Rose*, eds Joseph Baird and John Kane, North Carolina Studies in the Romance Languages and Literatures, Chapel Hill, 1978, pp. 116–44.

—. *The Book of the City of Ladies*, trans. Earl Jeffrey Richards, Picador, London, 1983 (1405).

—. 'An Epistle to the Queen of France' (1405) in *The Epistle of the Prison of Human Life*, trans. Josette Wisman, Garland Library of Medieval Literature, London and New York, 1984, pp. 70–83.

—. *The Treasure of the City of Ladies*, trans. Sarah Lawson, Penguin, London and Harmondsworth, 1985 (1405).

Plamenatz, John. *Ideology*, Pall Mall, London, 1970.

Plato. *Timeus*, trans. Francis Cornford, Bobs-Merrill Education Publishing, Indianapolis, 1959.

—. *The Republic*, trans. Desmond Lee, 2nd edn, Penguin, Harmondsworth, 1974.

Poovey, Mary. *The Proper Lady and the Woman Writer: Ideology as Style in the Works of Mary Wollstonecraft, Mary Shelley and Jane Austen*, University of Chicago Press, Chicago and London, 1984.

—. 'Feminism and Deconstruction', *Feminist Studies* 14 (1988), pp. 51–65.

Pope, Barbara Corrado. 'The Influence of Rousseau's Ideology of Domesticity' in *Connecting Spheres: Women in the Western World 1500-the Present*, eds Marilyn Boxer and Jean Quataert, Oxford University Press, New York, 1987, pp. 136–45.

Quilligan, Maureen. *The Allegory of Female Authority: Christine de Pizan's Cité des Dames*, Cornell University Press, Ithaca, NY, and London, 1991.

Rabinow, Paul, ed. *The Foucault Reader*, Penguin, Harmondsworth, 1984.

Rawls, John. *A Theory of Justice*, Oxford University Press, Oxford, 1973.

Reich, Wilhelm. *The Function of the Orgasm*, trans. Theodore Wolfe, Panther, London, 1968 (1942).

—. *The Invasion of Compulsory Sex-morality*, trans. Werner and Doreen Grossman, Farrar, Straus and Giroux, New York, 1971 (1931).

—. *The Sexual Revolution*, trans. Therese Pol, Farrar, Straus and Giroux, New York, 1974 (1930).

Reuther, Rosemary. *New Woman, New Earth*, Dove Communications, Melbourne, 1975.

Rhode, Deborah, ed. *Theoretical Perspectives on Sexual Difference*, Yale University Press, New Haven, CT, 1990.

Rich, Adrienne. 'Compulsory Heterosexuality', *Signs* 5 (1980), pp. 631–60.

Rorty, Richard. *Objectivity, Relativism and Truth*, Cambridge University Press, Cambridge, 1991.

Rose, Hilary. 'Hand, Brain and Heart: A Feminist Epistemology for the Natural Sciences', *Signs* 9 (1983), pp. 73–90.

Rousseau, Jean-Jacques. *Confessions*, trans. J.M. Cohen, Penguin, Harmondsworth, 1953.

—. *Politics and the Arts: Letter to M. D'Alembert on the Theatre*, trans. Alan Bloom, Free Press, Glencoe, IL, 1960 (1758).

—. 'Sur les Femmes' and 'Essai sur les Evénements dont les Femmes ont été la Cause Secrette' in *Oeuvres Complètes de Jean-Jacques Rousseau*, Peliade, Paris, 1961, pp. 1254–5, 257–9.

—. *The Social Contract*, trans. Maurice Cranston, Penguin, Harmondsworth, 1968 (1762).

—. *A Discourse on Inequality*, trans. Maurice Cranston, Penguin, Harmondsworth, 1984 (1755).

—. *A Discourse on Political Economy*, trans. Maurice Cranston, Penguin, Harmondsworth, 1984 (1755).

—. *Emile*, trans. Barbara Foxley, J.M. Dent and Sons, London and Melbourne, 1986 (1762).

Ruddick, Sarah. 'Maternal Thinking', *Feminist Studies* 6 (1980), pp. 342–67.

—. 'Preservative Love and Military Destruction' in *Mothering: Essays in Feminist Theory*, ed. Joyce Trebilcot, Rowman and Allenhead, Totowa, NJ, 1984, pp. 231–62.

—. 'Remarks on the Sexual Politics of Reason' in *Women and Moral Theory*, eds Eva Kittay and Diana Meyers, Rowman and Littlefield, Totowa, NJ, 1987, pp. 237–60.

de Sade, Marquis. 'Selections' in *The Marquis de Sade*, ed. Paul Dinnage, John Calder, London, 1962, pp. 85–205.

—. *Selected Letters*, trans. Margaret Crosland, Peter Owen, London, 1965.

—. *The Complete Justine and Other Writings*, trans. Richard Seaver and Austyn Wainhouse, Grove Press, New York, 1966.

Salzmann, Rev. C.G. *Elements of Morality*, trans. Mary Wollstonecraft in *The Works of Mary Wollstonecraft*, vol. 2, eds Janet Todd and Marilyn Butler, William Pickering, London, 1989 (1790), pp. 3–205.

Sanday, Peggy. *Female Power and Male Dominance*, Cambridge University Press, Cambridge, 1981.

Sapiro, Virginia. *A Vindication of Political Virtue: The Political Theory of Mary Wollstonecraft*, University of Chicago Press, Chicago, 1992.

Sartre, Jean-Paul. *Existentialism and Humanism*, trans. Philip Mairet, Methuen, London, 1948.

—. *Being and Nothingness*, trans. Hazel Barnes, Washington Square Press, New York, 1966 (1943).

de Saussure, Ferdinand. *Course in General Linguistics*, trans. Wade Baskin, Fontana/Collins, Glasgow, 1974 (1915).

Sayers, Janet. *Sexual Contradictions*, Tavistock, London, 1986.

Schwartz, Joel. *The Sexual Politics of Jean-Jacques Rousseau*, University of Chicago Press, Chicago, 1985.

Schwarzer, Alice. *After "The Second Sex": Conversations with Simone de Beauvoir*, Pantheon, New York, 1984.

Scott, Joan W. 'Deconstructing Equality-versus-difference; Or, The Uses of Post-structuralist Theory for Feminism', *Feminist Studies* 14 (1988), pp. 33–50.

Segal, Lynne. *Is the Future Female?*, Virago Press, London, 1987.

Seigfried, Charlene Haddock. 'Gender Specific Values', *The Philosophical Forum* 15 (1984), pp. 425–42.

—. '*Second Sex*: Second Thoughts', *Women's Studies International Forum* 8 (1985), pp. 219–29.

Sénéchal, Anicet. 'J.-J. Rousseau, Secrétaire de Madame Dupin, d'après des Documents Inédits, avec une Inventaire des Papiers Dupin Dispersés en 1957 et 1958', *Annales de la Société J.-J. Rousseau* 36 (1963), pp. 173–290.

Shanley, Mary and Carole Pateman, eds. *Feminist Interpretations of Political Theory*, Pennsylvania State University Press, University Park, PA, 1991.

Singer, Peter. *Hegel*, Oxford University Press, Oxford and New York, 1983.

Slama, Béatrice. 'Simone de Beauvoir: Feminine Sexuality and Liberation', in *Critical Essays on Simone de Beauvoir*, ed. Elaine Marks, G.K. Hall, Boston, 1987, pp. 218–34.

de Sousa, Ronald. *The Rationality of Emotion*, MIT Press, Cambridge, MA, 1990.

Spender, Dale. *Man Made Language*, Routledge and Kegan Paul, London, 1980.

Spiro, Melford. *Oedipus in the Trobriands*, University of Chicago Press, Chicago, 1982.

Tapper, Marion. 'Can a Feminist be a Liberal?', *Australasian Journal of Philosophy* 64 suppl. (1986), pp. 37–47.

Taylor, Charles. *Hegel*, Cambridge University Press, Cambridge, 1975.

—. 'Foucault on Freedom and Truth', *Political Theory* 12 (1984), pp. 152–83.

Thomas, A.L., Diderot, Madame d'Epinay, *Qu'est-ce qu'une Femme?*, ed. Elizabeth Badinter, P.O.L., Paris, 1989.

Thomas, Paul. 'Jean-Jacques Rousseau, Sexist?', *Feminist Studies* 17 (1991), pp. 195–217.

Thompson, William. *Appeal of One Half of the Human Race, Women, against the Pretensions of the Other Half, Men, to Retain them in Political, and hence in Civil and Domestic Slavery*, Virago, London, 1983 (1825).

Thucydides. *The Peloponnesian War*, trans. Rex Warner, Penguin, Harmondsworth, 1972.

Tiles, J.E. 'The Combat of Passion and Reason', *Philosophy* 52 (1977), pp. 321–30.

Trebilcot, Joyce, ed. *Mothering: Essays in Feminist Theory*, Rowman and Allenhead, Totowa, NJ, 1984.

Tyrell, W. Blake. *Amazons: A Study of Athenian Myth Making*, Johns Hopkins University Press, Baltimore, 1984.

Viroli, Maurizio. *Jean-Jacques Rousseau and the 'Well-ordered Society'*, Cambridge University Press, Cambridge, 1988.

Weiss, Penny. 'Rousseau, Antifeminism and Woman's Nature', *Political Theory* 15 (1987), pp. 81–98.

Wheeler, Samuel. 'Indeterminacy of French Interpretation: Derrida and Davidson' in *Truth and Interpretation: Perspectives on the Philosophy of Donald Davidson*, ed. Ernest LePore, Blackwell, Oxford, 1989, pp. 477–94.

Whitford, Margaret. 'Luce Irigaray's Critique of Rationality' in *Feminist Perspectives in Philosophy*, eds Morwenna Griffiths and Margaret Whitford, Macmillan, London, 1988, pp. 109–30.

—. *Luce Irigaray: Philosophy in the Feminine*, Routledge, London and New York, 1991.

—. ed. *The Irigaray Reader*, Blackwell, Oxford, 1991.

Willard, Charity Cannon. *Christine de Pisan: Her Life and Works*, Persea Books, New York, 1984.

Williams, Bernard. 'The Idea of Equality' in *Problems of the Self*, Cambridge University Press, Cambridge, 1973, pp. 230–49.

Wittig, Monique. 'The Social Contract', *Feminist Issues* 9 (1989), pp. 3–13.

Wollstonecraft, Mary. *Collected Letters of Mary Wollstonecraft*, ed. Ralph Wardle, Cornell University Press, Ithaca, NY, 1979.

—. *Mary and The Wrongs of Woman*, Oxford University Press, Oxford, 1980 (1788, 1798).

—. *Vindication of the Rights of Woman*, Penguin, Harmondsworth, 1983 (1792).

—. *The French Revolution* in *The Works of Mary Wollstonecraft*, vol. 6, eds Janet Todd and Marilyn Butler, William Pickering, London, 1989 (1794), pp. 1–235.

—. 'Hints' in *The Works of Mary Wollstonecraft*, vol. 5, eds Janet Todd and Marilyn Butler, William Pickering, London, 1989 (1798), pp. 271–76.

—. 'Letter on the Present Character of the French Nation' in *The Works of Mary Wollstonecraft*, vol. 6, eds Janet Todd and Marilyn Butler, William Pickering, London, 1989 (1798), pp. 443–46.

—. 'Letters to Imlay' in *The Works of Mary Wollstonecraft*, vol. 6, eds Janet Todd and Marilyn Butler, William Pickering, London, 1989 (1798), pp. 367–438.

—. 'On Poetry' in *The Works of Mary Wollstonecraft*, vol. 7, eds Janet Todd and Marilyn Butler, William Pickering, London, 1989 (1797), pp. 7–11.

—. *Original Stories from Real Life with Conversations calculated to Regulate the Affections and Form the Mind to Truth and Goodness* in *The Works of Mary Wollstonecraft*, vol. 4, eds Janet Todd and Marilyn Butler, William Pickering, London, 1989 (1788), pp. 357–450.

—. *Thoughts on the Education of Daughters*, in *The Works of Mary Wollstonecraft*, vol. 4, eds Janet Todd and Marilyn Butler, William Pickering, London, 1989 (1787), pp. 5–49.

—. *Vindication of the Rights of Men*, in *The Works of Mary Wollstonecraft*, vol. 5, eds Janet Todd and Marilyn Butler, William Pickering, London, 1989 (1790), pp. 7–60.

Wollstonecraft, Mary and William Godwin. *A Short Residence in Sweden, Norway and Denmark, and Memoirs of the Author of The Rights of Women*, Penguin, Harmondsworth, 1987 (1796, 1798).

Young, Iris. 'Humanism, Gynocentrism and Feminist Politics', *Hypatia: Woman's Studies International Forum* 8 Special Issue (1985), pp. 173–83.

Index